MODERN SOUTHEAST ASIA SERIES

Stephen F. Maxner, *General Editor*

ALSO IN THE MODERN SOUTHEAST ASIA SERIES

After the Killing Fields: Lessons from the Cambodian Genocide
by Craig Etcheson

Military Medicine to Win Hearts and Minds: Aid to Civilians in the Vietnam War *by Robert J. Wilensky*

Operation Passage to Freedom: The United States Navy in Vietnam, 1954–1955 *by Ronald B. Frankum, Jr.*

Vietnam and Beyond: A Diplomat's Cold War Education
by Robert Hopkins Miller

Vietnam Chronicles: The Abrams Tapes, 1968–1972
transcribed and edited by Lewis Sorley

Window on a War: An Anthropologist in the Vietnam Conflict
by Gerald C. Hickey

An Loc
The Unfinished War

★ ★

General Tran Van Nhut

with Christian L. Arevian

TEXAS TECH UNIVERSITY PRESS

This book is typeset in Arno. The paper used in this book meets the minimum requirements of ANSI/NISO Z39.48-1992 (R1997). ♾

Book design by Mark McGarry, Texas Type & Book Works

Library of Congress Cataloging-in-Publication Data
Tran, Van Nhut, 1935–
An Loc : the unfinished war / General Tran Van Nhut ; with Christian L. Arevian.
p. cm. — (Modern southeast asia series)
Summary: "The author, an officer in the military service of the Republic of Vietnam from the late 1950s on, participated in pivotal events including the North Vietnamese attack on the province capital of An Loc, April–May 1970. He discusses Vietnam's leadership, U.S. advisors, and South Vietnam's relationships with the United States"—Provided by publisher.
Includes index.
ISBN 978-0-89672-645-1 (clothbound : alk. paper) 1. Tran, Van Nhut, 1935- 2. Generals—Vietnam—Biography. 3. Vietnam War, 1961–1975—United States. 4. Vietnam War, 1961–1975—Personal narratives, Vietnamese. I. Arevian, Christian L. II. Title.
DS556.93.T727A3 200
959.704'3092—dc22
[B] 2008040973

Printed in the United States of America
09 10 11 12 13 14 15 16 17 / 9 8 7 6 5 4 3 2 1

Texas Tech University Press
Box 41037
Lubbock, Texas 79409-1037 USA
800.832.4042
ttup@ttu.edu
www.ttup.ttu.edu

Contents

Illustrations

MAPS

Series Editor's Preface

In this autobiographical account, Tran Van Nhut provides insight into his life as one of the longest-serving soldiers and highest-ranking general officers in the Army of the Republic of Vietnam. Beginning with the more seminal experiences of his early family life, Nhut describes the Japanese occupation of Vietnam and the imprisonment and torture of his father at the hands of Japanese captors. Almost as powerful in his young life was the influence of Western culture, especially popular depictions of Tarzan and Zorro, "heroic images of gallant warriors punishing the guilty and rescuing the innocent, . . . courageously sacrificing themselves to save the weak and defend justice, [which] gradually began to influence my character." Nhut recalls vividly the emergence of communism in Vietnam and how the Viet Minh harassed and threatened his father for collaborating with the French, compelling the family to seek safety in another village. Given such formative experiences, it is hardly surprising that Nhut would become one of South Vietnam's most patriotic nationalists and ardent anti-communists. Upon graduating from high school in 1953, Nhut entered Dalat Military Academy intent on becoming a combat officer. After rigorous training under French colonial officers, Nhut graduated on

July 1, 1954, and embarked on a twenty-one-year military career that ended only with the fall of Saigon in 1975.

As Tran Van Nhut entwines his personal history with that of his country and its relationship with the United States, he shares interesting insights into his nation's people and political leaders and the influence—or lack thereof—of U.S. decisions and policies over two decades. An excellent example is his critical examination of President Ngo Dinh Diem, whom he praises as a genuine nationalist who opposed both communist domination and French colonialism. Yet he criticizes Diem for excessive pride and for being "overly dependent on the gang of protégés and lackeys who surrounded him." Nhut criticizes Diem further as authoritarian and manipulative, noting that any South Vietnamese political and military figures who wished to be successful had to become Catholic and join Diem's political party. These are salient observations from a fellow Vietnamese nationalist, especially now, as American historians begin to reevaluate Diem's effectiveness as a leader.

Within his first year or so of military service, Tran Van Nhut held positions with units in Tay Ninh, in Rung Sat, off the coast of the Mekong Delta, in Nha Trang, in the Paracel Islands, and near Saigon. He served also in the campaign that defeated the Binh Xuyen Army. Later he went to the United States to attend the U.S. Marine Basic Officer Course at Quantico, Virginia. There he became convinced that South Vietnam should follow the example of the United States and not the Soviet Union or People's Republic of China.

General Nhut discusses some of the challenges faced by the United States and the South Vietnamese as the North Vietnamese received increasing support from the Soviet Union and China and honed strategies for fighting in South Vietnam. In particular he notes the Viet Cong's inexhaustible capacity for recruiting from the early 1960s into the American phase of the war when, "after every search and destroy mission, after every 'body count' of dead Vietcong, two new volunteers replaced each dead one." In contrast he observes that the Agroville and Strategic Hamlet Program "backfired and led to a decrease in support for the Diem regime" as well as to the attempted coup of 1960. Although Nhut's interpretations of the war may not posit anything particularly new, they are tellingly illuminated by his personal insights into such significant events as the Battle of Ap Bac, the Buddhist Crisis, and the successful coup against Ngo Dinh Diem in 1963. Nhut's chapter on that coup provides a stirring retelling of his participation in the events that led to the removal and assassination of Ngo Dinh Diem and his brother, Ngo Dinh Nhu.

Readers will be interested in Nhut's recounting of the coup as a very difficult personal decision, one with profound and lasting implications. Early on, Nhut had misgivings about Diem and questioned many of his policies. He describes the mistrust and suspicions that he and his contemporaries continued to hold for Diem's government, which had become, in his words, nepotistic and oligarchic. They especially detested Diem's brother Nhu. Approached in October of 1963, Nhut had to decide whether to support or oppose the attempt to overthrow Diem. Justifying his conclusion, Nhut writes, "Something had to be done to rescue our sinking ship of state. In the last few weeks there had been daily demonstrations by students and Buddhists in the streets of Saigon and a number of cities and province capitals. I finally decided to participate."

What I find rather striking in the author's perspective on these historical events is his assessment of the coup as thoroughly Vietnamese in both inception and leadership. These men realized the need to gather and maintain the support of fellow Vietnamese commanders within the different regions of South Vietnam. Although Nhut acknowledges the United States' approval of the coup, neither he nor his closest associates—nor the coup leaders and plotters—saw themselves as doing the United States' bidding. Instead they believed themselves driven by the best interests of the Republic of Vietnam and their fellow citizens. In the weeks and months that followed the coup, paranoia and tumult reigned as different groups and personalities vied for power. When General Nguyen Khanh surprised everyone by staging his own coup, Nhut found himself sent—ostensibly in exile—to the Philippines, where he served as an ARVN liaison officer to the Philippine Army. After Khanh was deposed and sent himself into exile, Nhut returned, but a string of uninspiring assignments would convince him that he was still not trusted by military and political leaders. It would be 1967 before Nhut was given the command that led to his performance during Tet 1968, which altered his military fortunes.

Tran Van Nhut eventually found himself in some of the highest positions of political and military authority in Vietnam. In 1969 and early 1970, he took command of the 43rd Infantry Regiment and then the the 48th Infantry Regiment. Then in 1970 he became the province chief and sector commander of Binh Long Province, located in northwest III Corps Tactical Zone (CTZ) along the Cambodian border. In this latter position, Nhut faced many challenges in managing the civilian and military responsibilities in the province. These included the Rural Forces/Popular Forces, People's Self Defense Forces, pacification programs, coordinating with U.S. advisors and U.S. and ARVN military units, as well as handling the civilian concerns of the province including education, transportation, communications, police and security, business, religious organizations, and ethnic minorities. During his tenure as province chief, Nhut also witnessed significant aspects of the Eastertide Offensive of 1972, including the battle of An Loc and the battle for Route 13. Readers will find his personal reflections and detailed recollections of these battles to be important and insightful contributions to our historical understanding of the war.

After the successful campaign at An Loc to halt the advance of the North Vietnamese Army, Tran Van Nhut was called to Saigon and assigned to take over the ARVN 2nd Infantry Division, a position he held until the war ended. As he discusses his unit's military operations from 1972 through 1975, Nhut also shares his perspective on the peace talks and his interpretation of the reactions of President Nixon and President Thieu, as well as Henry Kissinger and Le Duc Tho, as the peace process played out through early 1973. Nhut's is a powerful retelling of the decline of the ARVN forces during 1973 and 1974 and the chaos that ensued and resulted in the final collapse of South Vietnam in April 1975.

Readers will find in these pages a remarkable story that is simple, forthright, and convincing. In addition, there are subtleties in this narrative that readers might find equally intriguing. Tran Van Nhut is persuasive when he describes the political and economic hopes and aspirations of South Vietnam and the South Vietnamese people. But in his story we also see hints of some of South Vietnam's many challenges in establishing and accepting a democratic form of government. Many South Vietnamese wanted desperately to live in a democratic republic with a free-market economy. At the same time, various individuals, including some senior military leaders, faced personal challenges in accepting civilian control over the military and a military command subservient to civilian leadership. This was but one of the many challenges that South Vietnam might have overcome had the U.S. Congress not withdrawn support for the Republic of Vietnam. We will never know what might have been had U.S. support been maintained, but Tran Van Nhut's story helps us to better understand what did actually happen and why.

As the new series editor for the Modern Southeast Asia Series published by Texas Tech University Press, I find it a privilege to contribute a preface to *An Loc: The Unfinished War*. Regarding a couple of our editorial choices, most of the maps lend veracity to this edition as primary sources and are not adapted or redrawn. Also, the word *communist*, unless referring specifically to the Communist Party, is not capitalized.

I would like to thank my predecessor, Jim Reckner, for his many years of service and for his vision and dedication while working with Texas Tech University Press to establish and maintain this important series. This is also the first volume of the series published under the Press's new director, Robert Mandel. For that reason, I would like also to thank Robert's predecessor, Noel Parsons, for his tireless work and commitment to this series and to extend to Noel best wishes in his retirement. In a number of ways, *An Loc* is an excellent reflection of a shared vision for the Modern Southeast Asia Series to embrace, within its broader scope, incisive new interpretations of the Vietnam War. We are pleased to make this memoir available to a wide readership and look forward to issuing its worthiest complements.

STEPHEN F. MAXNER
Series Editor
Vietnam Center, Texas Tech University

AN LOC: THE UNFINISHED WAR

1

A Few Memories of My Childhood

I WAS BORN on December 17, 1935, in Saigon, to a middle-class Catholic family. I was named Paul Tran Van Nhut. Paul was my patron saint's name, but members of my family called me by my nickname—"Bom." My father, an official of the Bastos cigarette company, was from the Ba Tri district of Kien Hoa province southwest of Saigon. My mother was from the Cai Be district of Dinh Tuong province. I was the fourth child in a family of six sons and one daughter.

One of the most vivid memories of my early childhood was my great-grandfather's house. It was a very large house with many round and shiny wooden pillars. It had a high gate and two wooden gate pillars painted bright red. There was a row of Chinese characters along the top, painted in gold. To the left of the gate and beside the house were many stone grave-markers. Of these, the tallest was the marker belonging to my ancestors whose family name was To and who had emigrated from central Vietnam to Ben Tre in the early part of the nineteenth century.

My great-grandfather, about eighty years old, was strong and healthy, though with failing eyesight. He spent every day hobbling around on his cane, visiting relatives and friends in the neighborhood, returning home at sunset. When he reached the gate, he would call out loudly: "Where is that boy, Bom? Come here; let me see you." I would come running, and he would rub my head and hug me for a long time.

His fingernails were so long that they curled. His hair and beard were also long because he never shaved. He wanted to preserve everything from the time of his birth until he died. He practiced the Cao Dai religion. After dinner, he would go sit in front of the altar, praying for about an hour. Then he would get up, take his cane, limp over to his coffin, climb in, and go to sleep.

My great-grandfather had ordered a special coffin built to his own dimensions, carved and painted to his specifications. It was made of wood, engraved with ancient designs, and painted bright red. He had placed a number of his most prized possessions in it, with pieces of clothing from his childhood. He was to be buried in this coffin when he died. In the meantime, he slept in the coffin each night.

Whenever I woke up at night and saw my great-grandfather sleeping in the shiny red coffin under the light of an oil lamp, a gigantic eye (the symbol of the Cao Dai religion) staring down from the family altar, and his thin body looking like he was already dead, I would be terrified. I felt as if there was a ghost in the house. I would hug my grandmother tight in order to go back to sleep.

My great-grandfather had grown up in Ben Tre, the fertile land where coconuts and sugarcane grew. It was originally part of Cambodia and so abundant in fish that Cambodians named it "Fish Lake." The land was built up over the millennia by silt deposited by the mighty Mekong River. The Mekong never rests. It flows more than 2,500 miles from Tibet, through China, down through Laos and Cambodia, and finally across the lowlands of South Vietnam before reaching the Pacific Ocean. South Vietnam is a truly rich, fertile, and gentle land. Ben Tre grew to maturity during the course of our long, historic struggle to build a nation.

I do not remember my paternal or maternal grandfathers because they both had died before I was born.

My father was born, grew up, and went to school in Saigon. He refused to return to his father's home village to work. He had big dreams and sought adventure. He worked as an official in Saigon for a while, and then went to Phnom Penh, Cambodia, to set up a fishery company. When that company failed after a few years, he returned to Vietnam to work as an official in the vast Courtenay rubber plantation east of the district capital of Xuan Loc in Bien Hoa province. The entire family moved to Courtenay, living in a large house belonging to the plantation.

During the 1950s, malaria spread rapidly through the mountain jungles and rubber plantation. My mother came down with the debilitating disease and seemed to have a fever constantly. The mosquitoes of the rubber plantation did not neglect my father, but for some reason he escaped the high fevers. He often joked that it wasn't because he took quinine pills but because of his drinking sessions, when he ate wild jungle meat with hot peppers and washed the food down with copious amounts of alcohol.

* * *

By mid-1945, I was nearly ten years old and the realities of World War II began to catch up with me. At noon on a Sunday, I heard aircraft engines and guns firing overhead. I looked up and saw two aircraft chasing each other across the sky over the plantation, soaring high and then diving low, firing quick bursts from their machine guns. The entire village was in an uproar, people yelling and screaming in total confusion, running in panic, trying to find a place to take cover. My mother said it was a Japanese and an American plane shooting at each other. She called me to come in and hide in the bunker we had dug along the side of the house.

A few days after this incident, the Japanese occupation army ordered the French managers of the plantation and their families to move to Saigon. The senior Vietnamese employee of the plantation took over the management of the plantation.

One dark night, we were awakened by a knock on the door. We all arose and my father opened the door. Two Japanese soldiers, accompanied by a Vietnamese interpreter, arrogantly strode into the house and handcuffed my father. My mother pleaded with them, but they refused to release him, pushed him into their car, and drove away. The next morning, my mother ran all over the town trying to locate her husband. She finally learned that the Japanese were holding him at their headquarters in Hang Gon, six miles south of Xuan Loc.

The Japanese accused my father of being an informer for the French. They interrogated and beat him mercilessly and tried to starve him into confessing. Fortunately, a plantation worker who knew and admired my father managed to secretly bring him a little rice soup.

Several days later, senior Japanese officers conducted an investigation, decided that my father was innocent, and released him. When he got home, his shirt was covered with blood, his left eye swollen shut and caked with blood. He had been tortured repeatedly and had not been allowed to bathe. He stank. My mother and grandmother held his hands and sobbed; all the children hugged him and cried.

That scene was etched on my memory, and is still there to this day. I felt a strong revulsion for all colonialists, white or yellow, who abused their power and oppressed their helpless subjects. The sight of my father's suffering made me decide that I should always strive to help Vietnam become a stronger nation, capable of resisting the oppression of others.

The Vietnamese management of the plantation was a total failure, and production was paralyzed. My father had to quit his job. We moved to Xa Bang, a sparsely populated hamlet between Xuan Loc and Long Le. My father bought a dilapidated house and began to renovate it with the help of two of his brothers. It soon became one of the nicer houses in Xa Bang. At this point, though, the brutal Vietnamese communists now replaced the barbaric Japanese. The Viet Minh denounced my father for cooperating with the French and working against the anti-colonialists. He was harassed and threatened to such an extent that he had to flee to Ben Cat in Thu Dau Mot, and the rest of us had to abandon our home and seek temporary asylum in the village of Long Le.

* * *

Vietnamese communism had its real beginning in 1890 when Nguyen Sinh Cung was born, seven years after Vietnam had become part of the French colony called Indochina, which included Vietnam, Laos, and Cambodia. When he was ten years old, Nguyen Sinh Cung's father changed his name to Nguyen Tat Thanh, following general practice, and started lecturing him about devoting his life to free his country from French occupation. The young man studied French at the Royal Academy in Hue and focused on Europe instead of China or Japan, as most Vietnamese students did. At age twenty-one, he changed his name to Ba and signed on as assistant cook on a French ship. At age twenty-seven, he settled in Paris, became a socialist and a contributor to three left-wing newspapers, changed his name to Nguyen Ai Quoc (Nguyen the Patriot), and appointed himself leader of the Vietnamese independence movement. He prepared an official eight-point Program of Vietnamese Demands and tried to present it to President Woodrow Wilson who was attending the Versailles Peace Conference; he could not get nearer to Wilson than the outer door.[1]

At age thirty, Nguyen Ai Quoc found out that Lenin's anti-colonialism was stronger than the socialist version and decided to become a Marxist-Leninist; he wrote: "It was patriotism and not communism that inspired me." At age thirty-two, he started publishing a militantly communist magazine named *The Pariah,* which made him famous among both the communists and the Indochinese. Then he moved to the center of the communist world, Moscow, where he studied revolutionary tactics and the solidarity of oppressed people. He became a member of the Comintern (Communist International) and was sent to China and other Far Eastern nations as an agent of the Comintern.[2]

In China at age thirty-five, he changed his name to Vuong and founded the Indochinese Communist Party. In Southeast Asia at age thirty-eight, he changed his name to Thau Chin to elude French security service agents. In Hong Kong at age forty-one, he was using the name Tong Van So. Then, back in China at age forty-seven, he changed his name to Tran.

World War II convinced him that the time was ripe for the liberation of Vietnam. He moved to Indochina and set up his revolutionary headquarters in a cave near the Chinese border, by a mountain he named Karl Marx and a river he named Lenin. He considered the occasion important enough to change his name for the ninth and last time to Ho Chi Minh (He Who Enlightens).[3]

In a 1941 meeting presided over by Ho Chi Minh, the Indochinese Communist Party founded the Viet Minh (Viet Nam Cach Mang Dong Minh Hoi—Viet Nam Political Reform Groups) to fight a guerilla war against the Japanese occupation of Indochina. There were many other groups fighting French colonialism. Ho Chi Minh betrayed them by taking control of the anticolonial movement as though it was only a communist movement. The First Indochina War thus began in 1941 with the establishment of the Viet Minh.

The Viet Minh guerilla organization of five thousand men was entrusted to Ho's most faithful disciple, a former professor of history called Vo Nguyen Giap, whose friends called him The Volcano Under the Snow to portray a mixture of fiery intensity and cold determination. Giap referred to himself as a self-taught general. He studied the centuries-old Vietnamese tradition of fighting invaders: how to use deception and surprise to overcome enemy strengths, how to "defeat the greater with the lesser." He studied Lenin, Mao Tse Tung, Clausewitz, and Sun Tzu. He studied the Mongol campaigns from the point of view of the people whose country had been invaded. He developed rural and urban strategies, guided by the writings of Mao.[4]

In a short time, Giap became second only to Ho Chi Minh among the Vietnamese communists, and the most influential guerilla warrior in the world. He created an army based on the theory that "quality" was more important than "quantity" because his men would always be outnumbered by the major powers they were fighting. Indoctrination of the soldiers and civilians became essential. Ho and Giap aimed at the creation of a single-minded group of millions of military and civilian Vietnamese willing to fight with whatever arms were available, from a sharpened bamboo stick to an antiaircraft gun.

The indoctrination and motivation systems of these two men proved to be ruthless and effective.

At about the same time that I was witnessing the dogfight between the Japanese and American fighter planes, more precisely on August 13, 1945, Ho Chi Minh created the National Liberation Committee of Vietnam and proclaimed it to be the country's provisional government. Within a few weeks, the Japanese imperial delegate had fled and the Vietnamese emperor Bao Dai had abdicated. The Viet Minh controlled all of Vietnam and "Uncle Ho" rose from the underground and became president of the Democratic Republic of Vietnam.

Ho Chi Minh's mentor, Josef Stalin of the Soviet Union, did not even bother to recognize the newly created Democratic Republic of Vietnam.

From such an unpretentious beginning, but with a huge determination and a firm belief that "nothing is more precious than independence and freedom," Ho Chi Minh became one of the top statesmen of the twentieth century. Ho was the undisputed dictator, but he was flexible enough to allow Giap and the other members of the communist hierarchy to claim authorship of any successful endeavor. They all did; Giap even went on to become a prolific writer about his exploits in guerilla warfare, in the process painting a self-portrait that claimed he was eight feet tall.

But it was Ho Chi Minh in the background who was the chief policymaker and the chief strategist, approving or canceling any of Giap's creations, based on Ho's own vision of the future of Vietnam as well as the probability of success.

* * *

Meanwhile, back at Long Le, the Village People's Committee, a communist organization operating under the Viet Minh, had heard that my father had joined the French army and was stationed at Binh Ba. They arrested us and imprisoned us in one of their homes, waiting for the French army to leave so they could execute the entire family. Fortunately, a convoy of French army vehicles swept into Long Le, and the members of the Village People's Committee fled in all directions.

My father had in fact joined the French forces. He had been monitoring the situation and knew about our arrest. When he learned that the French army was going to conduct an operation into Long Le, he arranged for a neighbor from Courtenay to drive her horse cart to Long Le, pick us up, and deliver us to Binh Ba. We were thus saved from certain death.

In 1946, train locomotives were still steam-powered. My father went into the lumber business and received a contract to supply firewood to the railroad in Saigon. He moved our family back to Saigon, where I could enjoy a few relatively quiet years getting acquainted with new classmates and making new friends.

My greatest pleasure, though, came from the novelty provided by movies. I was infatuated and thrilled by the courage of Tarzan and Zorro. My friends and I never missed an episode of these epic serial movies. The heroic images of gallant warriors punishing the guilty and rescuing the innocent, then courageously sacrificing themselves to save the weak and defend justice gradually began to influence my character. I wanted to be a hero like Tarzan and Zorro.

The Japanese occupation had ended, but the French had no intention of abandoning sovereignty over the colonies of Indochina. France agreed to recognize the Republic of Vietnam provided Vietnam would accept to be part of the Indochinese Federation within a new entity called the French Union. But then France unilaterally decided that the Indochinese Federation consisted of five sectors: Laos, Cambodia, North Vietnam, Central Vietnam, and South Vietnam. It claimed that the Viet Minh represented only North Vietnam. Central Vietnam and South Vietnam could join the North only after a referendum.[5]

The year 1946 saw a series of conferences in France and Vietnam in an atmosphere of mutual distrust and hardening attitudes. By December, all hopes of a compromise had been dashed. To use Ho Chi Minh's imagery, the fight between the tiger and the elephant resumed: "If ever the tiger pauses, the elephant will impale him on his mighty tusks. But the tiger will not pause, and the elephant will die of exhaustion and loss of blood." Giap was even more resolute: "We shall not let ourselves be stopped by any loss, any violence, any destruction." The determination of the Viet Minh turned into extremism.

By 1947, the communist/capitalist competition had turned into the Cold War. The hot war between the Viet Minh and France had resumed. Ho Chi Minh's intimate contacts in the highest levels of the Soviet Union were helping provide arms to the Viet Minh, while the Truman administration came to France's rescue with financial and military assistance.

The National Security Council of the United States, created at the end of 1947, had reached the conclusion that the greatest threat to United States security came from the Soviet Union. Hence the domination of Asia and Europe by the Soviet Union was politically and strategically unacceptable. Based on this philosophy, President Truman decided that extending assistance to the French was in the American national interest. The policy of containment of communism was extended to Southeast Asia in general and Vietnam in particular. American involvement in Vietnam began with assistance to France.

In 1949, fate intervened in favor of the Viet Minh. The Chinese communists defeated the nationalists and took control of China. Peking recognized Ho Chi Minh's government, followed two weeks later by Moscow. The Viet Minh was revitalized by the Chinese supply of automatic weapons, mortars, howitzers, even old American trucks and Soviet equipment. Chinese aid to the Viet Minh increased from four hundred tons per month to more than three thousand tons, plus four thousand "volunteers." But direct Chinese involvement was not requested. Ho Chi Minh preferred the revolution to stay a purely Vietnamese affair; he wanted to avoid Chinese domination.[6]

The invigorated Viet Minh began harassing French garrisons. In 1950, after the summer rains subsided, General Giap took the initiative and the French lost so much territory and so many men that a CIA report described the French hold on Indochina as "precarious." A panicked French government reinstated Emperor Bao Dai as the head of a new government in Saigon, dismissed most of the French officials, and conferred both military and political responsibility of the colony on one of France's most prominent soldiers, Gen. Jean de Lattre de Tassigny. General de Lattre (helped by Giap's miscalculations) not only managed to blunt the Viet Minh advances, but he also used U.S. funds to expand the Vietnamese National Army to thirty-three infantry battalions. Later, Eisenhower continued Truman's policy of assistance to the French, even adding a human presence of four hundred military advisors. "The French soldier in Indochina and the American soldier in Korea are fighting the same thing," he declared.[7]

* * *

During 1951–52, as French police and secret service agents launched a series of sweeps to arrest opponents of their policies, life in Saigon became very turbulent. There were strikes and student demonstrations, one of which turned tragic when Tran Van On, a high school student leader of the protest movement, was shot and killed. The students of all the schools boycotted classes.

I began training in Binh Dinh martial arts for a while, with great enthusiasm. The Binh Dinh martial arts began with the Nguyen Tay Son brothers, who launched an uprising in the late eighteenth century. Their army marched north, waited until the Chinese soldiers were celebrating the lunar New Year, attacked and captured the outpost at Ngoc Hoi, recaptured Hanoi, and seized the throne of the emperor. Binh Dinh martial arts have become our national martial art, so widespread that even the women and young girls are adept at them. Anyone who visited Binh Dinh would be fascinated by the sight of young men and women wrestling one another along the banks of the An Khe River. There was an old saying: "If you visit Binh Dinh, go see the women and girls dance with whips and flashing fists."

When I returned to school, I learned that the French police had arrested our teacher Co Tan Van Luong. Professor Luong taught history and geography. He told stories that helped the students understand the roots of the Vietnamese people, telling us who our heroes and our enemies were. He described to us the wonderful battles fought against the Chinese oppressors by Emperor Quang Trung (Nguyen Hue), the clever stratagems of the heroic Le Loi, the valor of Tran Binh Trong, the outstanding naval strategy of our hero Tran Hung Dao during the battle of Bach Dang, the victories of Emperor Ngo Quyen, the heroic exploits of the Trung sisters and Madame Trieu, and the glorious victory of Dinh Bo Linh.

Luong was also good at creating vivid images of the geographic locations of Vietnam. We could easily imagine where the Gianh River was located and how the historic battles were fought there; where the Red River and the Thai Binh River could be found, carrying the sorrow and the courage of our nation as they flowed down to the sea. We could close our eyes and see the Tam Diep Mountains, the Annamite Chain, and the sacred Seven Mountains. We could watch as the waters of the Mekong flowed into the Upper and Lower rivers in the Mekong Delta, surrounding and nourishing millions of South Vietnamese.

Our teacher pined for the day when our nation would become independent. Vietnam, he told us, must deal fairly with the Cambodians and the Lao and Cham, with the Montagnards (mountaineers), and with the ethnic minorities. We listened to him, enthralled. We loved this teacher of Vietnamese nationalism. And the French arrested Co Tan Van Luong exactly because he had Vietnamese nationalist feelings.

At the end of the school year, my father took my brothers and me for summer vacation at Bu Dop, where he had his logging operation, employing more than one hundred laborers. The foreman of the operation was a wonderful character, Uncle Lam Ut, a former paratrooper corporal in the French army. After his discharge, Lam Ut returned to Loc Ninh to work for my father. The two men were very close and trusted each other like brothers. My father often loaned Lam Ut a hunting rifle to shoot large game animals for meat, of which we often shared the spoils. Although fish, shrimp, crab, and crayfish were the primary sources of protein for the people living along the rivers and the coast, wild game was the primary source of food for the tribal people living in the jungles of Loc Ninh and Bu Dop.

The tribal people had a wealth of experience in hunting and snaring different types of wild game, from small game such as squirrels, foxes,

CHINA
Gejiu
Wenlan
Kaihua
Xinjing
Gui Xian
Nanning
CHINA
Yulin
Simao
Lao Cai
Black River
Red River
Yen Bai
Lang Son
Phong Saly
NORTH VIETNAM
Dien Bien Phu
Viet Tri
Hanoi
Hon Gai
Zhanjiang
Luong Nam Tha
Muong Sai
Hoa Binh
Hai Phong
Samneua
Nam Dinh
LAOS
Nam Binh
Luang Prabang
Thanh Hoa
HAINAN ISLAND
Xiangkhoang
Sayaboury
Gulf of Tonkin
Mekong River
Vinh
Vientiane
Nong Khai
Dong Hoi
Udon Thani
Vinh Linh
DEMILITARIZED ZONE
Nakhon Phanom
Muong Xepon
Cam Lo
Quang Tri City
Phitsanulok
Savannakhet
Khe Sanh
Phu Bai
Khon Kaen
Hue
Da Nang
An Hoa
Saravane
THAILAND
Tam Ky
Chu Lai
Ubon Ratchathani
Si Sa Ket
Attopeu
Surin
Warin Chamrap
Pakse
My Lai
Nakhon Ratchasima
Dak To
Sara Buri
Kontum
Bangkok
Qui Nhon
Pleiku
Aranyaprathet
An Khe
Sisophon
Siem Reap
Stoeng Treng
Lomphat
SOUTH VIETNAM
Tuy Hoa
CAMBODIA
Battambang
Kompang Thom
Ban Me Thuot
Pursat
Nha Trang
Gia Nghia
Kompong Cham
Cam Ranh
Phnom Penh
Phuoc Binh
Gulf of Thailand
An Loc
Da Lat
Kompong Speu
Phan Rhang
Tay Ninh
Bao Loc
Saigon
Phan Thiet
Kampot
Kompong Sam
Long Binh
My Tho
Ha Tien
Vung Tau
Rach Gia
Can Tho
Bac Lieu
South China Sea
CON SON
Vietnam 1972

wild chickens, peacocks, birds, and porcupines to large game such as wild boar, deer, wild oxen, tigers, and even elephants.

They also grew jungle rice, which is soft and glutinous. They did not put rice in a pot and boil it as city people do. They put it in a hollow tube of bamboo, poured in a little spring water, and sealed it tight with leaves. They then buried the bamboo tube in a pile of hot ashes. When the rice was cooked, they split the bamboo tube and cut it into sections. Rice cooked in this manner is fragrant and delicious.

Corn was the primary source of carbohydrates for the tribes, not rice. They cooked the corn by burying a whole ear of corn under a pile of hot ashes for about ten minutes.

Another supplementary source of food was growing behind their houses, without the need for planting: bamboo shoots, which are soft and sweet. They dug deep into the soil and pulled the shoots off the roots of the mother tree. They did not eat them raw as city people do; they first roasted them under a pile of hot ashes, just as they did sweet potatoes and manioc.

Among the tribal laborers, I noticed some young girls working in the orange groves who were not wearing tops. Brightly embroidered sarongs covered their bodies only from the knees to the waist. The breasts of these fifteen- and sixteen-year-old mountain girls were round, firm, dark brown, and enticing. When they noticed me staring at their shapely, sexy bodies, they were not shy. They gave me smiles that were part dare and part invitation.

I later learned that mountain girls had to use every means at their disposal to attract men. Breasts were the magnets that attracted the most attention. As soon as one of these seemingly promiscuous but extremely faithful girls found a suitable mate and fell in love, she would cover her breasts to show that her "garden" had found an owner. No other man was then allowed to view these treasures; they belonged exclusively to her mate.

Who says tribal people are uncivilized? Who says tribal people are careless and easy in matters of love?

2

Entrance into the Armed Forces

OUR CLASS graduated in the summer of 1953, receiving the French *brevet* diploma. Ten of us decided to join the armed forces. Khuong, Cuong, and Tam joined the air force. Tran Le Tai and Dao Van Quang joined the navy. Tran Ngoc Tri, Le Quang Luong, Tran Van Thong, Le Hang Minh, and I joined the army. I was not yet eighteen years old and needed my father's permission to take the test for entrance to the Dalat Military Academy. With my father's permission, I entered the armed forces of the State of Vietnam on October 1, 1953.

On the morning of the day I was to report for transportation to Dalat, my mother could not hold back her tears. She was sending her son off to war, to a new life filled with danger. She was worried about me. There was heavy fighting between the French and the Viet Minh in North Vietnam, and the result of the fighting would create conditions favorable to one side or the other at the ongoing negotiations in Geneva. The fate of the three regions of Vietnam—North, Central, and South—lay in the hands of the dealmakers at the Geneva Conference, and each region tried to secure victory.

We left Saigon for Dalat on a bright autumn morning. Twenty students were packed into American-built GMC trucks. Route 14 took us into the highlands. After passing through Dau Giay, our convoy climbed the mountain slopes to Dinh Quan and Blao and skirted around the Prenn waterfall, reaching an altitude of 3,200 feet. We began to feel the cool climate of Dalat. When the convoy reached the gates of the academy, cadet officers dressed in crisp, starched uniforms were standing still as statues along the side of the road, waiting to greet us and escort us to our billeting areas.

The buildings and barracks were impressive, and the camp was immaculately maintained. Steel bunks stood in two lines along the sides of the rooms. We were divided into squads, platoons, and companies and issued uniforms and military equipment. Our class was the largest in the history of the Dalat Military Academy, 525 young men from all over Vietnam, including a number of cadets from the Cao Dai and Hoa Hao religious sects and from the private Binh Xuyen army. Our class was designated Class Ten, but some superstitious classmates were unhappy because the number ten was considered unlucky. A French major named Cheviotte commanded the academy and his assistant was Captain Lafayette. Most of the commanders and instructors were French officers or NCOs.

The most exciting moment was when we were allowed to pin the Alpha symbol on our shoulder boards to become full-fledged officer cadets. Our entire class marched up Langbian Hill at an altitude of 6,400 feet to mark the end of this challenging phase of our training. One by one the gold Alpha symbols were pinned on our shoulders by the upperclassmen and our commanders. For those cadets who were Regular Army, a gold dragon was pinned on beside the Alpha symbol to differentiate them from reserve officer cadets.

When we were allowed out on a pass for the first time, I had to make sure my cadet uniform was pressed and starched correctly and that my shoes sparkled. A line of buses took us to the city. It was only fifteen minutes from the academy into town, but it seemed to take forever. When I was a high school student in Saigon, I had heard older friends talk about the "fairies" of Dalat. The girls of Dalat were just as beautiful as everyone had claimed. They had voices like angels, soft and hypnotic, completely different from the haughty girls of Hue with their aristocratic backgrounds. We were all enchanted by the grace and beauty of these fairies of the land of a thousand pines.

As Regular Army cadet officers, we received the salary of a corporal, first class, 2,000 piasters a month. We spent our money rather freely, and the stores and restaurants greeted us warmly. We visited the famed sights of Dalat: the Lake of Sighs, St. Benoit near the academy, the Prenn waterfall, and Cam Ly waterfall with its muddy waters.

I had asked to be assigned to the combat branches, so I was sent to the Commando Training School at Vat Chay in Hon Gay, North Vietnam. We flew to Haiphong, and then sailed up the coast on French navy river gunboats. This was the first time I saw the beautiful scenery of Ha Long Bay, with its countless limestone mountains rising out of a deep blue sea, just as our teacher Luong back in Saigon had described it, a site of wondrous natural beauty, one of the wonders that God had given to Vietnam.

The instructors at Vat Chay were all French commando officers and NCOs who had had a great deal of practical experience. The training was dangerous and demanding. One exercise involved a cable stretched from the top of a high hill to a small tree below. A student was supposed to slide down the cable until almost the end, then would let go and drop into a sandpit. If he let go too soon, he would fall into the trees or into a deep pool of water. If he let go too late, he would smash into the trunk of the tree. He had to remain calm, listen for the sound of the siren, and watch for the signal flag telling him when to let go.

The mountain-climbing class was reserved for students assigned to assault teams. The students had to learn to use ropes to climb to the top of tall rock crags, and then to rappel down quickly and safely.

Quick-reaction marksmanship was one of the more exciting courses, based on the principle that one had to fire at the proper time. If a man were too fast and missed, he died. If he were too slow, he died. If he wanted to live, he had to shoot at the proper moment and pick the right target.

The climate in North Vietnam was harsh. It was winter and the cold cut to the bone. There never was any hot water. In the morning, we brushed our teeth with water that was so cold it hurt our teeth. In the evening, we had to shower in water so cold that a student's "manhood" shrank right out of sight.

Our commando training was over, but before returning to Dalat, I had the opportunity to visit my oldest brother, Tran Van Si, in Hanoi. He was attending the Thu Duc Reserve Officers Training School at Do Son.

* * *

We were glad to be back at our beloved academy in Dalat, but it had changed a great deal during the months we were away because the military and political situation had changed. The academy had expanded, and the number of reserve cadets had skyrocketed. We had to sleep in a long barracks in bunk beds stacked several tiers high. We were in phase three, the final phase of our cadet training.

Our class graduated on July 1, 1954. Four hundred of the 525 cadets were commissioned as active-duty second lieutenants in regular units, forty-two were commissioned as second lieutenants in the paramilitary forces, and the rest were given the ranks of sub-lieutenant, first sergeant, or sergeant, or returned to civilian life.

My brother and I graduated at the same time and had the same period of leave before reporting for duty. Before proceeding to my new unit, I accompanied him to Gia Dinh to visit his future bride, Tran Kim Phung. I knew nothing about his fiancée or her family other than her name. When we reached their home, though, I discovered that she was not the only girl in the house. I caught a glimpse of a young girl helping her mother cook in the kitchen. I heard sounds of giggling behind the door. After dinner, the girl accompanied her mother out into the yard. Realizing that I was interested, my brother led me to her and introduced us to each other. Her name was Lang and she was Phung's younger sister, sixteen years old. She was a lovely girl, indeed. I remembered a line from a classic poem:

What is the point of meeting?
It takes one hundred years to find out if our fates are intertwined.

During occasional visits to the family of my brother's fiancée, my days were filled with joy. Sometimes, Lang would sing me my favorite song, "Love My Country, Love My People," by Pham Duy. My brother and I sometimes joined the two sisters on shopping trips. Lang daintily skipped along the streets of Saigon on the arm of a sunburned young man wearing a shiny officer's uniform. The relationship between Lang and me grew warmer and warmer. I had not yet worked up the courage to tell her how I felt about her, but when I looked into her eyes, I could tell she already knew.

My parents urged my brother to hurry up and get married. They wanted grandchildren to play with in their old age. As for Lang and me, we hoped our siblings would get married soon, so it could be our turn. By ancient tradition, we could not precede our older siblings to the altar. While Lang and I contemplated marriage, momentous things were happening on the political front. A miscalculation by the French military had given the Viet Minh a major victory.

French general Henri Navarre, hoping to draw the Viet Minh guerillas into a conventional battle and destroy them, had set a trap: he had established a garrison in Dien Bien Phu near the Laotian border. The stronghold was in a vulnerable location at the bottom of a bowl-shaped river valley about ten miles long, whose only link to the outside world was an airstrip. It was an attractive lure for the Viet Minh. It was supported by a series of strongpoints on nearby hills to encircle and annihilate any attackers.

When American advisors looked at the terrain, they pointed out that artillery on the hills would have a devastating impact on the planned defense. The French officers answered that they knew their enemy well: "The Viet Minh don't have any artillery. Even if they manage to get some, they wouldn't know how to use them." The garrison had a force of thirteen to sixteen thousand, mostly members of the French Foreign Legion, plus black soldiers from the African colonies and some loyal Vietnamese.

The trap worked, but it was the French who were trapped. General Giap surrounded Dien Bien Phu with fifty thousand Viet Minh soldiers. They dragged disassembled artillery pieces up steeply forested hillsides and assembled them on site. Their assault on March 13, 1954, proved how flawed the French strategy was. The outlying strongpoints were overrun in only a few days. The main garrison was amazed to find itself under heavy, withering artillery fire and its airstrip destroyed. The distraught French artillery commander committed suicide by pulling the safety pin out of a grenade with his teeth. A barrage of Viet Minh antiaircraft fire frustrated resupply and reinforcement attempts by parachute. The parachuted supplies of food and ammunition had to be dropped from higher and higher altitudes and drifted into Viet Minh territory.

There were some claims that the Chinese had committed troops and artillery to this battle. The French tried to get the United States to provide air support; President Eisenhower was receptive at first, but was finally persuaded by Gen. Matthew Ridgway, the Korean War commander, to avoid getting involved in a lost cause.

After fifty-five days of stubborn but futile resistance, and after the death of 2,200 soldiers, the surviving ten thousand defenders surrendered on May 7, 1954. Viet Minh casualties were eight thousand killed and fifteen thousand wounded. For the French, it was a debacle of such magnitude that it spelled the end of the French colony of Indochina. General Vo Nguyen Giap was awarded the newly coined title "The Tiger of Dien Bien Phu."[8]

What the Viet Minh won on the battlefield was lost two months later at the Geneva Conference, where the French played the colonial game of "divide and conquer" even when they were losing the game. They proposed that Vietnam be divided into two halves—a communist north and a non-communist south. The Soviet Union and communist China, instead of backing their Vietnamese ally, accepted the French plan. The two communist powers were playing a game of geopolitics. They wanted to accommodate France in the hope that a grateful French electorate would vote the French Communist party into power during the upcoming elections. They put heavy pressure on the Viet Minh for a compromise peace. The Vietnamese were forced to let the French save face by accepting to divide Vietnam "temporarily" at the 17th parallel until a referendum in 1956. They even agreed that the ten thousand North Vietnamese fighting in the South would return north. These concessions by Ho Chi Minh caused a rebellion in the ranks of the Viet Minh. It took him some time to convince his followers that his allies forced him into this position. The division of the country that was supposed to last two years lasted twenty more years.[9]

In my opinion, the Viet Minh naively believed that the great powers of the Geneva Conference—France, the Soviet Union, China, and the United States—had come to Geneva to reward the Viet Minh for its victory at Dien Bien Phu instead of pursuing their own national interests.

1. France had not yet completely given up on colonialism. It was still trying to see what could be salvaged from its colonial empire under the new "French Union" label.
2. The Soviet Union feared that a Vietnam unified right after Chinese assistance at Dien Bien Phu would make Vietnam a satellite of China.
3. China, with a deep historical memory, preferred a weak, divided Vietnam as neighbor rather than a strong, unified Vietnam competing with China for influence in Southeast Asia.
4. The policymakers of the United States had already developed the "domino theory" that a communist Vietnam would be the first domino in a bunch of dominoes to fall to communism and thus push all of Southeast Asia into the communist camp.

It was because of these views that U.S. Secretary of State John Foster Dulles, backed by President Eisenhower, took a stand against the "disaster" of the Geneva Conference and the weakness of France. Even though it was Vietnam that was penalized by the collusion among France, Russia, and China, an aggrieved Dulles felt that the United States now had a chance to turn history around after the "loss of China." Almost single-handedly, Dulles changed Vietnamese history for the next two decades.

The United States undertook an experiment in nation building, believing that American financial assistance, American administrative know-how, and American military power would make the newly created country a model of capitalism. The idealism of this high-risk gamble left no room for either a thorough study of the magnitude and complexity of the problem or any doubt whether the South Vietnamese society was capable of justifying the anti-communist crusade of John Foster Dulles. The CIA stationed a team in Saigon, headed by Col. Edward Lansdale, to undertake sabotage missions in the North and conduct "psywar" operations against Hanoi, including the hiring of astrologers to predict hard times in the North and good times in the South.[10]

American policymakers overlooked one possibility that might have changed the geopolitical realities of Southeast Asia. Although a devout communist, Ho Chi Minh was also an admirer of the American Revolution. The proclamation of Vietnamese independence, dated September 2, 1945, declared: "All men are created equal. They are endowed by their Creator with certain unalienable rights; among these are life, liberty and the pursuit of happiness." Furthermore, Ho had never hidden from his comrades that his patriotism was superior to his communist ideals.

When the Soviets and the Chinese abandoned their Vietnamese ally at the Geneva Conference of 1954, Ho Chi Minh and the Vietnamese communist hierarchy were so bitterly disappointed that any friendly overtures by the United States would have been welcomed. But American policymakers never tried to drive a wedge between the Vietnamese and their communist overlords. Americans did not try to enroll Ho Chi Minh in the free world in 1954. Considering his aggrieved mentality of that period, such an attempt might have found success!

* * *

Although the French were ready to withdraw from Indochina, increasing American involvement turned the Franco-American friendship into a protracted conflict, while Emperor Bao Dai was attempting to take advantage of the situation for his own benefit. The United States prevailed.

The strongly anti-communist Ngo Dinh Diem, leader of an old court family and son of the grand chamberlain and minister of rites of the Emperor Thanh Thai, returned from self-imposed exile in the West and was appointed prime minister of South Vietnam by Bao Dai with the understanding that he would have total control over all civilian and military matters. Diem was a genuine Vietnamese nationalist. He opposed both communist domination and French colonialism. He was supported by nearly $400 million of American assistance annually. A French journalist snarled: "Diem has that one rare quality so precious in Asia. He is pro-American."[11]

There was a divergence of views about Diem in both Vietnam and the United States. Vietnamese Catholics were overjoyed; they began leaving North Vietnam and eventually nine hundred thousand of them resettled in South Vietnam. Diem's policies did in fact prove to be pro-Catholic and anti-Buddhist, alienating the 70 to 90 percent of the people who followed Buddhism, Confucianism, and Daoism. The Binh Xuyen organized crime syndicate that controlled gambling, opium trafficking, and prostitution, maintaining its own military, opposed Diem. In addition, the heavily armed Cao Dai and Hoa Hao religious sects also opposed the Diem regime.

I believe Diem suffered from excessive pride and a superiority complex. Although he was a good man, he was overly dependent on the gang of protégés and lackeys who surrounded him. He became famous for the successes he had when he first returned to Vietnam, but those successes were primarily the result of the resolute support he received from the United States, plus the enthusiastic support of political factions. Another contributing factor was that the military situation quieted down after the Geneva Agreement as Hanoi was busy consolidating its regime in the North and reorganizing its infrastructure in the South.

After Diem consolidated his authority, he became nepotistic. He removed many of those who had supported him. His National Revolutionary movement and his Can Lao party were founded in 1956 and run by his brother Ngo Dinh Nhu. His younger brother, Ngo Dinh Can, was put in charge of the Imperial City of Hue. Another brother, Ngo Dinh Luyen, was appointed ambassador to the United Kingdom and also put in charge of the Cham minority. His older brother, Ngo Dinh Thuc, was a Catholic archbishop aspiring to become a cardinal. Because Diem was a bachelor, his sister-in-law, Madame Nhu, became effectively South Vietnam's first lady. Political figures and generals who sought power and promotion had to become Catholics and join the government's own political party.

Meanwhile, back in the United States, the joint chiefs of staff thought it was "hopeless" to train a South Vietnamese army without a "reasonably strong, stable civil government in control." Defense Secretary Charles E. Wilson urged the United States to get out of Vietnam as "completely and as soon as possible," warning that he could see "nothing but grief in store for us if we remain in that area." The U.S. National Security Council, on the other hand, wanted to "make every possible effort . . . to maintain a friendly non-communist South Vietnam."

Ho Chi Minh and the Hanoi government remained committed to the reunification of the country under communist rule. The United States now replaced France as the main obstacle to their aims. They would therefore change tactics to meet the new challenge, without changing their protracted guerilla war strategy. One of their officials explained: "Americans do not like long, inconclusive wars—and this is going to be a long, inconclusive war. Thus, we are sure to win in the end."

Ultimately, official numbers of military losses for South Vietnam would rise to 224,000 killed and 1 million wounded. The Viet Cong and North Vietnam's casualties totaled 1 million dead and 600,000 wounded. The United States suffered 58,000 dead and 300,000 wounded. Ten million South Vietnamese were to become refugees.

3

Early Assignments

THE BRAND NEW military career of 2nd Lt. Tran Van Nhut began in 1954 in the brand new country of South Vietnam, a country trying to become part of the free world while being threatened by the communist dictatorship of North Vietnam.

Both Vietnams were freeing themselves from French colonialism. In North Vietnam, the French army was a vanquished army, being evicted. In South Vietnam, the departure of the French was more civilized; they were being replaced gradually as the corresponding officers of the South Vietnamese army became able to replace them. Meanwhile the French were dumping on South Vietnam all the obsolete armament they did not want to ship back to France. As the French were disappearing, the American presence was light. It was felt indirectly, mostly by equipment being used. For instance, the French MAS-36 rifle, weighing 7.7 pounds, was replaced by the U.S. M-1 Garand rifle, which was longer and weighed 9 pounds.

A dictatorship headed by Ho Chi Minh ruled North Vietnam. Emperor Bao Dai and Prime Minister Ngo Dinh Diem ruled South Vietnam. Everybody knew that Bao Dai's star was fading and Diem was the rising star of South Vietnam's pro-American future.

At this time, a major problem facing South Vietnam was the influx of nearly 1 million Catholic refugees who had left their homes in North Vietnam to come south. The North Vietnamese government was pursuing a policy of discrimination against Catholics, while the Diem government of South Vietnam favored Catholics in military promotions and tax concessions. The people of South Vietnam worked feverishly for the reception of this huge number of refugees and their dispersal to every province in the South, particularly the Saigon area.

* * *

When my graduation leave was over, I reported to the Military Region One headquarters. They ordered me to go to Trang Bang and report to the 68th Vietnamese Battalion. The battalion commander was Maj. Nguyen Van Nho, whose name suited him perfectly. *Nho* means little, and he was a rather short and pleasant armored branch officer. He was the son-in-law of Gen. Bay Vien, commander of the Binh Xuyen organized crime syndicate, which controlled a private army of forty thousand soldiers. The general was initially allied with the Viet Minh but switched loyalties to provide military and political support to the French in exchange for government protection of Binh Xuyen's illegal activities.

After signing into the battalion, I was ordered to report to 1st Lt. Thach Khay in Tay Ninh, commander of 1st Company. I was appointed deputy commander of 1st Company.

Before I had a chance to become acquainted with the company's soldiers, we were sent to conduct an operation in the area of Nui Ba Den (Black Lady Mountain). During that operation, my company had a firefight with forces loyal to Trinh Minh The's breakaway faction of the Cao Dai army.

This action was the first battle of my military career. My youth and inexperience made me an enthusiastic participant in the battle. Even though I had no combat experience, I used my commando training and led a platoon in an attack on defensive positions held by The's troops. Due in somewhat equal parts to sheer luck, youthful enthusiasm, and the enemy's weak defenses, we captured a number of enemy base camps with little difficulty. A number of Colonel The's soldiers were killed, and we captured some weapons. Colonel The later surrendered to the Diem government and was subsequently promoted to major general; he was killed in a battle with the Binh Xuyen and was promoted to lieutenant general posthumously.

My first military success was marked by a solemn military ceremony during which the chief of the joint general staff, Lt. Gen. Nguyen Van Hinh, pinned the Bronze Star for Heroism on my chest.

General Hinh's wife, a Frenchwoman, was the official sponsor of the 68th Vietnamese Battalion. Afterward, General Hinh frequently visited our battalion in an effort to "purchase" our loyalty and support. He himself was supporting Binh Xuyen commander general Bay Vien, who was using the police and the secret service to control Binh Khang village, which was notorious for prostitution and the International Casino. A short time later, Hinh departed for France, where he joined the French air force as a general, eventually becoming its deputy commander. He died in Paris in 2004.

Saigon had insufficient administrative personnel, cadre, and policemen to oversee the resettlement of the Catholic refugees from the North. The 68th Vietnamese Battalion was brought down from Tay Ninh to help the refugees, who were temporarily quartered hastily in a camp at the Phu Tho racetrack. We were assigned to maintain law and order, put up tents, dig latrines, and provide plumbing and electricity for the camp. After completing our mission, we returned to battalion headquarters at the citadel, which had just been turned over to Vietnam by the French army.

The political situation in South Vietnam was becoming unsettled. The religious and paramilitary factions were resisting Diem, who frequently visited units of the Vietnamese army and sought their support in isolating the armed factions. He came to visit the 68th Battalion and used this opportunity to meet the leader of Cao Dai, Pham Cong Tac. I was assigned to escort the prime minister and the Cao Dai pope to the top level of the citadel, where a number of gun positions had been constructed for observation and defense. Unfortunately, some soldiers had been too lazy to go the latrine; the smell of their urine was so strong that it made the two leaders and their entourage ill. Company Commander Thach Khay received a reprimand for this episode, and the meeting did not produce any results. The religious factions came out openly in opposition to the Diem government, and later the Cao Dai pope fled to Cambodia.

The Binh Xuyen army, after a failed attack on Saigon, retreated into the Rung Sat, a desolate jungle swamp southeast of Saigon. The 68th Battalion was ordered to conduct an operation in the area of Thi Vai Mountain in Phuoc Tuy province. We had only a few minor encounters with some Binh Xuyen remnants and did not inflict significant losses on them, but we easily captured a number of their outposts along Route 15.

In the middle of this operation, I received orders to report to the headquarters of the newly formed South Vietnamese marine corps, commanded by Lt. Col. Le Quang Trong. Three days later, I left for Nha Trang with orders to report to the newly formed 1st Marine Battalion, whose commander was the French captain Delayen. After Dien Bien Phu and after withdrawal from the North, many of our units were still commanded by French officers because we did not have enough officers to take their positions. Captain Delayen later became a lieutenant general and commanded all French army forces in the nation of Chad in Africa.

When he saw I was wearing the patch of North Vietnam Commandos, Captain Delayen immediately gave me command of the company-sized Corps Franc (force reconnaissance unit) replacing First Lieutenant Delanurien. The unit was directly subordinate to the new marine corps headquarters in Saigon, not to the 1st Marine Battalion. The primary mission of the force reconnaissance unit was to launch small-unit operations, using small boats to infiltrate into enemy territory and conduct reconnaissance and sabotage missions behind enemy lines.

The 1st Marine Battalion was a composite unit formed by combining together a number of commando companies that had been evacuated to South Vietnam following the signing of the Geneva peace agreement. The majority of the battalion's soldiers were members of the Nung ethnic minority tribe from North Vietnam. Life in Nha Trang was hard for the troops during the battalion's initial formation period. The soldiers and their families lived packed together in small thatch huts with sand floors and bamboo walls that had just been built in between the air force and navy training centers. Both of these centers had clean, elegant barracks and headquarters areas equipped with all the amenities.

In the process of the Vietnamization of the army, French commanders were, one by one, relinquishing command to Vietnamese officers. Captain Bui Pho Chi, Captain Delayen's deputy, moved up to take over as commander of the 1st Marine Battalion. Captain Delayen became an advisor to the battalion, together with Capt. James T. Breckinridge of the U.S. Marines, a member of TRIM (Training Relations and Instruction Mission). The TRIM team, established in February 1955, was part of the Franco-American effort to reorganize and train the South Vietnamese army. The program was initially commanded by French general Paul Eli, but was eventually turned over to the U.S. armed forces as part of the American nation-building program.

Captain Breckinridge was the first of many U.S. military advisors I had the privilege of working with during my twenty-one-year career. The American advisors sent to Vietnam were, as a group, extremely competent and dedicated. In my opinion, they represented the backbone of the armed forces of the United States and rated an overall A+ in performance.

* * *

Meanwhile, the situation in the Mekong Delta was heating up. Paramilitary forces loyal to the Hoa Hao faction were sweeping across the southern provinces under the command of Col. Le Quang Vinh, nicknamed Ba Cut (Three Finger) because he was the third child in his family and had had a finger amputated. The Hoa Hao, a Buddhist sect founded in 1939 by Huynh Phu So, with a private army equipped by the French, was now mounting a challenge against the Diem regime.

The 1st Marine Battalion, including my force reconnaissance unit, was sent to the Mekong Delta in the Dinh Tien Hoang Campaign, commanded by Col. Duong Van Duc, to destroy Ba Cut's forces.

Our battalion landed northwest of the Rach Gia province capital. My force reconnaissance unit was transported by Vietnamese navy LCU (landing craft, utility) to Son Rai Island, in the Gulf of Thailand, still inside Vietnam's territorial waters. This extraordinarily beautiful island was 2 miles long and 1.3 miles wide, surrounded by wonderful beaches of fine, white sand. It had an abundant supply of fresh water, from wells dug just twenty yards from the shoreline. The eastern side of the island was bordered by lines of coconut trees, leaning out and casting their shadows over the gentle surf along the beach. Several small, green mountain peaks could be seen against the horizon. It was a truly beautiful sight.

The residents of the island were fishermen. The waters were rich in fish and shrimp, and these shrimp were what made the Phu Quoc brand of fish sauce famous. The citizens of Rach Gia came here to fish. Every day motorized sampans transported bushels of fresh fish from Son Rai to Rach Gia. Son Rai was also known as Tamasu Island, a name that had been given to the island by the Japanese during World War II.

According to local tradition, when Prince Nguyen Anh was defeated in battle in the eighteenth century, he retreated to Son Rai. The island's otters kept him alive by offering him fish they had caught in the ocean. When he became emperor in 1802, Nguyen Anh named the island Son Rai (Otter Mountain).

Prime Minister Ngo Dinh Diem made an official visit to Son Rai Island. We provided security to our nation's leader because he had only recently taken power and had not yet formed his own security unit. The 1st Marine Battalion was one of the "refugee" units loyal to him.

The individual who greeted the prime minister on his arrival to the island was Maj. Lam Quang Phong, a former Viet Minh regimental commander who had refused to return north as required by the Geneva agreement. The people of Rach Gia and Son Rai held Major Phong in high regard and addressed him as Brother Tu, his old alias from the Viet Minh days. I kept in touch with him on several occasions, appreciated his perspective as a veteran Viet Minh soldier, and learned many valuable lessons from him. We later became as close as brothers, and the lessons I learned from him helped me a great deal when I had to conduct operations in the muddy rice fields and swamps of the Fourth Tactical Zone (IV Corps).

The Dinh Tien Hoang Campaign successfully eliminated the Ba Cut forces of the Hoa Hao armed bands opposed to the Diem regime. The 1st Marine Battalion and my force reconnaissance unit returned to our home base at Nha Trang to rest and regroup. But not for long. We were soon sent back south to participate in the Hoang Dieu Campaign to destroy the remnants of the Binh Xuyen forces.

The operation began when two marine river assault craft companies landed 1st Marine Battalion in the swamps of the Rung Sat, southeast of Saigon along the river to Vung Tau. The river assault companies, commanded by Capt. Nguyen Kien Hung, were composed of a number of landing craft, gunboats, and French torpedo boats. They were able to operate effectively in the dense thickets and heavy vegetation of the streams flowing through the Rung Sat low jungle area.

The Rung Sat was the main lair of the Binh Xuyen. The terrain was treacherous because it was a mangrove forest, a swamp with thick vegetation and water as high as a man's waist. Infantry could operate there only when the tide was out and the water level was low. When the tide came in, troops had to find a place of refuge. If we had time, we cut down mangrove trees to provide a place to rest. If we did not have time, we just climbed up into the mangrove branches and slept there like monkeys. The enemy could easily have ambushed us and blocked our advance at the twists and curves in the streams flowing through the forest.

The Binh Xuyen troops, however, were not professional soldiers. Most of them had no combat experience. They were not accustomed to adversity. Most of them had been "parade ground" soldiers who bribed their commanders and showed up only for parades and inspections. They were not combat soldiers like the soldiers of the Vietnamese National Army, like the 1st Marine Battalion, or like my force reconnaissance unit. Most of them brought their wives and children with them when they retreated into the Rung Sat, with its swamps, mud, and mosquitoes. When the tide came in, they, like us, had to hide in the trees like monkeys. There was no fresh water, and they did not make cooking fires for fear of giving away their positions. They lived under constant threat from our harassing artillery fire. Therefore, it was not long before they began to surrender, one by one.

Lieutenant Colonel Le Quang Trong, the commander of the Marine Corps, pulled my force reconnaissance unit back and stationed us at An Thit base, the former headquarters of the Binh Xuyen forces, to protect the marine headquarters. He sent for me one morning. When I entered his office, I noticed that Maj. Pham Van Lieu, chief of staff of the Marine Corps, was sitting next to him. Lieutenant Colonel Trong ordered me to select twenty of my most trustworthy men for a special mission. Each man was to carry an empty pack. Our mission was to recover money the Binh Xuyen had hidden in the jungles of the Rung Sat. He ordered that when we found the money, we were to place it in the empty packs we carried. Each man would be allowed to keep a few bills for himself, and each man would also receive a separate reward afterward. He emphasized that I must maintain control of my men and make sure that they did not become so greedy as to start shooting one another, as had happened to other units.

This was a truly unexpected and interesting mission. In keeping with the strict discipline of the force reconnaissance unit, none of the soldiers asked me where we were going or what we were going to do. I ordered them to eat an early breakfast, pack a meal of cooked rice for the trip, and each carry an empty pack. Early the next morning, Lieutenant Colonel Trong and I, together with the twenty handpicked soldiers, boarded two river assault boats and sailed into the Rung Sat. The two riverboats wove their way through the trees and bushes, pushing ever deeper into the swamp. When we reached the head of a stream, the tide was out and the water was shallow.

Lieutenant Colonel Trong and I jumped into the waters of a large stream that emptied into the Long Tao River. After verifying the location, I ordered the twenty soldiers to spread out in a line and move up the stream from the mouth and pass one, two, three, and then four smaller streams that fed into it. Because the tide was out, it was easy to locate the smaller streams. We waded back and forth four times but found nothing. My men were becoming discouraged. To keep them interested, I told them exactly what we were looking for. When they heard what our mission was, they perked up immediately. We made several more sweeps but still found nothing. With darkness approaching, Lieutenant Colonel Trong gave up hope and ordered the troops to board the riverboats and return to base.

The next day my force reconnaissance unit was ordered to set up perimeter security around the area we had searched the day before. We were informed that Col. Duong Van Minh had ordered Maj. Nguyen Van Nho, the son-in-law of Binh Xuyen commander general Bay Vien, to lead us to the money cached in these swamps. Trong and Nho were close friends and classmates. Trong wanted to get to the money before anyone else did. Colonel Minh now ordered Major Nho to lead us to where the money was hidden. Without even looking at the map, and after wading past the four streams we had searched the previous day, Major Nho continued for another two hundred yards. There we found another stream that was not on the map. Major Nho soon located several dozen steel boxes, each with a capacity of fifty gallons, sealed in green nylon bags. When he opened the crates, he pulled out an enormous quantity of Vietnamese 100 piaster notes, folded into quarters, small and crisp, as was the custom at the International Casino and the other casinos in Cho Lon and Saigon.

Colonel Minh ordered the soldiers to take the money out of the boxes, place it in large canvas sacks, and load it aboard the riverboats for transport back to campaign headquarters. After we returned to our base, my soldiers talked about how they had each kept a little money for themselves. They wanted to share it with me, but I thanked them and told them to keep it all for their families. I said I was still single and did not need the money as much as they did.

* * *

October 23, 1955, was an important day for the Diem regime and marked a turning point in the short history of South Vietnam. A referendum was held on that day on whether South Vietnam was to turn into a republic. Observers said that fraud was obvious. Diem's troops guarded the polls, and those who attempted to vote for the Emperor were assaulted. In Saigon, Diem claimed more votes than there were registered voters in the entire area.

Diem, backed by the United States, forced former Emperor Bao Dai out of the political arena, bringing an end to the Nguyen dynasty. The First Republic was born. South Vietnam had a new political structure. In place of the monarchy, the nation now had a republican form of government.

While claiming victory, Diem, still prime minister, came to visit the marine headquarters at the An Thit base to reward us for our performance during the campaign. We had to stand at attention for hours with our uniforms soaking wet from the heavy downpour of a late autumn rain. Diem pinned the Gallantry Cross with Palm on my breast and shook my hand.

On October 26, 1955, Diem became president of the Republic of Vietnam. The Vietnamese National Army became the Army of the Republic of Vietnam (ARVN). Bao Dai was deposed and continued to live as an exile in France until his death.

On the same date, one year and five months after my graduation from the Dalat Military Academy and before my twentieth birthday, I received a battlefield promotion to the rank of first lieutenant. When a magnificent parade was held in Saigon to celebrate Maj. Gen. Duong Van Minh's victory in the Rung Sat campaign, I led my Marine force reconnaissance unit. As we marched past the National Assembly building, I saw Lang standing in the front row watching me and waving at me as her face glowed with affection and pride.

The military situation quieted down, temporarily at least, during the initial days of the First Republic. South Vietnam worked feverishly to establish itself. The army played an important role in the efforts to draw the boundaries of authority of the infant South Vietnamese government. The soldiers and civilians of the nation were determined to develop and defend the southern half of the S-shaped nation of Vietnam, exhausted after years of constant warfare.

The army was modernized in accordance with a new strategy. A plan to reorganize the armed forces from an administrative form of organization into a combat organization was vigorously implemented with support from the United States. I moved up to become commander of 1st Company and concurrently deputy battalion commander when the force reconnaissance unit was transformed into 1st Company, 1st Marine Battalion.

Beginning in 1955, when France turned the Paracel Islands over to us, once every three months my 1st Marine Battalion sent one company out on a rotational assignment to guard one of the Islands, where we had an early weather warning station. Because the island had a pool of fresh water, communist Chinese fishing boats would occasionally anchor at the island to barter with our marines for fresh water.

In 1956, Ngo Dinh Diem announced that the elections called for in the Geneva accords would not be held. The Vietnamese of the South had not signed the accords; only France and the Viet Minh had signed the agreement, so Diem did not have to honor it. In fact, however, Diem and the Americans knew that the communist infrastructure in South Vietnam was so strong that Ho Chi Minh, not Diem, would be elected if elections were held. Furthermore, the North Vietnamese had agreed in Geneva to withdraw their ten thousand fighters from the South, but never did. Thus, when the United States and Diem did not allow elections and North Vietnam did not withdraw its fighters from the South, both sides were violating the Geneva accords.

During this time, I continued to serve as a company commander in the marines. Meanwhile, American advisors helped to reorganize and train our army, navy, and air force. On the personal level, after waiting impatiently for three long years, the most important day in our lives finally arrived; Lang and I got married on November 27, 1957. The groom was twenty-two and the bride just nineteen.

* * *

The new South Vietnam and its American advisors had some ambitious programs for the advancement of Vietnamese officers. In 1956, I attended the air support course on Okinawa. More important, though, I was sent to Quantico, Virginia, in mid-1958 to attend the U.S. Marine basic officers' course. The goal of the marines' basic school program was to train young ROTC students to become platoon leaders, although I was already a first lieutenant. It was a big advantage for me that my roommate, Lovejoy, was an ROTC candidate; he helped me improve my English and learn about American traditions.

The training program was basically the same as the Vietnamese, except that the U.S. Marine facilities were better organized, very well equipped, and much superior to the Vietnamese in firepower and mobility—helicopters, airplanes, tanks, artillery, and naval vessels. Furthermore, the tactics of conventional warfare taught at Quantico were completely different from the Vietnamese courses.

But that memorable year in the United States went further than the military aspects of my training. I thought Vietnam was at a crossroad in 1958, and my visit to the United States would help me decide if a future tied to the United States was the right road for my country to follow.

For most of my twenty-three years, I had lived within a French colonial system based on French values called *la civilisation française.* Dien Bien Phu had put an end to the myth of French civilization. It had become certain that Vietnam would not and should not continue to imitate the French logic of being receptive to all kinds of ideas. This mentality had weakened France and French politics for the decades before and after World War II. It was not a good road for Vietnam to follow.

The crossroad of 1958 was a choice between a path to the left—the communism of the Viet Minh, or to the right—the capitalism of the United States.

I saw communism as an illusion that some dictators insisted was the wave of the future. The Soviet people were starving, but Nikita Khrushchev wanted us to see only the results of their space program and their Sputnik satellite in the sky. The Chinese were starving, but Mao Tse Tung wanted us to see it as the "great leap forward." North Vietnam was starving, but Ho Chi Minh wanted us to see only his determination to unite the two Vietnams and to become the dominant power in Indochina and Southeast Asia. But I wondered: Was I right in thinking that South Vietnam would be better off as part of the free world led by the United States? With nearly a year at my disposal, living in Virginia, a typical American state, I was going to find out.

There was no doubt that the United States was in fact a wealthy country. Its people were so used to its wealth that they took it for granted. An American would walk to the sink, turn on the hot water faucet, and get hot water. It did not occur to him that constantly available hot water was an unusual event in the rest of the world. Electric lights and electric signs were on all the time; nobody thought that this was a waste of money.

For somebody like me, born in the colonial world, the superior attitude of the English or the French was to be expected. It was such a relief to be treated as an equal by all the Americans I dealt with. There was no condescension.

I was surprised to visit a town of fifty thousand inhabitants and learn that it had fifty churches. Americans did not seem to be as devout Christians as the French, and yet I realized soon that they were better Christians.

Another thing that impressed me was the general truthfulness of Americans. There is lying in all societies, but the level of lying in America was much lower than in the East. People gave me honest answers to my questions, and life became easier because they did not have to remember how they had misled you. Because of this truthful atmosphere, honesty was more prevalent. It was assumed that a person was innocent until proven guilty. Therefore, life in general was full of trust. When I was asked to pay a dollar for something, I automatically paid a dollar; I did not question its value.

It seemed that everybody in the United States was well educated, even when I knew that this was not possible. Their intelligence level was high, their reasoning was solid, their arguments logical, with no need to become shrill. Naturally, there was some poverty, there were some disadvantaged people, but I had no doubt that the majority of the people belonged solidly to the middle classes.

As would be expected from the economical and industrial giant of the world, Americans were highly competitive. But they had reached such a level of abundance that they did not need to suck the blood out of every underdeveloped country to become even wealthier. They had developed an American set of values, an American set of priorities, which did not aim to take advantage of poor countries like Vietnam. On the contrary, they constantly asked themselves what they could do to make the world a better place for its entire population to live in.

I was impressed! I went to Virginia believing that South Vietnam would be better off as part of the free world led by the United States. I left Virginia *convinced* that all Vietnam, North and South, would be better off as part of the free world led by the United States.

* * *

In 1960, I was promoted to captain and appointed commander of the 1st Marine Battalion, a typical marine battalion, which had a table of organizational strength of more than one thousand men and would likely go into battle with about eight hundred men.

By this time, the United States had become the main obstacle to Ho Chi Minh's aims. He, therefore, had to change his strategy to meet the new challenge. He created a hydra-headed monster called the NLF (National Liberation Front), better known as the Viet Cong (Vietnamese communists). American generals were to learn to their chagrin that after every search-and-destroy mission, after every "body count" of dead Viet Cong, two new volunteers replaced each dead one.[12]

In early 1961, I was sent to attend the marine command and staff course at Quantico. Captain Nguyen Ba Lien replaced me as battalion commander. I returned in mid-1962 and took back my position when Captain Lien was injured in a traffic accident.

In the United States, I noticed a change in the mentality of American youth from what I had seen only three years earlier. Their search for freedom of thought had gone to such extremes that it had turned into anarchy. They had turned against the American values of their parents, claiming that Castro represented the wave of the future and that Che Guevera would soon turn South America into a new continent. What was equally surprising was that most of the parents agreed with their children. Furthermore, the new generation claimed that the older generation was addicted to cigarettes. The new mentality was that tobacco was harmful to people's health and should be replaced by marijuana.

On the other hand, I was well impressed with the idealism expressed by President Kennedy, particularly the unforgettable line of his inaugural address: "Ask not what your country can do for you. Ask what you can do for your country." His concept had such a strong influence on me and remained with me for such a long time that I decided to use it in 1975 to remind my soldiers of their responsibility to South Vietnam. I translated it into Vietnamese, had it painted as a sign, and displayed it in front of my ARVN 2nd Division Training Center in Chu Lai.

* * *

The North Vietnamese communists resumed their aggression against South Vietnam, claiming that the conflict was a popular uprising of the South Vietnamese masses opposed to Diem's dictatorial regime. Military clashes between communist and ARVN forces at the platoon, company, and even the battalion level broke out throughout the country. After the communists overran and captured Phuoc Thanh province, the fighting became particularly intense.

In 1959, President Diem instituted the Agroville program based on a similar program by the British to suppress an insurgency in Malaya. Its aim was to separate the Viet Cong "fish" from the "ponds" of the rural population. To separate the people from the Viet Cong and to prevent them from providing assistance and supplies to the Viet Cong, Diem ordered the relocation of peasants of rural communities into large Agroville communities, controlled and protected by the government.

By 1961, when there were twenty-three Agrovilles, it was reformed into the strategic hamlet program, but failed to achieve the desired results. I believe the concept was successful in Malaya because the majority of the population lived in concentrated areas on the rubber plantations. In Vietnam, it was only successful in the land reclamation plan, the objective of which was to resettle a large number of refugees who had fled south after the 1954 Geneva agreement.

For the people already in the South, the strategy should have been more carefully studied and researched before forcing people to abandon their ancestral homes, ancestral tombs, and livestock and move to resettlement areas far from their fields and gardens, without adequate supplies or fresh water, making them convenient targets for Viet Cong shelling and ground attacks. Furthermore, the strategic hamlets were built in haste, with emphasis on outward appearance only because the local governments were simply trying to reach the goals set by Saigon. In the end, the strategic hamlet program backfired and led to a decrease in support for the Diem regime.

As the Viet Cong became more active, there were disagreements about how to defend South Vietnam. This situation planted seeds of military and political dissension in the country. The Caravelle group of political and military figures spoke out in opposition to the oligarchy that Diem's government had become, laying the groundwork for a failed coup attempt in late 1960.

The shots fired during that coup should have served as a warning to Diem and his family to amend their methods of governing the nation. It was hoped that President Diem would wake up and change his leadership style. He did not.

* * *

South Vietnam had grown to fifth among recipients of American foreign aid. The U.S. mission in Saigon was the largest in the world. President Kennedy dispatched his military advisor, Gen. Maxwell Taylor, to Vietnam to assess conditions and recommend a new course of action. Taylor's report was pessimistic. He found the ARVN in a defensive outlook and the Diem government disorganized and inefficient. He thought there was a crisis of confidence that demanded urgent measures.

Taylor had already provided the Kennedy administration with a new strategy in the conduct of armed conflict against communist expansionism. As the Soviet Union's nuclear arsenal grew in the 1950s, Taylor reached the conclusion that Eisenhower's "massive retaliation" could not be invoked for low-intensity wars like the insurgency in Vietnam. He convinced President Kennedy to adopt instead a "flexible response" strategy to meet a wide range of threats from nuclear war to guerilla insurgencies.

In my opinion, the "flexible response" strategy, later called the "limited war" strategy by U.S. Secretary of Defense Robert McNamara, was flawed. It was in fact a "no win" strategy.

President Kennedy was receiving conflicting advice about Vietnam from General Taylor and other advisors, from the Defense and State departments, and from the National Security Council. He finally decided that sending sixteen thousand military advisors to Vietnam would be a temporary solution to the problem. This number included a contingent of four hundred Green Berets who were to teach the South Vietnamese how to fight a counterinsurgency war against the Viet Cong. Simultaneously, the United States initiated MACV (Military Assistance Command, Vietnam), headed by Gen. Paul D. Harkins, and supplied it with armored personnel carriers and three hundred military aircraft.

The situation did not improve though but became worse. In January 1963, in the village of Ap Bac in the Mekong Delta, a contingent of 350 Viet Cong defeated the poorly led ARVN 7th Division of ten thousand. The Viet Cong commander expected to be crushed and wrote in his diary: "Better to fight and die than run and be slaughtered."[13]

But the ARVN, to the dismay of their American advisor, Lt. Col. John Paul Vann, did everything wrong until five helicopters had been downed, then moved their armored vehicles slowly and separately, making them easy targets. Then they hesitated until dusk when it became difficult to distinguish friend from foe and found themselves shooting at each other in confusion. Three American helicopter crew members and sixty-one ARVN soldiers were killed and a hundred wounded. The Viet Cong evaporated into the darkness, leaving three bodies behind.

The Buddhist crisis became a major problem for the government when Bishop Ngo Dinh Thuc, Diem's older brother, ordered the police to lower the Buddhist flags flying on Buddha's birthday. The Buddhists accused the Diem regime of discrimination and the government responded with mass arrests and raids on Buddhist temples. Some monks decided to set themselves on fire and die in protest. They wanted the world to be aware of their plight, so the members of the foreign media were invited to "a protest meeting" whenever a monk was about to sacrifice himself by fiery suicide. The worldwide distribution of television pictures of monks immolating themselves became a powerful anti-Diem propaganda spectacle.[14]

It seemed, however, that Diem's strengths and weaknesses were in the eye of the beholder. Kennedy sent two officials on a fact-finding mission to Saigon. General Victor Krulak of the Defense Department advised the president that the war could be won if the United States firmly supported Diem. Joseph Mendenhall of the State Department reported a virtual breakdown of the civil government and warned that there was no chance of defeating the guerillas unless, at a minimum, Diem's brother Nhu withdrew or was removed from the government.

"You two did visit the same country, didn't you?" asked the bewildered president.

Eventually, Kennedy sided with the State Department and authorized the American ambassador in Saigon to arrange a coup d'etat. It should be pointed out that the Kennedy administration and the American public were affected by the extremely negative reporting of the U.S. news media about Ngo Dinh Diem, Ngo Dinh Nhu, and Madame Nhu.

4

Participating in the Coup of November 1, 1963

ONE AFTERNOON in early October 1963, Maj. Nguyen Ba Lien visited me at my battalion headquarters. He raised the question of a coup against President Ngo Dinh Diem and asked if I would be willing to participate. I was hesitant because this was an extremely important and dangerous decision. I had heard rumors of an impending coup, but this was not a decision I could make on the spur of the moment.

I thought long and hard and considered seriously all the pro and con arguments for such a move. The political situation had in fact reached the final stages of dissatisfaction. Something had to be done to rescue our sinking ship of state. In the last few weeks, there had been daily demonstrations by students and Buddhists in the streets of Saigon and in a number of cities and province capitals. I finally decided to participate.

After each military operation, my 1st Marine Battalion was recalled to Saigon to help maintain security and to stop the demonstrations and street riots. We had set up our battalion headquarters in the museum next to the entrance to the city zoo. The building had telephones, making it easier for me to contact my units. It was easy for us to move our troops and dispatch reaction forces from this location because we did not have to cross the Thi Nghe bridge and the main highway bridge. I had stationed one squad in every high school in the city.

One day, while visiting one of my units stationed at a high school in Tan Dinh, a young female student spat at my feet. This incident showed me the depth of the people's anger toward Diem. At the academy, we had been taught: "The army was formed by the people, to serve the people." I told myself that I had to do something to avoid being forced to betray the people.

That night, I stepped out into the hallway. Looking at the sleeping faces of the officers and men of the headquarters staff as they lay on the concrete floor of the museum, my stomach tightened. For more than eight years, we had shared hardship and adversity together. We had faced life and death side by side on the battlefield in the fight against the enemy, from the swamps of Ca Mau to the arid Quang Tri; in the remote passes and mountains of Ban Me Thuot, Pleiku, Kontum, Ara Salour, and Ba To; in the jungles of War Zone D and the Duong Minh Chau base area; and on the tiny islands of the Paracels, Phu Quoc, and Ly Son. Today or tomorrow or the next day, I would lead them into a new battle, a battle they had never anticipated, a battle against their supreme commander, against their own president. It was so sad, but one must choose decisively when faced with a difficult choice in a historic moment.

Why did I continue to ponder this decision? Was I justified in being wary? Nguyen Ba Lien was one of the officers with whom I had had a close friendship and the man I respected the most. When I was executive officer of the 1st Marine Battalion in Nha Trang, he was the battalion S-3. We had exchanged command of the 1st Marine Battalion several times. He had replaced me when I attended the Marine Command and Staff College in the United States. We had no reason to be suspicious of each other, but he was the nephew of Col. Do Mau, President Diem's "favorite," serving as director of the Military Security Service.

My lingering suspicions vanished two days later when Lien, accompanied by Capt. Nguyen Phuc Que, chief medical officer of the Marine

Brigade, came to tell me that Col. Do Mau had joined the coup. The colonel had established close contacts with generals Tran Van Don, Le Van Kim, Ton That Dinh, Duong Van Minh, and Tran Thien Khiem, chief architects of the plot against Diem.

During this period, the chief of the joint general staff, Gen. Le Van Ty, was undergoing medical treatment in the United States. Lieutenant General Tran Van Don was serving concurrently as army commander and as chief of the joint general staff. General Khiem was chief of staff of the joint general staff. Taking advantage of this fortuitous circumstance to facilitate preparations for the coup and, using as its excuse the deteriorating military situation, the joint general staff asked the president to place 7th Infantry Division from IV Corps under the command of the III Corps, which was commanded by Maj. Gen. Ton That Dinh. General Dinh was a trusted follower of Diem (and overall military chief of the Can Lao Party), so the request was quickly approved. Dinh was an important man in the coup. He was the commander of the forces in the Saigon area and also the commander of the capital military district.

Three days before the coup, Col. Nguyen Huu Co was sent down to Dinh Tuong province to replace Col. Bui Dinh Dam as 7th Division commander. Bui Dinh Dam had been commander when the 7th Division forces were defeated at Ap Bac; he was also one of Diem's supporters. Colonel Co was to block the road north of My Thuan ferry to prevent Gen. Huynh Van Cao, IV Corps commander and a Diem man, from sending forces to save Diem.

Nguyen Ba Lien suggested that I try to recruit Capt. Le Hang Minh, commander of the 4th Marine Battalion, to join the coup. Minh was an old schoolmate of mine from Huynh Khuong Ninh high school. He had served as S-5 of 1st Marine Battalion while I was the battalion's executive officer. No one ever suggested contacting the 2nd or 3rd Marine Battalions. Captain Nguyen Thanh Yen, the 2nd Marine Battalion commander, was an older officer and very experienced, but he was a heavy drinker. Everyone was afraid he would disclose our secret while he was drunk. As for the 3rd Marine Battalion commander,

Capt. Ma Viet Bang, he was a member of Diem's Can Lao party, so we could not trust him.

In the end, only the 1st and 4th Marine Battalions participated in the coup. To avoid the watchful eyes of Ngo Dinh Nhu's henchmen and spies, when we wished to exchange information or assess the situation, we usually did so in my own personal automobile as I drove Lien and Que around Saigon.

By early October 1963 we had completed work on our plan. We intended to make our move on National Day, October 26. On this holiday, my 1st Marine Battalion would march in a parade past a reviewing stand on which President Diem would be standing. I, as battalion commander, 1st Lt. Le Ngoc Chau, my 3rd Company commander, and twenty trusted marines would fire our weapons to threaten and overpower Diem's bodyguards and the military police teams maintaining security on the reviewing stand. We would take President Ngo Dinh Diem and his brother, Ngo Dinh Nhu, prisoner and force them to dissolve the government. Ordinarily, all weapons had to be checked before any parade. Since the 1960 coup attempt by elements of the airborne brigade, however, when the marines intervened and rescued Diem, he trusted the marines more than any of his other forces. As a result, the Military Security Service allowed each marine unit commander to inspect his own unit's weapons before a parade. This provided an excellent opportunity for my unit to overpower the president's bodyguards. All arrangements had been made to carry out this plan, but in the end we were unable to execute it.

As we were preparing for the upcoming coup, my 1st Marine Battalion and Le Hang Minh's 4th Marine Battalion were ordered to conduct an operation in the Ho Bo Woods secret zone. Confused, I asked Lien what was going on. He told me this was part of a plan to position our forces before the coup. During the operation in the Ho Bo Woods near Cu Chi, the 1st Marine Battalion discovered an extensive, multi-level Viet Cong tunnel system inside a rubber plantation. I ordered the engineers to pump gas into the tunnels, but the gas was not as effective as I had hoped. After 1975, Hanoi improved this tunnel and made it a tourist attraction.

* * *

On October 31, 1963, we were ordered to leave the VC secret zone and return to Ben Cat to await orders. That afternoon a helicopter picked up Lien and took him to 5th Infantry Division headquarters at Bien Hoa to attend an urgent meeting. Que, Minh, and I sat up all night waiting, but Lien did not return. We became suspicious, thinking that perhaps our planned coup had been discovered. As the night wore on, we grew more and more worried.

Early the next morning, November 1, 1963, the sound of a helicopter woke us up. It was Lien, returning after an all-night meeting. Giving us no details of the meeting, he ordered the 1st and 4th Marine Battalions to move out and reassemble at the Bien Hoa wild game restaurant on the banks of the Dong Nai River, from where we would launch a new operation into the Thi Vai Mountain area of Phuoc Tuy province.

As soon as our truck convoy arrived at the Bien Hoa wild game restaurant, Lien held a quick, private meeting. Que, Minh, and I sat waiting for him to speak. His expression became stern. He spoke clearly and distinctly, as if reading an order: "The coup will be launched this afternoon!"

Captain Que was ordered to change into civilian clothes and return to Saigon for one last check of the capital's defenses. All company commanders were ordered to go to the residence of the 5th Division commander to receive their orders.

When my jeep arrived at the home of the 5th Division commander, my men were not there. I waited for some time, but none of my company commanders showed up. I was surprised and began to worry. When I called them on the radio, I learned that they had gone to the wrong house. Instead of going to the home of the 5th Division commander, they had gone to the province chief's house. The province chief lived in a spacious villa. During Diem's rule, the province chief, a major or a colonel who was the symbol of Diem's authority in the province, lived in a better house than the division commander, who was a general. That situation changed after Diem was overthrown.

At the province chief's house, the company commanders ordered the household staff to bring them some drinks. Fortunately, Maj. Tran Van Dinh, the Bien Hoa province chief, was not home that day. If he had been home, he would certainly have become suspicious, and the course of Vietnamese history might have been changed.

When all the company commanders finally gathered in the conference room of the division commander's house, Major Lien informed us that the coup would begin at precisely one o'clock that afternoon. The other units participating in the coup included Col. Nguyen Van Thieu's 5th Division, airborne forces under Maj. Ho Tieu, armored forces under Maj. Ly Tong Ba, and a number of air force and navy units. The marines, however, would make the main effort. The 1st Battalion would occupy and defend the Saigon radio station, while 4th Battalion would take control of National Police headquarters. Once this was accomplished, depending on the situation, our two battalions would launch a coordinated attack on the Gia Long Palace to capture Diem and Nhu. Republic barracks, where the tanks and infantry of the Presidential Guard Brigade were housed, would be a secondary target.

As I gazed at the faces of the company commanders, I saw signs of both happiness and worry.

There was happiness because we were acting at last. For almost six months, we had confided in one another about the unrest in the country. We knew something had to be done to stabilize the political situation, otherwise it would not be long before the Viet Cong would seize control of all of South Vietnam. The company commanders all favored a coup and were glad when they heard there would be one.

There was worry because they were concerned. They knew they would have to fight their own comrades-in-arms, the soldiers assigned to protect the president. They did not want to commit fratricide; they had no desire to hurt their own friends.

Carrying out Major Lien's orders, I immediately gave each of the units their missions. First Lieutenant Hoang Tich Thong, commander of 1st Company, would lead our truck convoy. Thong's company would turn left after crossing the Phan Thanh Giang bridge and seize control of the intersection of Hong Thap Tu and Nguyen Binh Khiem streets. The company's mission was to stop the Presidential Guard Brigade when it moved out to recapture the radio station after our forces had secured it. Second Company, under 1st Lt. Nguyen Kim Phuong, would follow 1st Company. After reaching the intersection of Nguyen Binh Khiem and Phan Dinh Phung streets, however, 2nd Company would proceed directly to the radio station and seize control of this key facility. Second Company would also provide security for my battalion headquarters. First Lieutenant Nguyen Kim Thinh's 4th Company would follow 2nd Company. When it reached the northern end of Dinh Tien Hoang Street, 4th Company would turn left to take control of the intersection of Dinh Tien Hoang and Hong Thap Tu streets, where it was to block any attempt by Presidential Guard Brigade troops to reach the radio station from that direction. Third Company, under 1st Lt. Le Ngoc Chau, would bring up the rear. Third Company would move to the intersection of Phan Dinh Phung and Dinh Tien Hoang streets and set up positions there to protect the right flank of my battalion headquarters.

As soon as I finished issuing my orders to each unit, Capt. Nguyen Phuc Que, our chief medical officer, who had been sent out to make one last check on the situation in Saigon, returned and told us there was no change in the disposition of the forces defending Saigon. After hearing Que's report, the company commanders all felt more confident.

On November 1, 1963, at exactly one o'clock, the plan was carried out. Second Company occupied the radio station without encountering any resistance. While I went around checking on all the units, Captain Que began to record a message from the coup leaders for broadcast in both Vietnamese and French. About a half hour later, after I returned, the recording was finished and we were about to begin broadcasting in English when I heard volleys of gunfire coming from the intersection of Hong Thap Tu and Nguyen Binh Khiem. Led by tanks, the Presidential Guard Brigade had penetrated 1st Company's defense line. Guard Brigade soldiers surrounded the radio station. Even though there had been a lot of shooting, both sides had only fired into the air. No one on either side had been hurt.

As I was preparing to make the broadcast in English, Lt. Col. Pham Ngoc Thao strode into the room. He told me he had come to broadcast an appeal to the nation from the Revolutionary Military Council.

Lieutenant General Tran Van Don, former vice premier and secretary of defense, later told me that the Revolutionary Military Council had never instructed Thao to make this broadcast. In 1965, when Gen. Nguyen Khanh exiled me to Manila, Thao was in Washington serving as military attaché, while Gen. Tran Thien Khiem was forced out, to become South Vietnam's unwilling ambassador to the United States. Later, apparently with permission from Khiem, Thao returned to Saigon and took part in several coup attempts by both Gen. Duong Van Duc and Gen. Lam Van Phat. After these failed coup attempts, Prime Minister Nguyen Cao Ky ordered the arrest of Thao. He was killed a short time later. After the fall of South Vietnam in 1975, the communists exhumed and reburied Thao's body with great honors, as if he were a martyr for their cause. Suspicions still continue to swirl around these events.

Realizing that the Presidential Guard Brigade troops surrounding the radio station outnumbered my men two to one and that the Guard Brigade was equipped with tanks and armored personnel carriers, I contacted Major Lien to ask 3rd Corps headquarters to send tanks to support us. Apparently, no one at 3rd Corps headquarters could make a decision, however, because no tanks were ever sent, even though a number of tanks from the Van Kiep Training Center were deployed around the Phan Thanh Gian bridge waiting for orders. I do not know what they were waiting for, unless it was to see which side was winning before deciding which side to join.

While monitoring the frequency being used by the armored

branch, I heard the Presidential Guard Brigade request permission from President Diem to destroy the radio station with their tank guns, but the request was refused. If the radio station was destroyed and then the coup forces were defeated, Diem's government would not be able to use the radio to appeal to the people for calm.

Occasionally, a few Presidential Guard soldiers would lay ladders against the building and climb up to look in through the windows, but the marines inside the radio station reacted quickly, forcing them to pull back.

As I stood on the second floor, looking out the rear windows of the radio station, I saw an air force A-1 Skyraider fighter-bomber, flying high, fire a few machine-gun bursts at Republic barracks. But then it flew away, apparently after antiaircraft guns fired back at him. I became worried, thinking: *This coup is not well organized. If this is the kind of support we are going to get from our tanks and our air force, how can we ever hope to succeed?*

I felt responsible and afraid of what would happen to my men if the coup failed, as the coup of November 1960 had failed. I thought of my wife and children. Had my wife followed my instructions to hide out at the home of Ms. Hieu, one of her closest friends, to avoid the harassment that had been experienced by the families of those who opposed Diem in the past?

As for myself, I was not concerned. If worst came to worst, I would get a chance to see my old friend and classmate from the academy, 1st Lt. Nguyen Ba Manh, who was serving a sentence of sixteen years at hard labor and three years in exile. Manh and Maj. Phan Trong Chinh were being held on the prison island of Con Son for their participation in the 1960 coup. Both had been tried under provisions of Law 10/59 by a special military tribunal on charges of violating domestic security.

The standoff continued until about five o'clock in the afternoon, when the 3rd Company commander, 1st Lt. Le Ngoc Chau, walked out to ask for a meeting with First Lieutenant Xuan, commander of the Guard Brigade's tanks. When Lieutenant Chau got close enough to the Guard Brigade commander, he whipped out his pistol, pointed it at the tank commander, and ordered him to tell his men to lay down their weapons and surrender. My marines moved in, collected the weapons of the Guard Brigade, and regained control of the situation.

The radio resumed its regular broadcast programming after a four-hour struggle in which many shots were fired but no one was injured on either side. This proves that both sides had been careful. The soldiers followed the orders of their commanders to make the greatest possible effort to avoid any unnecessary bloodshed.

At about six o'clock, when the situation had already turned in our favor, 1st Lt. Le Dinh Que, the Marine Brigade S-3 who had previously been my communications officer in 1st Marine Battalion, broke in on my radio frequency to ask if I needed any help. While I seethed with anger inwardly, I thanked him politely for his generous offer. Only later did I learn that the marine commander, Lt. Col. Le Nguyen Khang, and a number of senior commanders of other services who had not participated in the coup planning were detained at the joint general staff throughout the time the coup was taking place.

At about seven o'clock, as the sky grew dark, a battalion from 5th Infantry Division under the command of 1st Lt. Lau Venh Quay moved up to the radio station. Lieutenant Quay was glad to see me because we had been classmates at the academy. Quay said he had been ordered to attack Republic barracks. I gave him a detailed briefing on the situation and told him he had nothing to fear. Most of the Presidential Guard Brigade's armored vehicles were now being guarded by 1st Marine Battalion at the radio station, and we had confiscated all the weapons of the Guard Brigade's infantry unit before releasing the troops to return to the military families' quarters, adjacent to Republic barracks, to care for their loved ones. If it became necessary for Quay to attack Republic barracks, I said, he would have no difficulty and there would be little bloodshed.

Things were also going well for Capt. Le Hang Minh and his 4th Marine Battalion. During the afternoon of November 1, after completing the occupation of the National Police headquarters, he released a number of political prisoners. He then received orders to attack and occupy Gia Long Palace early on the morning of November 2. A marine artillery unit and a company of armored personnel carriers under the command of Maj. Ly Tong Ba supported Captain Minh's attack. Nguyen Ba Lien phoned my headquarters to order me to send two companies to occupy the Ministry of Justice to protect 4th Battalion's rear during the attack on Gia Long Palace.

By the morning of November 2, 1963, the coup had achieved total success after President Ngo Dinh Diem and his brother Ngo Dinh Nhu surrendered. Then, however, both men were murdered. This was a brutal act to which Lien, Que, and I would never have agreed because during the coup planning we had been promised that President Diem would be sent abroad and that Nhu would face trial by the people.

Much later, after 1975, Mr. Cao Xuan Vy, who at the time of the coup was director general for youth, told me that during the afternoon of November 1 he had personally driven Diem and Nhu from Gia Long Palace to Cho Lon. At that time, he said, there were no coup forces anywhere around the palace. Apparently, the coup leaders did not know what to do throughout the course of the coup. If 1st Marine Battalion had not defended the radio station so effectively, and if the Presidential Guard Brigade had managed to recapture the radio station, things might have worked out much differently.

After the coup, Major Lien was promoted to lieutenant colonel. To avoid offending Lieutenant Colonel Khang, and on Lien's recommendation, Khang was promoted to the rank of colonel. Lien was appointed to command the marine corps. I was promoted to major and appointed deputy marine commander and concurrently marine corps chief of staff. Colonel Khang was sent to Manila as military attaché at our embassy in the Philippines.

On November 22, 1963, President Kennedy was assassinated. At the time of his death, he had not yet reached a firm decision about the form of American commitment to South Vietnam. President Johnson believed that Kennedy would not abandon Vietnam and that, on the contrary, he planned to commit ground troops for the successful conclusion of the American experiment in South Vietnam. However, some of Kennedy's assistants claimed that he was considering the end of American involvement and the recall of U.S. military advisors by 1965.

* * *

Lien and I had planned to hold a party for our marines to celebrate the victory. The party was to be attended by the generals of the Revolutionary Military Council. But on February 1, 1964, before the party could be held, Gen. Nguyen Khanh took control of the government with the support of the Tan Dai Viet party, which was led by Col. Huynh Van Ton, the province chief of Gia Dinh. The senior Tan Dai Viet leaders, Dr. Nguyen Ton Hoan and Professor Nguyen Ngoc Huy, were out of the country on a visit to France.

The generals who led the November 1 coup were so intoxicated by their success that they never suspected General Khanh, flying down from II Corps, would conduct his own coup. I am certain that Khanh's coup received more than a little support from Gen. Tran Thien Khiem, who wanted to ensure continued U.S. confidence in and support of our country. At the time there were rumors that the chief of state, Gen. Duong Van Minh, and other pro-French generals, such as Le Van Kim, Mai Huu Xuan, and Tran Van Don, intended to allow several officers who had led the failed coup attempt of 1960 to return from France and drum up support for the neutralization of all of Indochina.

After the coup against Ngo Dinh Diem, as a result of power struggles between the leading generals, things became chaotic and the nation's military and political situation deteriorated even further. There was a widespread feeling that the individuals who assumed the leadership of South Vietnam were merely pawns of the Americans. There was a scenario of constant change and a cast of characters moving quickly on and off the stage in a succession of "revolving door" governments.

Just before Khanh's coup, I had taken the 2nd Marine Battalion commander, Maj. Co Tan Tinh Chau, and the 3rd Marine Battalion commander, Maj. Nguyen Thanh Yen, to the headquarters of the 7th Infantry Division for a meeting with Gen. Lam Van Phat, who had replaced Maj. Gen. Nguyen Huu Co, to organize a sweep operation at Thanh Phu in Kien Hoa province. However, as we were preparing to move our troops the next day, I was informed that there had been a coup and that 2nd Battalion was protecting General Khanh and Gen. Tran Thien Khiem.

A few days later, I led Capt. Ton That Soan's 1st Marine Battalion and Maj. Nguyen Thanh Yen's 3rd Marine Battalion down to conduct the planned sweep operation fifty miles south of Saigon. Another incident occurred that both angered and saddened me greatly. Even though the military situation in Dinh Tuong was deteriorating because of the frequent changes of leadership in the area, changes made for political reasons on orders from Gen. Nguyen Khanh, I received an order from General Khanh directing me to place 2nd and 3rd Marine Battalions under the operational control of 7th Infantry Division. The orders directed that neither my headquarters nor I were to accompany our battalions on this operation. This fundamental error in the principles of command made Lt. Col. Wes Noren, the U.S. advisor to the Marine Brigade, who was with me on this operation, extremely upset. Because of this error, and because of 7th Division Commander Huynh Van Ton's lack of combat experience (Colonel Ton had just replaced Col. Bui Huu Nhon, who in turn had replaced Maj. Gen. Lam Van Phat, who had replaced Maj. Gen. Nguyen Huu Co, who had replaced Col. Bui Dinh Dam, *everything happening in less than three months*), our two marine battalions suffered heavy casualties during the Dinh Tuong operation. Among those killed were Captain Thich and a number of American officers from the 3rd Marine Division in Okinawa who were visiting to study combat operations in Vietnam as part of an on-the-job training program.

This incident reminded me of the time 2nd Marine Battalion was ambushed at Cai Nuoc in Ca Mau province in 1961. I was immediately sent back to Cai Nuoc, even though I had just turned command of 1st Marine Battalion over to Capt. Nguyen Ba Lien and was preparing to leave to attend the U.S. Marine Command and Staff College in the United States. I was ordered to re-assume command and conduct an operation to rescue and evacuate Capt. Nguyen Thanh Yen, the 2nd Battalion commander who had been seriously wounded, and a number of other casualties. I was also ordered to recover the bodies of a number of 2nd Marine Battalion personnel trapped inside the hulk of a ferry that had been sunk at Cai Bat hamlet on the Bay Hap River. Meanwhile, the Marine Brigade headquarters, commanded by Major Khang and with 1st Lt. Bui The Lan serving as chief of staff and 1st Lt. Le Dinh Que as S-3, was just sitting in the Ca Mau province capital, trying to exercise command from there, just as the headquarters staff had done during many other previous operations in Kontum and Tay Ninh.

5

The Ups and Downs of a Military Career

IN DECEMBER 1963, the Central Committee of the Vietnamese Communist party met in Hanoi to discuss the future strategy of the war. They were evenly divided between the overconfidence of the ideologues and the caution of the military. They waited for their leader to decide the issue. Ho Chi Minh believed that Ngo Dinh Diem was the only person who could have held the South Vietnamese government together. His assassination and the ensuing chaos presented an opportunity for North Vietnam to change the nature of the war by supporting the Viet Cong more intensely. Ho overrode the objections of Giap and ordered thousands of northern soldiers to the South. He rearmed the Viet Cong with new weapons. He ordered the southern insurgents to escalate their terrorist attacks, especially against American personnel and installations. The Hanoi high command set in motion a vast and ambitious scheme to turn the primitive trails running from North Vietnam, Laos, and Cambodia into South Vietnam into a modern logistical system that came to be called the Ho Chi Minh Trail.

On the other side of the globe, as Lyndon Baines Johnson (LBJ) took over the government of the United States, he held on to the

Kennedy cabinet. Because Dean Rusk stayed on as secretary of state and Robert McNamara stayed on as secretary of defense, it became clear that U.S. policy regarding Vietnam would stay unchanged. LBJ was not going to abandon Vietnam. But 1964 was a presidential election year; he was not going to make any drastic moves before the first Tuesday of November, Election Day. He was going to devote most of the year developing an internal legislative agenda and running for election. Foreign affairs would have to wait for 1965.[15]

Johnson appointed Gen. William C. Westmoreland as commander of MACV to prepare the ground for that day. He told the joint chiefs of staff during a White House reception: "Just let me get elected, then you can have your war." Later in the year, Gen. Maxwell Taylor retired from active military duty and was appointed ambassador to Saigon, with full responsibility for the policy of the U.S. government in South Vietnam. Although Taylor did not interfere with Westmoreland's everyday running of the war, Westmoreland was really only Taylor's deputy for military affairs.[16]

LBJ's Vietnam policy had one major flaw. It was a negative policy; its only aim was *not* to lose South Vietnam to the communists. He was so afraid of prodding China into becoming a direct participant of the Vietnam War (as in Korea in 1953) that he did not allow any planning to unify the two Vietnams and to make the new nation a part of the free world. As a result, the bad guys—the communists—found themselves in the enviable position of being the ones working for the positive course of ending the unnatural division of Vietnam.

* * *

In mid-March 1964, General Khanh recalled Col. Le Nguyen Khang from the Philippines. Lien and I received orders sending us to serve as military attachés in the Philippines. I, however, had to remain behind for a time to turn over my duties as deputy marine corps commander to Maj. Nguyen Thanh Yen (commander of 3rd Marine Battalion) in Go Cong, and to turn my duties as marine corps chief of staff over to Capt. Bui The Lan. Captain Lan was attending the U.S. Marine junior course at the U.S. Marine Training Center in Quantico, Virginia; he was ordered to return to Vietnam before he finished his course.

The most regrettable order, however, was the one that sent Capt. Nguyen Kien Hung, former commander of a river force company, who had no experience in infantry and had just returned from exile in Cambodia, down to the Ong Doc River in Ca Mau to replace Maj. Le Hang Minh as commander of 4th Marine Battalion right in the middle of an operation against the Viet Cong U Minh Battalion.

Colonel Khang also asked me to accompany him on a visit to marine units conducting an operation in Long An province, even though by then I had been stripped of all my duties in the marine corps. I did not understand why he did not just go by himself, but Khang had never commanded a marine battalion in the field and he needed me to go with him to introduce him to the men.

After this visit, I left Vietnam for the Philippines. I was essentially exiled because I was the senior Vietnamese marine officer, having joined the marine corps at the very beginning of its existence, and had the loyalty of my marines. General Khanh was afraid I would lead a coup against him, so I was being sent out of the country. Later, I was transferred to the army.

* * *

In November 1964, Johnson was elected to the presidency of the United States by a landslide vote of 61 percent. He began building his Great Society program. He pushed Congress to enact a large variety of new legislation. Medicare was established. The Voting Rights Act outlawed literacy tests and removed other obstacles that prevented blacks from voting. The Department of Housing and Urban Development was set up. Federal aid to schools increased substantially. Unemployment compensation was liberalized. The food stamp program was expanded.

After all these accomplishments, it was time for LBJ and his secretary of defense, Robert McNamara, to tackle the Vietnam problem. They decided to introduce ground forces into Vietnam in a flawed "limited war" strategy, which was in fact a "no win" strategy. At that time, there were two groups of Americans. The "hawks" wanted to solve the Vietnam problem by war and the "doves" wanted to solve it by negotiation. LBJ's favorite middle-of-the-road consensus strategy tried to satisfy both camps: a measured increase in involvement coupled with calls for negotiations. And a limited escalation, avoiding the bombing of areas too close to China, would serve the purpose of not instigating the Chinese to enter the conflict. Johnson wanted to "keep control of the war in my own hands" in order to be able to make sudden changes if the Chinese showed signs of getting involved.

Gradually, intensified air attacks called Flaming Dart were initiated against North Vietnam just north of the demilitarized zone (DMZ), and ground troops were introduced with an increase of twenty thousand in American forces. On March 8, 1965, two battalions of marines, with tanks and 8-inch howitzers, splashed ashore near Danang, the first step in the buildup of U.S. ground forces. The South Vietnamese government had not been consulted, but a Pentagon press release declared that the marines were being sent at their request. In a speech at Johns Hopkins University on April 7, Johnson stated that the United States was prepared to enter into "unconditional discussions" with Hanoi.

The United States was playing poker with North Vietnam with all its cards on the table and seeing none of the opponent's cards, saying: "I show twenty thousand troops. If you can beat that, you win the pot."

Of course they could, with a fierce offensive on May 9, 1965, against Bao Trai, Song Be, and Ba Gia. American forces had to be increased to fifty thousand in May and to seventy-five thousand by July, plus allied forces from South Korea, Australia, Thailand, New Zealand, and the Philippines. The enemy matched the American escalations. On July 28, 1965, LBJ announced an authorization to one hundred twenty-five thousand and promised more.

The buildup of U.S. forces overwhelmed the South Vietnamese economy. The people rushed to meet the demands that American money was creating. Saigon became a "boom town" clogged with traffic, its restaurants bursting with soldiers, its bars crowded. New bars and brothels sprang up overnight around base areas. Much of the urban population was employed providing services for the Americans and in their turn becoming buyers of consumer goods. Prices increased; crime and corruption flourished. American soldiers became black marketers: garbage trucks left PXs loaded with stolen goods.

The "Second Indochina War," or "the war without frontlines," was in full swing.

* * *

In mid-1965, while I was serving as assistant military attaché in the Philippines, the embassy requested that I be allowed to return home to brief the Ministry of Defense and the Foreign Ministry on the Philippine Civilian Service Battalions that were about to be sent to work in Vietnam. Although the embassy recommendation was approved, the briefings were cancelled when I arrived back in Vietnam. I took the opportunity to visit my family and a number of friends. I also visited the Marine Corps headquarters at Cuu Long Camp. There I met with Capt. Duong Hanh Phuoc, commander of the Marine Corps Headquarters Service Support Company, who had previously served as a company commander and deputy battalion commander under me. In addition to being a classmate from the academy, he was also my brother-in-law.

I confided in Phuoc my concerns about the disruptions General Khanh had caused for our nation by his coup. I said, half in jest, that if we wanted to become national heroes, we should arrest General Khanh. My statement was based on the knowledge that, whenever Khanh faced a threat or when there was disorder in Saigon, he would board a helicopter at the marine corps amphibious landing training facility next to the naval shipyard to fly out to Vung Tau until things settled down. Phuoc listened carefully but we were unable to meet again because, after one short week of temporary duty in Saigon, I had to return to the Philippines.

In mid-1966, just after I returned from the Philippines, I received the sad news that my friend, Duong Hanh Phuoc, had been killed in battle in Quang Ngai, and that another friend, Le Hang Minh, was ambushed and killed on Highway 1, Quang Tri, immediately thereafter.

General Khanh was no more successful at turning back the Viet Cong than Diem had been. He declared a national emergency in August and instituted press censorship and prohibited mass meetings. On August 16 he issued a new constitution, which became known as the Vung Tau Charter. This document gave Khanh considerably more power. He had great faith in Col. Le Nguyen Khang, promoting him to brigadier general, along with most of the other colonels like Nguyen Cao Ky who made up the so-called Young Turks. Khang and the others had given their total support to the Vung Tau Charter.

When it became clear that the charter could not conceal the militaristic character of the government, the masses and the students who had earlier supported Khanh took to the streets to denounce him. In the face of such pressure, Khanh backed down. He praised the spirit of those who opposed him and "democratically" ripped the charter in full view of the public.

Ultimately, Khanh developed a confrontational relationship with U.S. Ambassador Maxwell Taylor. He requested that the United States replace Taylor, but the Johnson administration refused. Khanh installed Phan Huy Quat as premier, hoping to retain real control of the government as chairman of the Armed Forces Council, but the "Young Turks" removed him from that position and forced him to leave Vietnam to live in exile abroad. Khanh, ever the dramatic actor, just before boarding the plane, melodramatically picked up a handful of the sacred soil of our Fatherland to take abroad with him.

General Khang withdrew his support of Khanh and became the favorite of Gen. Nguyen Cao Ky, who promoted him again in an effort to buy Khang's support in Ky's power struggle against Gen. Nguyen Van Thieu. Ironically, Khang later smartly switched sides yet again by supporting Thieu (at that time all three other corps commanders [I, II, and IV] had already declared full support of Thieu for the presidency), thereby earning General Ky's eternal hatred.

Before I was recalled to Vietnam to work in the Ministry of Defense, I made some good friends in the Philippine General Staff Liaison Office, such as Capt. Fidel Ramos, who later became president of the Philippines. I was able to help Ambassador Pham Dang Lam and Maj. E. Golez, chairman of the Philippine Veterans' Association, to form the Philippine-Vietnamese Association. Actually, this was the kind of job that should have been the responsibility of the embassy secretaries, Robert Don, half-brother of Lt. Gen. Tran Van Don, and Second Secretary Le Huy Nam.

Sometimes I handled other small matters. The Vietnamese Air Force often flew planeloads of Vietnamese officers to Malaysia for training courses before flying the aircraft to the Philippines for maintenance. Flight crews used these flights to smuggle black-market cigarettes, especially Salem brand cigarettes, hidden under the steel seats of the C-47 aircraft. The Philippines had a heavy tax on imported cigarettes; Salem cigarettes produced in the Philippines were the only ones that could be sold. On the return flight, the crews would smuggle cloth purchased in the Philippines to sell in Saigon. I warned the flight crews on several occasions about smuggling cigarettes. They ignored my warnings. When they were caught, I had to work with Philippine general staff liaison officers to secure their release. I do not know if the crews were disciplined after their return to Vietnam.

I did not feel isolated while living in the Philippines because I was able to monitor the situation in Vietnam closely and because living conditions were good in the Philippines. When Vietnamese Air Force aircraft came to the Philippines for maintenance, we often asked the crews to carry packages of fruit back home as gifts for our families. In turn, our families would send us Vietnamese foods such as rice paper, Sa Dec shrimp cakes, and even herbal leaves for seasoning. I planted some of these herbs and distributed them to the Vietnamese community in Manila to eat with fertilized duck eggs (Filippinos eat fertilized duck eggs with soy sauce). Although my salary was small, I took good care of the flight crews, even letting them stay at my house and thus saving the money they were given for hotel accommodations.

Ambassador Lam often asked me to send fruit back on these flights as gifts to his loved ones, including both his wife and the well-known classical singer, Thanh Nga. Everything went smoothly because the flight crews would personally deliver the gifts to each recipient's house. One day we were out at the airport to meet Mrs. Lam, who was coming from Saigon to join the ambassador. The entire diplomatic corps was assembled in the VIP lounge at the airport to greet the incoming flight. Mrs. Lam was very cold toward her husband, holding her newborn baby and sitting across the room from Ambassador Lam, even though Lam was scurrying around trying to appear warm and affectionate. Surprised at her attitude, my wife asked me what was going on, but I didn't know the reason for the chill in Mrs. Lam's demeanor.

That night, Ambassador Lam phoned and said in an anguished voice: "Nhut, you've ruined me!" Shocked, I asked him what he meant. "Why did you send Miss Nga's present to my wife?" Lam wailed in an accusatory tone. I learned later that the weather had been bad, with strong headwinds, and the normal six-hour flying time from Manila to Saigon had taken ten hours. When the plane landed at Tan Son Nhut Airport at two o'clock in the morning, the flight crew was exhausted, so they made a call to the duty officer at the Foreign Ministry to come to the airport and pick up the ambassador's presents. The duty officer did not bother to look at the labels on the gifts and delivered both baskets of fruit to Lam's house. Sooner or later, the guilty must pay for their sins.

* * *

In May 1965, Johnson asked Congress to approve an appropriation of $700 million for the Vietnam War. He believed this appropriation was adequate because U.S. involvement in Vietnam would be over in twelve to eighteen months. He said: "It will be like a filibuster—enormous resistance at first, then a steady whittling away, then Ho Chi Minh hurrying to get it over with."

Some filibuster! A year later, his miscalculations and faulty strategies had backfired and he had gone from being a beloved president with huge domestic accomplishments to a reviled president who was considered a failure in foreign policy. The intellectual community was treating him with contempt, and college professors were encouraging their students to disobey. LBJ's reaction to intellectual elitism was "I didn't realize you had to look down your nose to understand foreign policy." But there was a growing antiwar movement in the United States, student demonstrations against the military draft, and a credibility gap between the public and the Johnson administration.

On January 12, 1966, Johnson assured Congress: "I believe that we can continue the Great Society while we fight in Vietnam." Hence, his budget did not provide adequate funds for the war, creating long-range inflationary pressures beyond his control.

In Vietnam, General Westmoreland began a "war of attrition" against the Viet Cong. The stubborn Ho Chi Minh decided that he would confront Westmoreland with his own war of attrition. The entire North Vietnamese economy was put on a war footing. Thousands more North Vietnamese were added to the infiltration groups heading south. Westmoreland cabled Washington: "Whereas we will add an average of seven maneuver battalions per quarter, the enemy will add fifteen." He asked for an additional two hundred thousand troops in 1966 and possibly another two hundred thousand in 1967.

By October 1966, infiltration of fighters from North Vietnam was continuing at the rate of 8,400 a month. The number of new Viet Cong recruits was 3,500 a month and rising.

Westmoreland's search-and-destroy strategy was shattered by Ho Chi Minh's flexible strategy of avoiding combat against superior forces just for the sake of holding on to a given piece of territory. Westmoreland was forced to conduct the war according to Ho Chi Minh's guerilla rules and was bound to fail. American technology and American firepower could achieve only a stalemate on the ground.

In the United States, in the 1966 midterm elections, Johnson's Democratic party lost forty-seven seats in the House and three seats in the Senate.

* * *

In mid-1966, after I completed my tour of duty in the Philippines and returned to Vietnam, Lt. Gen. Nguyen Huu Co, deputy chairman of the National Administrative Council and concurrently minister of defense, appointed me assistant director of cabinet for the Ministry of Defense. I was promoted to lieutenant colonel on November 1, 1966, three years after receiving a battlefield promotion to major. I now understand that the reason General Co retained me at the Ministry of Defense was that at the time Thieu, Ky, and Co were struggling for power against one another, and Co needed my support. He wanted me in particular because I still had a great deal of support and standing within the marine corps. After thinking it over, I agreed to serve at the Ministry of Defense. I knew I had made great sacrifices in the course of the war, especially during the November 1, 1963, coup against Diem. I had wanted to improve the life of my country, but after the coup I was considered such a "bad apple" that I was mustered out of the marine corps and sent into exile abroad.

After two years abroad, I found the situation in our country worse than when I left. While I was gone, a number of "apple-polishers" and "brown-noses" had been promoted from first lieutenant and captain to colonel. Others had been promoted from lieutenant colonel all the way up to lieutenant general in the space of only two years. Some of the generals who had participated, to some extent at least, in the coup, had indiscriminately promoted their protégés to important positions even though these protégés had never commanded any unit, not even a platoon, in battle. Those who had sacrificed themselves by taking the lead in the coup had not done so merely to overthrow one dictatorial, factional government in order to replace it with another government even worse than Diem's.

While serving at the Ministry of Defense, I had the opportunity to talk to many generals and political figures, including Generals Don, Dinh, Mau, Kim, and Xuan, lawyer Tran Van Tuyen, and Buddhist leader Venerable Thich Tri Quang (whom I usually met at Nguyen Ba Lien's house), to discuss the national situation and possible courses of action for the future. In all these discussions, however, I never heard anyone present a workable plan capable of providing Vietnam with a better future.

One morning in early 1967, Nguyen Ang Ca, publisher of the newspaper *Tin Som* (Early News), called and asked me to go to his office right away. When I arrived, Ca showed me several press bulletins from Reuters and AP reporting that General Co had been detained while on an official visit abroad. On my return to the Ministry of Defense, I informed Col. Nguyen Dinh Vinh, director of cabinet at the Ministry of Defense, of these reports. He was as surprised and shocked as I was.

At about eleven o'clock in the morning, Col. Do Kien Nhieu, assistant for military affairs at the Ministry of Defense, and I received orders to report to the chief of the joint general staff at his office at the Joint General Staff headquarters at one o'clock. I quickly went home to have lunch and pack my bags. Then I picked up Colonel Nhieu and we went to the headquarters building. But there was no one there to meet us. Orders had been left with the duty officer that we were to report to the VIP lounge at Tan Son Nhut airbase. There, a C-47 was waiting to transport Nhieu north to I Corps. An H-34 helicopter was waiting to take me to III Corps headquarters, where I was to report to Lt. Gen. Le Nguyen Khang, a member of the Council of Government, commander of the III Corps, as well as Military Region Three, the Capital Special Zone, concurrently governor of Saigon, and last, but not least, commander of the South Vietnamese Marine Corps. This last position was the most surprising because General Khang had never once commanded a marine battalion in battle.

General Khang was sitting at his desk, reading a Chinese martial arts novel written by Kim Dung. When he saw me, he stuck out his hand to shake mine, with an arrogant expression on his face. All camaraderie from the old days when we served together was gone. But I did not find his current attitude out of the ordinary because in just less than three years he had risen from the rank of major to lieutenant general, with a vast array of responsibilities and duties.

Like a number of other generals who were classmates of Gen. Nguyen Cao Ky, chairman of the National Administrative Council,

General Khang had been given responsibilities far beyond his capabilities and experience. Even after the Tet Offensive of 1968, when the communists slipped into Saigon and other cities to ravage them and slaughter innocent civilians, none of the generals responsible for the security of those areas who were cronies of Ky were fired or reprimanded.

After exchanging a few pleasantries, Khang sent for Lieutenant Colonel Khuyen, director of the Military Security Service for III Corps. After a whispered dialogue with Khuyen, Khang ordered that I be placed aboard a U.S. helicopter and, escorted by Khuyen, flown to Xuan Loc in Long Khanh province, to report to 18th Division. I felt like a prisoner of war! Apparently, I was still under suspicion and Khang was still afraid of my intentions.

In Xuan Loc, the division commander, Col. Do Ke Giai, sent me to Binh Tuy, a small province that had no access road. One could get there only by plane or by boat, so I would not be able to drive to Saigon. Once I got there, I just sat around with nothing to do, drawing my salary and contemplating how bleak my career prospects had become. Occasionally, my family was able to hitch a ride up from Bien Hoa aboard one of the U-17 observation aircraft that supported the various province sector headquarters in the region. I will never forget the fact that my wife always supported me; she sacrificed for our children and me through even the most difficult periods. Ignoring all hardship and danger, she often visited me at remote locations from Ban Me Thuot all the way down to Ca Mau.

Another event from this period will remain etched forever in my memory. When I learned that a dog had bitten my second child, I hurriedly caught an observation aircraft to 18th Division headquarters to request permission to go home to see my child. Colonel Giai was not in. He was in Saigon, making arrangements for the wedding of one of his children. I could find only the deputy division commander, Col. Phan Dinh Niem, who was getting a haircut. He told me to go visit my child and return the next day.

I quickly changed into civilian clothes and boarded a bus for Bien

Hoa, then took a taxi to my house in Gia Dinh. At about midnight there was a knock on my door. Captain Hay, a Military Security Service officer assigned to the Ministry of Defense, and several soldiers were standing outside. They asked me to accompany them to the Military Security Service headquarters for the Capital Special Zone. For some reason that I did not understand, I was detained there. Even the officers who brought me in did not know why. They could not have thought I was AWOL because the deputy commander of 18th Division had given me permission to come home. It was the eve of the Tet lunar New Year, 1967. I later learned that the entire Military Region Three area and the Capital Special Zone had been placed on a state of alert because of a report that I was contacting the marine corps to organize a coup.

After the coup of November 1, 1963, I often thought that overthrowing President Diem might have been a mistake. We seemed to have replaced him with a bunch of unworthy leaders who cared only about their own interests and their own factions. They were leading the nation into a situation no better than what we had before. If it had not been for the arrival of massive allied forces to support us in the conflict, South Vietnam would actually be in a worse position than it was under Diem.

I was detained at the Capital Special Zone headquarters for two nights. Perhaps they held me that long to allow their superiors to celebrate Tet without any worries. I was then sent to the Military Security Service office in Bien Hoa. Colonel Phan Dinh Niem personally picked me up there and took me back to Binh Tuy, after confirming to corps headquarters that he had authorized me to go to Saigon to see my child, who had been bitten by a dog.

In September 1967, I was appointed commander of the 18th Division Training Center at Gia Ray, twenty miles north of Xuan Loc. According to the table of organization chart, this position should have been given to a major, not a lieutenant colonel. Rather than being discouraged, however, I was elated. I happily set to work organizing the training of our troops. In addition, using the assistance of an American engineering unit, I set out to strengthen the defenses of the training center. Everything that we did, from building exercise fields, obstacle courses, and firing ranges, to the expansion of the training center to allow us to establish a professional training course for noncommissioned officers, was done without any help from 18th Division headquarters.

* * *

On January 31, 1968, the communists launched the Tet Offensive, the battle of all battles for North Vietnam, a synchronized nationwide surprise attack during a truce for the celebration of Tet. It targeted more than one hundred South Vietnamese cities and towns, plus numerous specific targets such as the Joint General Staff headquarters and the headquarters of all four military regions of South Vietnam.

The communist command committed 67,000 of its troops to the initial assault. Ranged against them were 492,000 American fighting men, 342,000 Vietnamese government regulars, 284,000 Vietnamese men of the regional and popular force militia, 61,000 Allied troops (mainly South Korean), for a total of 1,179,000. The communist command did not have a single airplane or helicopter. The United States had 2,600 airplanes, 3,000 helicopters, and 3,500 armored vehicles.[17]

These numbers did not need any elaboration as to who would prevail militarily. The value of a surprise attack had dissipated within hours. American forces were in control and proved their superiority. Their only weakness was their commander in chief, but he was confined to the White House, worrying about intelligence reports that General Giap planned to attack the outpost of Khe Sanh and make it another Dien Bien Phu. He summed up his feelings in his inimitable style: "I don't want any damn Dinbinphoo."

This "general offensive" was a total failure, and the "general uprising" that North Vietnam expected in the South never took place. The people of South Vietnam showed where their loyalty was; there were no uprisings against the government. The urban masses were not interested in the "liberation" offered by the communists. They rallied to the government and even asked to be armed so they could join the fight in case the communists struck again. The ARVN soldiers did not mutiny or desert. On the contrary, they fought with exceptional bravery.

The enemy launched 155 attacks on January 31, 1968. Nearly 90 percent of them failed, some in less than one hour of fighting. At the end of the day, they did not control a single town. They had some degree of control in several towns, but not for long. By February 11, 1968, the Tet Offensive had sputtered to an end. Only the imperial city of Hue, not defended by the Americans, remained in communist hands until February 24, 1968. During those twenty-five days, the enemy executed 2,800 "reactionaries," the most extensive, purely political slaughter of the war. Another 2,000 residents were also presumed murdered because they were on the "enemies list" of the communists. These 4,800 premeditated murders were a foretaste of the bloodbath the communists would unleash soon in South Vietnam and Cambodia.

Throughout the Tet Offensive, local Viet Cong cadres were on the frontlines because of their familiarity with the terrain; hence they were the first ones to die. They were irreplaceable. But for the North Vietnamese planners, they were expendable. The North Vietnamese armed forces were held in reserve and saved. The planners insisted on this "rear base area" strategy of Lenin; as Giap explained: "The rear base area is always necessary for success because it is a source of supply for human and material resources for the war and a source of political and spiritual motivation and encouragement for the front line. Without a stable rear base area, the front line cannot defeat the aggressor. This is the general law for every war."[18]

Viet Cong units were decimated and would never completely recover. The northerners had pushed them to the front of every firefight. The Viet Cong was no longer a viable force. Westmoreland claimed that the communists had lost thirty-seven thousand killed and 5,800 captured. To replace the depleted ranks of the Viet Cong, Hanoi began to move so many of its own troops to the South that by May 1968 nearly 80 percent of communist soldiers in the South, even in traditional Viet Cong units, were northerners. Most South

Vietnamese believed that this was exactly what Gen. Vo Nguyen Giap, the chief planner of the Tet Offensive, wanted to accomplish. Whoever reads Giap's books will notice that he is callous about the number of Vietnamese lives lost for the noble cause of an independent Vietnam ruled only by communist ideology. I claim that he went beyond his usual lack of compassion for human life and planned for the elimination of southerners from the Viet Cong for political reasons. He preferred northerners to dominate the political decisions of a unified Vietnam after a successful Tet Offensive.

Regarding the results actually achieved by this episode of the war, as Bernard Brodie pointed out in his book *The Tet Offensive,* it was "probably unique in that the side that lost completely in the tactical sense came away with an overwhelming psychological and hence political victory."

The reason for this anomaly was that North Vietnam and the Viet Cong had a powerful ally: the U.S. news media. During the 1960s, American newsmen were suffering from a bad case of virulent anti-Americanism.

The U.S. embassy in Saigon was a symbolic target. A group of less than twenty men were assigned to attack it. They breached the wall with explosives at three o'clock in the morning, raced across the lawn carrying rocket launchers, and began firing at the building. They took positions in or behind flowerpots on the lawn and fought until they were killed or captured by the rescue squads of U.S. Marines and Military Police. Six and a half hours after the first call for help, the embassy was declared secure.

But the Associated Press reported that the Viet Cong were *inside* the embassy. United Press International reported: "There were unconfirmed reports the Communists had taken over the first five floors of the modernistic white building." Chet Huntley of NBC News announced to 14 million viewers that the Viet Cong were inside the building, the Americans were in the rest of the compound, and the Viet Cong were firing at them from outside the walls, exactly the opposite of what was happening.

Westmoreland arrived at the embassy at 9:30 a.m., inspected the damage, and gave the press a strictly military view of the situation and how the enemy had deceitfully taken advantage of the Tet truce. What the journalists saw was Westmoreland "standing in the ruins saying everything was great." AP reporter Peter Arnett portrayed the attitude of his colleagues: "We had little faith in what General Westmoreland said." Arnett claimed that, according to dozens of persons on the scene, the Viet Cong had entered the chancery and that Westmoreland's version of the story was a lie.[19]

The next day, Westmoreland held a news conference "dressed in starched fatigues," as the media reported. He gave an analysis of the enemy's plans, then read a list of the cities attacked and the situation at each. He announced that the enemy had suffered five thousand killed, compared to 530 allied troops. If the enemy continued their attacks, their losses would be so staggering that it would take them several months to rebuild their strength. Tom Buckley of the *New York Times* insisted that the guerillas had penetrated the chancery and had held it for seven hours. Beverly Deepe of the *Christian Science Monitor* found reasons to believe that the United States faced the possibility of military defeat. Saigon had suffered only light damage, but TV viewers in the United States were convinced that it had been reduced to a smoldering ruin. TV commentators ignored any facts that did not fit into their preferred "disaster image" or "action and drama," such as strafing jets, devastated neighborhoods, crying women, and orphaned children.

At that time and later, the TV networks adopted Arnett's attitude that Westmoreland's reports could not be believed, that they were just attempts to put a good face on a bad situation. The enemy was treated with awe, praised for his intelligence, bravery, tenaciousness, boldness, careful planning, skill of execution, and willingness to die for a cause. Giap was wily, bold, crafty, brilliant, a master planner, a brilliant tactician, and a tactical genius. Giap did not win on the Vietnamese battleground, but he won the hearts and minds of the press, the TV networks, the war critics, and, through them, eventually the U.S. public and the U.S. Congress. Senator Eugene McCarthy said that Westmoreland and Johnson had been deceiving the American people and themselves.

The chasm between the American government and the American news media had become so deep that the afternoon briefings for correspondents in Saigon were known as "the five o'clock follies." At one point, an exasperated Secretary of State Dean Rusk exclaimed: "There gets to be a point when the question is: Whose side are you on?"

Only a handful of journalists had the courage to admit that the reporting of the Tet Offensive was biased and distorted. Howard K. Smith, the eminent TV commentator, resigned in disgust from ABC News. "Vietcong casualties were one hundred times ours," he angrily told an interviewer, "but we never told the public that. We just showed pictures day after day of Americans getting the hell kicked out of them." Robert Elegant, a correspondent in Vietnam, wrote: "Never before Vietnam had the collective policy of the media—no less stringent term will serve—sought by graphic and unremitting distortion the victory of the enemies of the correspondent's own side." Peter Braestrup, former correspondent of the *Washington Post,* wrote: "Rarely had contemporary crisis-journalism turned out, in retrospect, to have veered so widely from reality. . . . To have portrayed such a setback for one side as a defeat for the other . . . cannot be counted as a triumph for American journalism." Peter Braestrup's book entitled *Big Story: How the American Press and Television Reported and Interpreted the Crisis of Tet* won the 1978 Sigma Delta Chi Award for research in journalism.

Walter Cronkite, anchor of CBS News, was the most trusted commentator of the television age. In 1965, he had praised "the courageous decision that Communism's advance must be stopped in Asia and that guerilla war as a means to a political end must be finally discouraged." Had the situation changed? He decided he owed it to his loyal listeners to find out firsthand what was going on in Vietnam.

He visited Vietnam on February 11, 1968, interviewed several generals, and reported his conclusions on a CBS News special, *Report from Vietnam by Walter Cronkite,* on February 27:

> Who won and who lost the great Tet Offensive against the cities? I'm not sure. The Vietcong did not win by a knockout, but neither did we. . . . It seems now more certain than ever that the bloody experience of Vietnam is to end in a stalemate. This summer's almost certain standoff will either end in real give-and-take negotiations or terrible escalation; and for every means we have to escalate, the enemy can match us, and that applies to invasion of the North, the use of nuclear weapons, or the mere commitment of one hundred or two hundred or three hundred thousand more American troops to battle. . . . To say that we are closer to victory today is to believe, in the face of the evidence, the optimists who have been wrong in the past. To suggest we are on the edge of defeat is to yield to unreasonable pessimism. To say that we are mired in stalemate seems the only realistic, yet unsatisfactory, conclusion.[20]

The oracle had spoken. The word had not been uttered, but the word was *disengagement*. His view became the view of the American public. And the view of the American public became the policy of the senators and congressmen of the United States. When LBJ listened to Cronkite, he knew that he had lost the American public, that election to the presidency for a second term was out of his reach.

Lyndon Baines Johnson had reached the point in his presidency when he realized that becoming chief executive officer of the United States of America, without dictatorial powers, was a humbling experience. He was not as powerful an individual as he imagined himself to be. In the true democracy of the United States, he could not survive a "no confidence" vote from the American public.

On March 31, 1968, he addressed the nation on the new medium of television and announced: "I shall not seek, and I will not accept, the nomination of my party for another term as your president."

The next day, the stock market reached a new high.

According to some accounts, Giap viewed the Tet Offensive as a failure and was prepared to negotiate surrender. Then he heard Walter Cronkite proclaim a stalemate. News reports of riots and protests in

America were "inspirational" to Giap and the North Vietnamese hierarchy. They reversed their plans of a negotiated surrender and decided instead that they needed to persevere only one more hour, day, week, month, and eventually American protesters would help them achieve a victory they knew they could not win on the battlefield.

On February 27, 1968, Walter Cronkite of CBS News decided, on behalf of the American public, that the United States was going to abandon Vietnam. The only things left to decide were when and how.

In 1968 and throughout the Vietnam era, the treatment of the U.S. military by the U.S. news media was abominable and inexcusable. After World War II, the armed forces of the United States had become the backbone of American supremacy in this world. An institution as powerful as that deserved more respect than it received, perhaps even the right to demand that the chairman of the joint chiefs of staff automatically assume the post of secretary of defense.

* * *

One night in mid-1968 the 275th Regiment of the Viet Cong 5th Division attacked our training center. The VC troops greatly outnumbered the ARVN defenders, who were young recruits with no combat experience. However, because I had refurbished and strengthened the center's defensive fortifications when I first arrived, and with powerful fire support provided by American helicopter gunships, my young recruits repelled the enemy regiment, forcing it to leave behind more than fifty bodies and a large quantity of weapons. The MACV commander, Gen. Creighton Abrams, visited the battlefield and awarded me an American Silver Star medal for this action. Eighteenth Division headquarters recommended me for the South Vietnamese Gold Star medal for valor.

After repelling the attack, I moved the training center to Phuoc Le, in Phuoc Tuy province, southeast of Saigon, because our facilities had been heavily damaged during the attack. At Phuoc Le, I requested the general commanding the Australian Brigade base in the same province to provide Australian engineering equipment to help us build firing ranges and obstacle courses for the trainees.

In 1969, after Gen. Cao Tri replaced General Khang as commander of III Corps, I was appointed commander of the 43rd Infantry Regiment. Under my command, my regiment defeated the enemy in a number of major battles at Tuc Trung, Kiem Tan, La Nga, Dinh Quan, and Cay Gao (War Zone D). A major communist supply route ran from Cambodia, through this area, and into the area where the Australians were based. Using information gleaned from POW interrogations, we located and destroyed a large number of communist ammunition and rocket caches in northern Long Khanh province. Through these actions, the 43rd Regiment drove the VC 5th Division, which had been based in the province, back to War Zone D, shattering the enemy plan to capture the province capital of Long Khanh. If not for our actions, Xuan Loc and 18th Division headquarters would have suffered heavy losses.

In early 1970, I replaced Col. Nguyen Cong Vinh as commander of the 18th Division's 48th Infantry Regiment. The 48th Regiment was mediocre and the division commander wanted me to shape it up. Colonel Vinh would later command the 9th Regiment of the 5th ARVN and would be captured during the battle for Loc Ninh in 1972.

During my time as regimental commander, I was surprised to find that American advisors were pressuring ARVN units to make maximum possible use of American capabilities and resources. For example, artillery units were forced to use the maximum amount of ammunition they could, hundreds of rounds every night, to fire H&I (harassment and interdiction), which were artillery fired at suspected enemy positions to disrupt their activities and movements. Every night, before going to sleep, American units would fire a "mad minute," firing indiscriminately all around their position, just in case the enemy was trying to sneak in to launch an attack. In addition, each infantry battalion was required to conduct two helicopter assaults each week. Confused, I asked my American advisors why they insisted on these measures. They told me they were just following instructions. MACV had requested an excessive level of logistics support in their yearly plan. If we did not use all the aid provided, the advisors would be reprimanded and our aid for the following year might be reduced. I believe these American demands helped create and foster bad habits among ARVN units, making them overreliant on excessive and wasteful expenditures of resources.

Meanwhile, Johnson's abdication had led to negotiations in Paris, which had led to a halt in the bombing of North Vietnam in October 1968, neither of which was good for South Vietnam. Richard Milhous Nixon's election as the new president of the United States was considered good news for us because he was a genuine friend of South Vietnam, but he was so restricted by Congress that he had no choice but to continue the policy of American disengagement.

American negotiators tried hard to convince the North Vietnamese to accept a plan of both sides withdrawing their forces from South Vietnam. When the proposal of mutual withdrawal was rebuffed by Hanoi, there was nothing left for the United States to do than to begin a unilateral withdrawal and pretend that this was part of a "Vietnamization" strategy.

On June 8, 1969, Nixon and Thieu met at Midway Island in the Pacific and announced the withdrawal of twenty-five thousand American combat troops from Vietnam. On July 20 Ho Chi Minh addressed his people and told them: "The Americans are beaten," instead of his usual "The Americans will be beaten."[21]

Ho died on September 3, 1969, his lifelong dream still unfulfilled. His successors had no other choice than to become even more intransigent. Anyone who veered slightly from Ho's directives and communist principles would pay for his deviation with his life. But they did not have to make any concessions anyway because the American system was creating its own contradictions.

On September 16, 1969, Nixon announced that the troop ceiling would be lowered by another forty thousand. Unilateral withdrawals would continue on a quarterly basis, reducing American forces from a peak of 543,400 in April 1969 to 475,200 by the end of 1969, to 334,600 by the end of 1970, to 156,800 by the end of 1971, to 24,200 by the end of 1972, to total evacuation shortly thereafter. There was no need for Hanoi to reciprocate.

As the withdrawal progressed, aid to Vietnam was cut by almost 50 percent, ammunition was in short supply, and the support provided by American air, armor, and naval forces was no longer available. The ground troops included seven U.S. combat divisions, three Korean and Thai divisions, three separate brigades, and most importantly, logistics and support units, air force units, 7th Fleet and marine units, and B-52 strategic bombers.

ARVN, however, was still expected to defend the same amount of territory. During the last years of the Republic of Vietnam, the joint general staff issued ridiculous instructions limiting the use of ammunition. For instance, each 105mm howitzer could fire only five rounds per day and each 155mm howitzer only three rounds. Soldiers had to retrieve and turn in all their ejected rifle cartridges after every engagement with enemy forces.

Nixon believed Vietnamization would work. Some experts had convinced him that South Vietnam, with large-scale military and economic assistance, would become strong enough within two years to resist a communist takeover without external help. But not everybody shared Nixon's optimism. General Abrams called it "slow surrender." Some Vietnamese dismissed it as a "U.S. dollar and Vietnamese blood sharing plan." Most saw it as a fig leaf to cover U.S. abandonment. North Vietnamese negotiator Le Duc Tho taunted American negotiator Kissinger about the futility of Vietnamization: "If the United States could not win with a half million of its own troops, how can you succeed when you let your puppet troops do the fighting?"[22]

I believed that Vietnamization was an excellent plan, but it should have been started much earlier, in 1960.

Supplies to the communist armies by the communist bloc were not interrupted. And their trucks, tanks, and infantry were able to move about more freely than before because of the "cease-fire in place" clause of the agreement, which resulted in a "leopard skin" situation on the battlefield (spots under communist control scattered through South Vietnam in between and in the rear of ARVN-controlled positions).

6

Province Chief

A PROVINCE CHIEF, normally an ARVN colonel, headed each of the forty-four provinces in the Republic of Vietnam. The province chief was responsible for administration and security within the province. He had at his disposal governmental administrators that dealt with myriad areas such as agriculture, civil affairs, medical support, and education, among others. He also served as the military sector commander and controlled the regional forces (RF) and popular forces (PF), who provided security for the province. Each of the provinces was further subdivided into a number of districts, which were administered by district chiefs appointed by the province chief. The province chief was assisted by an American advisory team under the auspices of the Civil Operations and Revolutionary Development Support (CORDS) program, organized by MACV Deputy Commander Robert Komer in 1967. This program brought together U.S. military, State Department, Agency for International Development, U.S. Information Agency, and Central Intelligence Agency pacification experts in an effort to assist the province chief to meet the needs of the people and spread the influence of the Saigon government.

* * *

In early 1970, I received a phone call from Brig. Gen. Lam Quang Tho, commander of the 18th Division, informing me that Lt. Gen. Do Cao Tri wanted to appoint me to the post of province chief and sector commander of Binh Long province. I was confused for a moment because I did not know where the province was. I quickly learned that it was the former Hon Quan district, a place where I had spent the happiest summers of my youth.

Binh Long (Peaceful Dragon) province was located in the northwestern portion of Military Region Three. It was bordered on the east by Phuoc Long province, on the north by the Cambodian border, on the west by Tay Ninh province, and on the south by Binh Duong province. Our province consisted of the districts of Chon Thanh, An Loc, and Loc Ninh. The capital was An Loc, a city that sat astride Highway QL-13, which ran from Snoul, Cambodia, through An Loc, to Saigon sixty-five miles away.

General Tho suggested that I stay on as regimental commander because I had a better chance of being promoted to colonel as a regimental commander than as a province chief. After thinking it over, though, I decided to accept the post as Binh Long province chief, for two reasons. First, the appointment brought back many pleasant personal memories. Second, my father had built a business in this province and always remembered this area with great affection (he had named my half-brothers and -sisters Tran Thi Loc Ninh, Tran Thi Bu Dop, Tran Van Hon Quan, and Tran Van Chon Thanh—the names of towns and districts in Binh Long); accepting the Binh Long post would be a way for me to honor his memory.

There was another reason, hidden deeper, that lurked in the recesses of my brain. It was my dream to follow the example set by the Vietnamese national hero Nguyen Cong Tru, who was famous both as a wise governor and as a ferocious warrior against foreign aggressors, a man who brought peace and happiness to our people. The post of province chief and military sector commander, which encompassed both governmental and military functions, would allow me to fulfill my dream. I promised myself that I would turn Binh Long into a quiet, peaceful province and bring prosperity and happiness to its citizens.

I had never met Gen. Do Cao Tri. When I reported to corps headquarters, I met Col. Dao Duy An, the chief of staff. Colonel An told me that General Tri had reviewed the files of all nine regimental commanders of the corps' three divisions—the 5th, 18th, and 25th—before selecting me as province chief and sector commander of Binh Long. I should point out that my duties made me a full colonel, albeit only on a temporary basis; when President Thieu visited An Loc in 1972, I was awarded a medal and my rank as colonel became permanent.

After the change of command ceremony in January 1970, presided over by the 5th Division commander, Maj. Gen. Nguyen Van Hieu, I convened a meeting of the province's senior officials, both civilian and military. After listening to briefings by the deputy province chief for administration, the chiefs of the different province governmental offices, and the sector headquarters operations staff, I told the assembled officials: "I am no stranger to this province. My father ran a logging business here from 1947 to 1955." I noticed pleasure and affection in the eyes of the older province officials and members of the province council.

I shook hands with each of them, making sure I remembered their names. I told them my thoughts about my job and about the assignment of responsibilities in the province. I said:

> I have little experience in civilian government, so Deputy Province Chief for Administrative Affairs Vo Tan Vinh and my office manager will have to explain to me all important documents before I sign them. From this moment on, Maj. Nguyen Thong Thanh, deputy sector commander, will be responsible for organizing and deploying our RF and PF units and for ensuring that we don't have any "ghost" soldiers or "parade ground" soldiers.

"Ghost" soldiers were soldiers who were dead or had never existed, but who were kept on the books of a unit so the commander could siphon off their salaries. "Parade ground" or "flower pot" soldiers were those who bribed their commanders to allow them to avoid participating in military operations and military details. They only showed up for parades and inspections.

I then asked Major Thanh to drive me around the province capital to inspect its defenses. If the enemy should attack that night, I wanted to be familiar with the defenses so I could react more effectively. I also set to work to carry out a number of measures to win over the people of the province.

I asked Raymond Perkins, the province senior advisor, to persuade MACV to let us have two old buses to provide transportation for the local population, officials, and troops. MACV approved our request; the province was given two buses, each of which could carry sixty passengers. Because the buses had been scrapped, we had to repair them before putting them back into service. Mr. Hoanh, the director of our machine shop, and Capt. Nguyen Van Pham, director of the Sector Administrative and Logistics Center, agreed to take on the task of rebuilding the buses. Under the skilled hands of our machinists and mechanics, parts from these two buses were used to assemble one relatively serviceable bus. We had to wait for approval from the joint general staff because there were rules against civilians traveling on military vehicles. We also had to obtain the agreement of the local province bus employees union before the bus could be put into service.

Leaving from An Loc, the province capital, every morning at eight o'clock, the bus provided free transportation to Saigon for families of soldiers, cadre, civil servants, and disabled veterans to enable them to go shopping or to take care of personal and family business in the city. The bus left Saigon at three o'clock every afternoon to return to An Loc.

To encourage students of the province to study hard, I was able to persuade local businessmen to provide financial support for a new program. The Province Youth Office was ordered to select, in coordination with local school boards and parent-teacher associations, one hundred outstanding students to be sent to Vung Tau on vacation every summer. Our "new" bus provided transportation for the trip. Local businessmen and the parent-teacher associations provided food.

For housing in Vung Tau, I purchased an apartment on the back beach of Vung Tau. Lieutenant Colonel Nguyen Van Tinh, the mayor of Vung Tau and my former executive officer at 1st Marine Battalion, made special arrangements that enabled me to pay for the building on an installment plan.

Many of the students, especially those from ethnic minority tribes, had never been out of the province before and did not even know what an ocean was. Through these vacations, the children were able to enjoy themselves thoroughly and to learn more about the beauty of our nation. Before their departure and after their return, I assembled the students in front of the province headquarters and counseled them to work hard, to be good, to obey their parents and teachers, and to strive to become outstanding students.

I also organized many tours for the children to visit scenic areas in the province, including trips to swim in the stream at Chon Thanh and races across the Be River. These day-tours provided recreation and helped the children learn about the history and geography of their province. My own children joined them during these trips. Their ancestors had passed down this land to them, and they had to learn to preserve it and make it even more beautiful.

Security was an important issue. The People's Self Defense Forces (PSDF) were the part of the province forces that fought communist guerillas, sappers, and underground communist agents. The PSDF was a national program begun in 1968 in which men and women too old or too young to serve in the ARVN or the RF/PF performed part-time self-defense duties. The PSDF was the most neglected, ill equipped, and underfunded of our units. PSDF personnel had to pay their own way when they were sent away for military training. The government would not even provide a subsidy to buy food for their meals during training. PSDF soldiers were frequently the ones who had worked to provide a living for their families. These poor families who had no money to buy their own food were now expected to pay for the meals of the PSDF soldiers.

I discussed this problem with my senior advisor, Raymond Perkins.

He analyzed the situation and arranged to use a portion of the advisory office's "special fund" to help pay for food rations for PSDF soldiers from our province. Each class received 50,000 piasters before leaving for the training center. The PSDF soldiers of Binh Long did not need to worry about monetary problems during their training classes, which lasted more than one month.

I tried to provide a foundation of knowledge for the people, and especially the cadre of Binh Long, to understand what was going on around them in order to develop good programs for the future. To keep up with developments in the province, a monthly pacification and development conference was held, attended by all levels of command. During these conferences, district chiefs, village chiefs, and province chiefs briefed the conference on their specific areas of responsibility, made recommendations based on identified strengths and weaknesses, and brought up problems that needed to be resolved.

I constantly stressed the duty of RF (regional force) companies to provide security for their village chiefs and of PF (popular force) platoons to provide security for their hamlet chiefs. In return, village and hamlet chiefs had to coordinate with and provide resources for these units to operate more effectively to provide security in their areas.

To resolve citizen complaints in outlying areas, we formed a special committee to go out and talk to the people directly. This committee consisted of the province chief, the deputy province chief for administration, and all province office and bureau chiefs. The Sector Culture and Entertainment Troupe usually accompanied us to provide entertainment. Sometimes a military-civilian medical team came along to examine and treat local civilians. To avoid wasting the people's time during the day, when they had to work and make a living, the committee held its sessions and answered questions and complaints at night. Through these missions to "spend the night in the hamlets," the people became more sympathetic toward their local officials, and the relationship between the people and the government grew stronger.

To provide better security, I altered our tactics and deployment of forces as part of a new province defense plan. I reduced the proportion of RF and PF troops assigned to defend the individual outposts to one-third of each unit, while the other two-thirds were sent out into the field to conduct mobile operations. Whereas in the past everyone spent all day inside their bases, making them so crowded that in some cases there was not enough room for all the troops to lie down, now the units were busy sending their troops out to conduct patrols, mount ambushes, and clear roads.

Through these operations, the RF and PF units gained confidence and gradually grew bolder. I ordered the PF units, our province reconnaissance teams (especially those who were members of ethnic minority tribes), and PSDF soldiers to don civilian clothing and go out into the fields to work and pick up information about the enemy. In this manner, our brave PF and PSDF soldiers became useful and productive eyes and ears for the province's intelligence staff.

Every time we had a success in battle, I would go to the scene of the fighting to award medals and battlefield promotions that were within my authority as sector commander. I was assisted in this effort to build the fighting spirit of the province security forces by Maj. Gen. J. J. Wagstaff, senior advisor for III Corps, who immediately gave his approval every time I recommended an outstanding soldier for a U.S. medal. He and I would go out to the unit to personally present the award in order to bolster the morale of our soldiers. As for those who gave their lives for the nation, I always went out myself, along with the district military commander, the headquarters staff, and the sector military band, to award posthumous decorations and promotions and to comfort and provide monetary assistance to the families of those who died.

* * *

On March 18, 1970, while the Cambodian head of state, Prince Norodom Sihanouk, was visiting Moscow, a pro-American clique headed by Prime Minister Lon Nol overthrew him in a bloodless coup. The media claimed that America was complicit in the coup, which the administration denied. However, the United States quickly recognized the new Cambodian government. Shortly thereafter, South Vietnamese units started conducting raids across the border into Cambodia with American air support, followed by American ground forces against North Vietnamese sanctuaries on the Cambodian/South Vietnamese border. These sanctuaries, approved by Sihanouk and pretending to be neutral, were in fact used by the communists for infiltration and to launch attacks on South Vietnam. They had storage facilities containing enough weapons to equip eighty NVA (North Vietnamese Army) battalions and enough food to feed every communist soldier in South Vietnam for six months. The communists could no longer launch their customary spring offensive in the South.

Direct U.S. involvement in Cambodia did help the military situation in South Vietnam and the Vietnamization program. But it had a shattering effect in the United States. Even within the administration, the secretaries of state and defense were opposed to the move. A letter of protest by the secretary of the interior addressed to the president was going out over the AP wire before it was delivered to the White House. Three members on the staff of the president's assistant for national security affairs, Dr. Henry Kissinger, resigned. Nixon announced that he would rather be a one-term president than preside over America's first defeat.

Reaction to the Cambodian incursion exceeded Nixon's worst fears. To the *Washington Post* this was a "self-renewing war supported by suspect evidence, specious argument and excessive rhetoric." Lawyers, architects, doctors, academicians, and corporate executives descended on Washington and lobbied to end the war. Even Secretary of State Rogers distanced himself from the administration by refusing to speculate on his own attitude during an interview with the *New York Times*.[23]

Antiwar students found arson to be a useful tool in their vicious fight against "the system." The University of California library at Berkeley was damaged by fire. Books were burned in the basement of Yale Law School. Stanford University's Center for Behavioral Studies was set on fire. The ROTC building at Kent State University was burned down.

An unruly demonstration at Kent State University first turned ugly when students pelted the National Guard with stones, then tragic when four students were shot dead. This sad incident created a huge uproar throughout the country. The mayor of New York City ordered the flag on city hall to be flown at half-staff. In response, hardhat construction workers and one hundred thousand of their sympathizers marched on city hall in support of the president.

The Cambodian incursion provoked a serious congressional challenge to presidential authority. There was outrage at Nixon's broadening of the war. In a symbolic act of defiance, the Senate voted to terminate the Tonkin Gulf Resolution of 1964. It also tried to cut off funds for military operations in Cambodia and to withdraw all U.S. forces from Vietnam by the end of the following year.

The North Vietnamese and Viet Cong delegates boycotted the Paris negotiations until the withdrawal of U.S. troops from Cambodia. The North Vietnamese presence in Cambodia and their support of the Khmer Rouge communist insurgency against Lon Nol deepened. Furthermore, the uproar in the United States reinforced the North Vietnamese conviction that domestic pressures would force more American withdrawals and weaken the American bargaining position.

U.S. troops were removed from Cambodia by the end of June 1970, but the divisiveness within the United States increased beyond the level of 1968 until it reached an unfortunate siege mentality of "us" against "them" in the White House that would eventually become fatal to the Nixon presidency.

* * *

When I assumed the post of province chief, I told everyone, during the change of command ceremony and during my meeting with the directors of the province and district offices, that Binh Long was my father's second home. My father had begun logging operations in this border province in 1947. I had come up to the province to spend summer vacations with my father. He had taken me hunting in the jungles all the way from Loc Ninh and Bu Dop to Snoul in Cambodia, crossing the border without need for a passport because back then the territory was all part of French Indochina.

My father frequently spent the night with a number of Vietnamese or Montagnard families, in the most remote villages and hamlets in the province. Binh Long was sparsely populated but a large province in area. My father knew almost everyone who lived in the province, including the Frenchmen who managed the vast rubber plantations in Cexso and Terre Rouge.

As province chief, I went out to the villages and hamlets to see for myself what the life of the people was like and to hear with my own ears what the people thought about the government. I met and talked to many Vietnamese and ethnic minority tribesmen who had worked with or known my father. Because of this connection with my family, they felt comfortable with me and were willing to give me many useful ideas in building and developing the province.

Among those who had known my father as a close friend was the chairman of the Province Council, Pham Van Qua. This relationship helped make the relationship between the province government apparatus and its elected representatives, who were similar to county supervisors, very friendly. We helped one another in every possible way to improve the security and the standard of living of the people of the province.

When I came to An Loc, a fire had recently destroyed its market area. The absence of a market to exchange goods and purchase their daily food caused great difficulties for its people. After personally inspecting the area, I contacted Doctor Tran Nguon Phieu, the minister of social welfare in Saigon, to request assistance. Although the ministry was not supposed to provide assistance for fire damage, Doctor Phieu, a personal friend, immediately provided me materials. The Province Public Works Office and the Province Social Welfare Office, working together, rebuilt the market and made it larger and better organized than before. The An Loc market expanded rapidly, with new buildings and houses sprouting up along all the streets around the market area.

The previously deserted streets became busy and active. The lives of the people became brighter.

As we worked to develop the provincial economy, we also paid attention to the needs of the people, making a special effort to raise the standard of education. We built or improved a number of parks. The stadium was refurbished to meet the sports and physical education needs of the young. We established programs to reconstruct and expand pagodas, temples, and churches, and provided assistance to help the minority tribes build their own temples. The province government asked U.S. units that were being withdrawn as part of the Vietnamization program to donate to us some of the supplies and equipment from their soon-to-be abandoned bases to build additional classrooms for the high school and housing for the families of our troops.

Every month the sector and province headquarters sent delegations of military officers, civilian officials, and local businessmen to visit the hospitals to comfort and provide assistance to wounded soldiers. The delegations were also helping to resolve the problems the wounded and sick soldiers were having with things such as military leave, awards, decorations, pay, and allowances. The sector headquarters drew up and monitored the implementation of a leave program for all units. Each unit was required to allow leaves twice each year, with each leave period lasting fifteen days. Ten percent of the unit's soldiers were permitted to be on leave at any one time. The unit commanders carried out the leave plan very strictly. If they did not, I did not allow the unit commander himself to take leave.

The improved security situation in the province enabled the local rubber plantations to increase production significantly. We were able to widen Highway 13, making the transportation of rubber easier. Taxes collected from these two plantations covered up to 60 percent of the province's budget.

The real result of our working to improve the security situation in the province would not become completely apparent until the enemy launched his massive invasion in 1972. An Loc would be defended not only by the soldiers in the province, but also by the entire population who, united as one, fought resolutely to defend our nation and prevent the loss of even one single citizen or one single inch of our sacred soil to the North Vietnamese communist aggressors. The proselytizing efforts made by the citizens, soldiers, and civil servants of Binh Long province, and the efforts made by me personally as the individual responsible for the entire province, played a role in this victory. The spirit of unity between the soldiers and civilians of An Loc throughout ninety-four days of savage fighting would play a major role in our ability to finally halt the communist aggression.

One-third of the population of Binh Long was Montagnards belonging to different tribes, such as Stieng, Mien, and so on. These tribal people were scattered around the province, with the largest numbers living in the Loc Ninh district, which shared a border with Cambodia. It was extremely important to persuade the ethnic minority tribes to cooperate with the government, and I naturally thought of Uncle Lam Ut, the foreman of my father's logging operation who had treated me like his little brother and of whom I had many happy memories almost thirty years before. I learned that Lam Ut had changed his name to Lam Cong and had become the chief of Loc Khanh village, where he was greatly respected and loved.

Uncle Lam Cong was happy to get reacquainted with me. For almost three years, I relied heavily on him in my efforts to persuade the minority tribes to cooperate with the government, to join the PSDF and the RF and PF units, and particularly to supply us with intelligence information. Thanks to the assistance of Uncle Lam Cong, our work in rural development, public health, and public education achieved great success in the villages and hamlets inhabited by the Montagnard tribesmen.

The coordination of my province's efforts with friendly military forces in the area was not so successful, however. When Gen. Do Cao Tri appointed me to the post of province chief and sector commander, I believed his primary tactical goal was to prevent communist forces from advancing from the Snoul and Fishhook areas of Cambodia to the approaches of Saigon. The commanders of the U.S. 1st Air Cavalry and 25th Infantry Divisions demanded that I send my forces out to conduct military operations in these areas. They were not happy when I told them the Binh Long sector was not capable of conducting such operations. This disagreement went on for a full month.

When General Tri and Ambassador Charles Whitehouse, senior U.S. advisor to III Corps/Military Region Three, came to visit me at sector headquarters, I briefed them on the capabilities and responsibilities of the sector. The National Pacification and Development Plan clearly stated that the responsibility of the sector was to conduct support operations to defend populated areas within the range of our support capabilities, which meant within a two-mile radius (because the sector's largest fire support weapons were 81mm mortars). Areas beyond that range were the responsibility of the ARVN 5th Division. General Tri and Ambassador Whitehouse accepted my arguments, and from that time forward I had no further problems with the U.S. 1st Air Cavalry and 25th Infantry Divisions when they operated in Binh Long province.

Meanwhile, as the U.S. and ARVN forces invaded Cambodia and destroyed communist sanctuaries and supply bases, in our province we damaged the National Liberation Front (NLF) infrastructure using the Phoenix program, and the situation became easier to maintain so we could focus on developing the province.

I hope I will be forgiven for skipping ahead of my narrative, but after such great exertions to achieve my goals, I was extremely pleased when the National Pacification and Development Center's annual report on the security situation for 1971 and 1972 placed Binh Long province at the top of its ranking of all forty-four provinces in South Vietnam.

* * *

Nixon's national security advisor, Henry Kissinger, advanced the attractive concept of a 1971 dry season offensive by the South

Vietnamese, aimed at cutting the Ho Chi Minh Trail in Laos near the DMZ. Such an operation would disrupt the flow of supplies of North Vietnam to the south and become a devastating blow for the enemy's 1972 strategy. The operation would have U.S. air support but no American advisors and no U.S. ground forces. Both governments approved.

In operation Lam Son 719, two South Vietnamese divisions crossed the Laotian border on February 8, 1971, and proceeded cautiously. After penetrating eight to twelve miles, halfway to their target, they stopped and dug in. On February 12 President Thieu ordered his commanders to be careful and to stop the operation altogether as soon as they had suffered three thousand casualties.

Giap hurled forty thousand troops into the battle, supported by two hundred of the newest Russian-made tanks, two hundred antiaircraft guns, and some long-range artillery. After six weeks of the bloodiest fighting of the war, the South Vietnamese retreated, with 3,800 dead and 9,775 wounded, raising serious doubts about the success of the Vietnamization program. The United States lost 108 helicopters and another six hundred were damaged. Two hundred and one American pilots and crewmen were killed and 1,200 wounded. The enemy losses were nearly twenty thousand killed.

A similar offensive in Cambodia achieved some good results in the beginning, but when its commander died in a helicopter crash, it bogged down and petered out. The aim of the dry season offensive of 1971—to foreclose an assault by Hanoi in 1972—was not realized.

On the contrary, the political situation in the United States was the one that deteriorated. Between April 1 and July 1 there were seventeen House or Senate votes to restrict the president's authority to conduct the war. On June 22 the Senate adopted Senator Mansfield's Sense of the Senate resolution that "it is the policy of the U.S. to terminate . . . all military operations in Indochina and to provide for the prompt and early withdrawal of all U.S. forces . . . subject to the release of American POWs." (It should be pointed out that Sense of the Senate resolutions are not legally binding.) Former officials of the Johnson administration, such as Clark Clifford and Averell Harriman, pressed for a total, unilateral withdrawal.

By the summer of 1971, there was a pervasive antiwar mood throughout the United States:

1. Seventy-one percent of the public agreed that the United States had made a mistake by sending troops to Vietnam.
2. Fifty-eight percent thought the war was immoral.
3. Nixon's approval rating on Vietnam dropped to 31 percent.

7

The 1972 Easter Offensive

THE FAILURE of operation Lam Son 719 encouraged the communist leadership in Hanoi to launch a massive invasion of South Vietnam. They had been discussing such an operation for some time, but had been undecided on the actual timing of the attack. They had watched the U.S. troop withdrawals closely and did not believe that the remaining American forces could influence the strategic situation once the general offensive was launched. Furthermore, they did not think that the political situation would permit Nixon to commit any new troops or combat support to assist the South Vietnamese forces. Additionally, they believed that a resounding NVA military victory would humiliate the president, destroy the Vietnamization program, and perhaps foil his bid for reelection in November. They hoped to convince Nixon that "he has everything to lose except an honorable exit."

Both ARVN and U.S. intelligence knew the communists would mount attacks during this time frame, but neither knew the exact dates or targets of the attacks. It was not until the first artillery barrages on the northern front that we finally realized that the enemy had selected Friday, March 30, 1972, the first day of Easter week, as the date for the launching of their massive offensive.

North Vietnamese Army Offensive, 1972.

Three NVA divisions attacked south across the DMZ toward Quang Tri. The attack, led by tanks, achieved surprise, and the enemy captured many artillery pieces as the ARVN and South Vietnamese Marines fell back in front of the enemy onslaught. Other forces threatened Quang Tri and Hue from the west. Meanwhile, there were indications that the North Vietnamese were maneuvering for an assault on Kontum.

The first four days of the attack, under heavy monsoon cloud cover, went well for the NVA. The 3rd ARVN Division fell back in disorderly retreat and gave up ten miles of territory immediately. Only the South Vietnamese Air Force A-1s and A-37s were able to work under the five-hundred-foot overcast, but they helped to contain the initial attack. After the weather broke, the North Vietnamese were exposed and the U.S. Air Force and the U.S. Navy came into play.

President Nixon rose to the occasion magnificently. He went all out in applying military pressure on North Vietnam and diplomatic pressure on the Soviet Union and China. He became the personification of American might, and all three adversaries had to bend, acknowledging the fact that, even together, they could not match American power.

Nixon felt that the North Vietnamese action had moved the war into a final stage. Only a forceful response by the United States could pave the way for a satisfactory conclusion. There was only one detail he could not control. If the South Vietnamese Army collapsed, as some American news reports suggested, the war would be lost. But the South Vietnamese were holding.

He approved the plans for a weekend of heavy B-52 raids aimed at destroying the oil depots around Hanoi and Haiphong, aware of the possibility that the Soviets might cancel the planned American-Soviet summit meeting in Moscow. They did not. Even when four Soviet merchant ships were accidentally hit, the Soviets' reaction was mild. They also accepted Nixon's assertion that the North Vietnamese actions were against the interests of both the Soviet Union and the United States. Simultaneously, Nixon ordered a major buildup of air power in the region. The U.S. Air Force and the U.S. Navy redeployed fighter squadrons, B-52s, and attack carriers to Southeast Asia.

* * *

The decision to seek a military victory had already been made by the Vietnamese Communist party during its 19th Congress in late 1970 through early 1971. The ongoing Paris negotiations and secret negotiations were only a means to buy time to replace their losses and stockpile weapons and ammunition for a new offensive. The strategy of "talk-fight" was their traditional strategy. The strength of their cadre and infrastructure had deteriorated badly during the years following the Tet Offensive. I believe the North Vietnamese had intentionally destroyed the Viet Cong by pushing them to the front during Tet 1968. They were afraid the Viet Cong would compete with them for political control whenever Vietnam was reunited. So their plan during Tet was to annihilate the NLF forces and then send their own cadre down from North Vietnam to take control of the South.

General Secretary Le Duan journeyed to Moscow in early 1971 to ask for more aid. The Soviets approved the request and supplied their most modern weapons to the North Vietnamese. Ships flying the flags of the Soviet Union and its Eastern European satellites unloaded a steady stream of weapons at the port of Sihanoukville in Cambodia. This fact contradicts the assertions made by Gen. Nguyen Dinh Uoc, a communist military historian, during a talk he gave at the Vietnam Center at Texas Tech University in July 1999. He claimed that, beginning in 1971, communist military aid to North Vietnam decreased by 60 percent. I pressed him closely on this point, saying that if his claims were true, then where did the North Vietnamese get all the modern weapons, such as 130mm guns, T-54 tanks, BTR-60 armored personnel carriers, SA-7 SAM missiles, and AT-3 antitank missiles that they used in 1972 during their massive attacks against Quang Tri, Kontum, and An Loc? His answer was that the North Vietnamese had stockpiled these weapons over the course of many years. This is the kind of stale argument the communists always make. If we are to believe them, the

North Vietnamese were stockpiling weapons their masters had not shipped to them yet.

In July 1971, the upcoming attack was given the code name the "Nguyen Hue Campaign." In December 1971, the communists withdrew Vietnamese units from Laos, regrouped and consolidated their forces, and re-equipped their army. General Giap briefed the 20th Party Congress, held in late 1971–early 1972, on the details of the planned attack. Giap told the Congress that they would attack simultaneously on three fronts, although the strategic objectives would be different for each of the three fronts.

The first front was the northern front. General Giap planned to send the 304th and 308th Divisions and five independent regiments, supported by two hundred tanks and four artillery regiments, across the DMZ to attack Quang Tri province. Division 324B would attack from Laos into western Thua Thien and besiege the ancient capital of Hue. After the attack succeeded, the communists would expand the territory of North Vietnam south to include the city of Hue.

The second front was the highlands of central Vietnam. Giap would commit the 2nd and 320th Divisions, supported by armor and artillery, to the offensive on this front. The two primary objectives were Kontum and Pleiku provinces. In addition, Giap planned to order the North Vietnamese 3rd Division to attack and capture Binh Dinh province along the coast, tying down ARVN forces and preventing them from sending reinforcements to save Pleiku and Kontum. Giap planned to cut central Vietnam in two, cutting the central highlands and the coastal lowlands at the intersection of Route 1 and Route 19. Their 711th Division would then be free to attack and overrun the city of Danang.

The third front was the southwestern front. Giap assigned responsibility for this front to three divisions, the 5th, 7th, and 9th Divisions. The 5th and 9th Divisions claimed to be Viet Cong units, but by this time in the war, they were really main force PAVN divisions. These three divisions, supported by more than one hundred modern Soviet-made tanks and long-range artillery pieces, would attack the tiny district capital of Loc Ninh and the province capital of An Loc. After capturing An Loc, the communists would announce that the city was the "capital of the provisional revolutionary government of South Vietnam." They would then advance down Highway 13 to take Saigon, the capital of South Vietnam. There was also a newly formed division called the Binh Long Division, consisting of units recruited locally.

The third front had the more important symbolic objective of capturing Saigon by May 19, Ho Chi Minh's birthday. Hence, the initial targets of Loc Ninh and An Loc, providing control of Highway 13, the highway that led to the capital, were of prime strategic importance. Highway 13 was needed for routing supplies to Saigon or for evacuation and return to the safe havens of Cambodia in case of failure.

In the Mekong Delta, hoping to pin down ARVN forces to prevent them from being sent to reinforce the other fronts, Giap assigned the 1st NVA Division to attack South Vietnam's richest rice-growing areas and to cut Route 4, a vital line of communications. The communist plan called for the maximum use of firepower to launch powerful attacks and to move as quickly as possible in order to neutralize our air power.

Although the plans for the offensive were complete, the actual date for launching the offensive was still dependent on the weather. The communists could conduct such an attack only during the dry season. If they attacked during the rainy season, they would not be able to transport the supplies for such a massive and wide-ranging campaign. The targets were spread throughout the territory of South Vietnam, and each had its own peculiar weather characteristics. In the northern provinces, the weather was dry from early January until the end of August. In the southwest, however, the rainy season began in mid-November and lasted until May of the following year. In order to mount simultaneous attacks, they had to select a date sometime between January and the end of April. This period was dry throughout the territory of South Vietnam.

* * *

As these attacks unfolded, the South Vietnamese province chiefs and ARVN corps commanders were attending a conference in Vung Tau on pacification and rural development, organized by Lt. Gen. Cao Hao Hon and presided over by President Thieu and Prime Minister Khiem. The province chiefs from Military Regions One and Two were ordered to leave the conference and return immediately to their provinces.

The province chiefs of Military Regions Three and Four were directed to remain in Vung Tau. On April 5, 1972, at eleven o'oclock, Lieutenant General Hon summoned me to his office and said: "Nhut, the president has ordered you to return to Binh Long immediately. The military situation in your province is extremely serious."

At that time, the South Vietnamese troops in the Loc Ninh district consisted of the 9th Regiment and 1st Armored Cavalry Squadron from the 5th ARVN Division. In addition to the troops from the 5th Division, there was a contingent of RF and PF soldiers under the command of the Loc Ninh district chief and 74th Border Ranger Battalion. Located at Hung Tam base camp just west of Highway 13 between Loc Ninh and An Loc was Task Force 52, a two-battalion task force from the 52nd Regiment of the 18th ARVN Division, which was under the operational control of the 5th ARVN Division commander, Brig. Gen. Le Van Hung.

Although I was away from my province, I had been telephoning Lt. Col. Nguyen Thong Thanh, my deputy sector commander, every day to monitor the situation. I had been informed of a number of scattered clashes between communist troops and RF and PF units along Highway 13 north of Can Le bridge and south of Tan Khai. Sector intelligence was monitoring the situation and had noted an increase in enemy traffic along the road north of the bridge, so Thanh had ordered the district military headquarters to intensify ambush operations in the area. These ambushes had resulted in a number of armed clashes on the nights of April 3 and 4, during which RF and PF units had killed more than twenty communist troops and captured a significant number of weapons. Of particular interest was the fact that the communist dead, based on their uniforms and equipment, were main force regu-

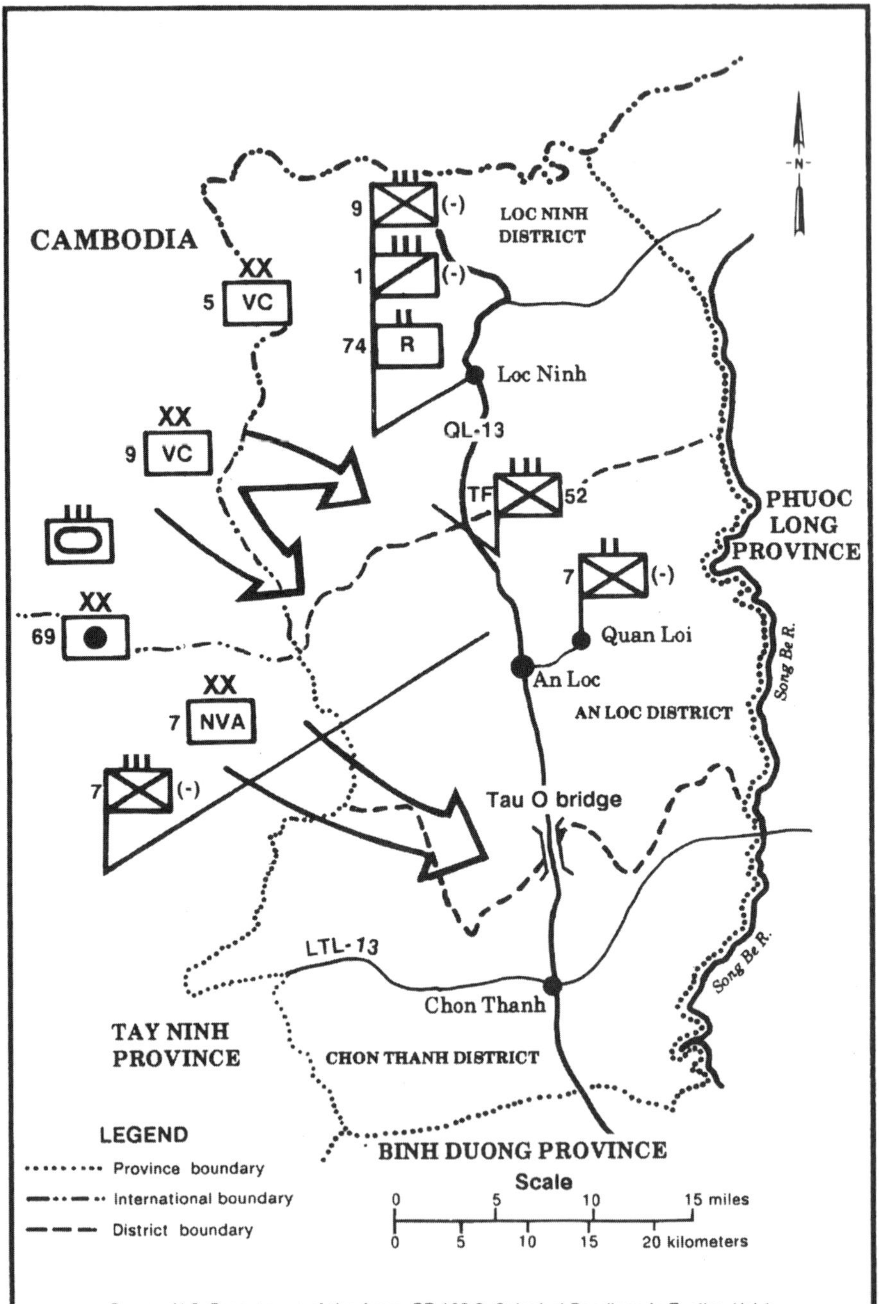

Source: U.S. Department of the Army, RB 100-2, *Selected Readings in Tactics*, Vol.1 (Fort Leavenworth, KS: U.S. Army Command and General Staff College, April 1974).

North Vietnamese Army Plan in Binh Long Province, April 5, 1972.

lars, not the local force VC troops we usually encountered. This fact caused me a great deal of concern.

To make matters worse, Mr. E. Gaudeul, director of the Cexso Rubber Plantation at Loc Ninh, informed us that many field telephone wires had been set up in the northwestern part of Loc Ninh. The military commanders in Loc Ninh had not paid attention to this report, though, and had not sent out reconnaissance troops to verify the report and to destroy the enemy's communications network.

As soon as Lieutenant General Hon told me of the president's order, I hurried back to my room, packed my bags, and returned to Binh Long by jeep. We drove from Vung Tau through Di An in Binh Duong, and reached Lai Khe at four in the afternoon.

As my jeep drove past the helicopter refueling station along Highway 13 inside the Lai Khe base, I saw someone motioning us to stop. As we slowed down, I recognized Thanh and Lt. Col. Robert E. Corley, senior advisor to sector headquarters. They had recognized my jeep because of the small green flag flying from my radio antenna (it was a Vietnamese Marine Corps flag, even though I had been out of the marines since 1966). I got out and shook hands with Thanh and Corley. Before I could ask a single question, Thanh gave me a quick briefing on the situation in the province. He said 122mm rockets had shelled the sector headquarters and one of our barracks was on fire; Loc Ninh district military headquarters was under siege; and the communists had set up a fortified roadblock on Highway 13 at Tan Khai south of An Loc, cutting off all vehicular traffic into the city.

As soon as Thanh finished his briefing, the three of us boarded a helicopter and flew to Chon Thanh to meet with Lt. Col. Pham Quang My, the district chief and district sub-sector military commander. After My briefed us on the situation in his district, I reboarded the aircraft and flew to An Loc. I convened a quick staff meeting at sector headquarters to obtain a better understanding of the situation, both enemy and friendly. Then Corley and I flew up to Loc Ninh to contact Maj. Nguyen Van Thinh, district chief and military commander of the Loc Ninh district, which was now surrounded and under heavy artillery attack by North Vietnamese forces.

Just after my helicopter took off, communist antiaircraft guns located north of An Loc directed a ferocious barrage at us. Luckily, not one round hit our helicopter, but when we tried to land at Loc Ninh, the curtain of North Vietnamese antiaircraft fire was so thick my American pilot was unable to land there.

Looking down on Loc Ninh from above, my heart sank. Smoke curled skyward from the town. Heavy artillery barrages rained down on district military headquarters and the headquarters of 9th Regiment, 5th Division. I told the pilot to circle over the town to allow me to contact Major Thinh on the radio. Many U.S. observation aircraft reported they had seen many communist trucks towing heavy artillery moving toward the district capital. They said a number of these trucks were deployed in the area of the bus station and recommended that air strikes be called in to destroy them. I delayed approving such strikes because I suspected these were actually logging trucks evacuating back to Loc Ninh. To be certain, I contacted Major Thinh. He confirmed that these were logging trucks pulling trailers transporting logs, which looked exactly like artillery pieces when viewed from the air.

We continued to fly toward the northern portion of Loc Ninh. As I looked down at the Loc Tan area, I became extremely worried. This area, the base area for 1st Armored Squadron, 5th Infantry Division, was being shelled and attacked, and many of the squadron's armored vehicles had been destroyed. Burned-out tanks and armored vehicles were scattered throughout the area. The military situation was beyond both the authority and the resources of a sector commander like me. In addition, at that time my forces actually located in Loc Ninh were quite weak.

In this situation, I tried to do those things that were within my capabilities. I ordered Major Thinh to maintain close radio contact and coordination with Col. Nguyen Cong Vinh, commander of 9th Regiment, 5th Division. I told him that, as of that very moment, the Loc Ninh district military headquarters was being placed under the operational control of Colonel Vinh to simplify command and control of the defending forces. Switching to Colonel Vinh's command frequency, I notified him that the district forces now belonged to him.

Then I flew back to the Chon Thanh military headquarters to monitor the situation. In the district conference room, I met the deputy province chief for administration and my province office and bureau chiefs, who had just arrived by road from Vung Tau. They told me that, after my departure from the conference, all Military Regions Three and Four province chiefs and office and bureau chiefs would return to their headquarters. After briefing them on the military situation in the province, the entire party boarded my helicopter to fly back to An Loc with me.

Although it was now after seven o'clock in the evening, the April sun was still high in the sky and it was still light. I ordered my driver to take me on a tour around the city in order to calm the civilian population. When the residents of the city saw that I had returned, they ran out onto the streets waving at me happily, their confidence restored.

When I returned to my residence, I saw a familiar orange jeep speeding into the courtyard. The jeep belonged to Bui Huu Tai, the chief of the province Public Works Office. He leaped out of his jeep, shouting with excitement: "Colonel! Why did your men shoot at me when I drove through Tan Khai?" Looking at Tai's ashen face, I could not help laughing. Bui Huu Tai, who went by the artistic name of Phung Trang, had a pleasant personality, but he drank cognac as though it was water. I teased him: "Did you drink so much at Vung Tau that when you drove through Chon Thanh you weren't sober enough to read the sign banning all traffic on Highway 13?" I told him the Viet Cong had set up a roadblock at Tan Khai early that morning. He was the only person with guts enough to drive through the communist roadblock. I invited him to have a glass of cognac to celebrate his brush with death.

I spent the entire day of April 6, 1972, flying over Loc Ninh to maintain radio contact with Major Thinh and Colonel Vinh. With my limited military resources, however, I was unable to do anything to help the Loc Ninh forces. Fortunately, the district military command post was located in a deep, heavily fortified bunker originally built by the Japanese Army during World War II, so we were able to maintain communications with one another despite the desperate fighting that was going on throughout Loc Ninh.

During the night of April 6, Regimental Task Force 52, commanded by Lt. Gen. Nguyen Ba Thinh, left Hung Tam base to reinforce Loc Ninh, but it was soon hit by extremely heavy artillery and ground attacks. The task force suffered heavy losses, leaving it with no more than three hundred troops still capable of fighting. The communists captured a tremendous amount of equipment from the task force, including six 105mm howitzers, two 155mm howitzers, and a large quantity of ammunition. The enemy used these captured guns and ammunition to shell An Loc city throughout the rest of the battle. After Task Force 52 withdrew back to An Loc, I ordered that the Can Le bridge be destroyed in order to slow the enemy advance and to delay the forward movement of his tanks.

By this time, the defenders in An Loc included 7th Regiment (-), commanded by Lt. Col. Ly Duc Quan, and 8th Regiment (-), commanded by Lt. Col. Mach Van Truong, both from Le Van Hung's 5th ARVN Division, the 3rd Ranger Group, the remnants of Task Force 52, and two battalions of RFs and PFs. PAVN forces vastly outnumbered the ARVN troops in Binh Long province. While the 5th VC Division finished off the defenders at Loc Ninh, the 9th VC Division prepared for a direct assault on An Loc. Meanwhile, the 7th PAVN Division was maneuvering to cut Highway 13 south of An Loc.

On April 7 Major Thinh asked me to confirm reports that communist tanks had appeared on the battlefield. I contacted General Hung, the 5th Division commander. He told me there were no indications that communist tanks were participating in the battle, with the possible exception of a few of our tanks that the enemy had captured from 1st Squadron at Loc Tan.

While the fighting continued at Loc Ninh, I decided to use all the resources of the province Public Works Office to strengthen the southern perimeter of An Loc, building our defensive wall higher and making it thicker and sturdier. I ordered RF, PF, and PSDF troops to string additional barbed-wire barriers across the streets and to build additional defensive positions on every block. The civilian residents of the city also began reinforcing their own bunkers and shelters. I had to use all the resources of the province public works office for this task because some of 5th Division's engineer vehicles had been destroyed at Loc Ninh, while many of the rest were in Lai Khe, unable to reach An Loc.

Reports that enemy tanks were attacking Loc Ninh caused fear among the troops because they had never before faced enemy armor and were not prepared materially (with weapons) or emotionally to combat tanks.

When Loc Ninh finally fell to the communists, An Loc would be next. I immediately convened a meeting to deal with the situation. I made several critical decisions at this meeting.

First, Mr. Vo Tan Vinh, deputy province chief for administration, was given responsibility for coordinating with the An Loc district chief and with the province Social Welfare and Information Offices to consolidate all rice and food stocks in the city; for making public address announcements telling the civilian population how to dig bunkers capable of withstanding artillery barrages; for concentrating all refugees in safe refugee centers far removed from our military bases; and for organizing the distribution of food to the refugees.

Second, the deputy sector commander was given responsibility to revise our plan for defending the province, in close coordination with friendly units. He was directed to appropriate all materials needed for preparing our defenses, such as barbed wire, iron stakes, steel mesh, and sandbags from the Logistics Administrative Center, including materials belonging to the Public Works Office, and to distribute them to all defensive units, including units of 5th Infantry Division. He was also ordered to expand and reinforce foxholes and fighting positions and to strengthen our defensive perimeter.

Third, I recommended to General Hung that he reinforce our defenses on Dong Long Hill, which was 420 feet high and located about three-quarters of a mile north of An Loc as the crow flies. The province sector headquarters service platoon, under the command of Second Lieutenant Nha, held the hill. From the top of this hill our troops could observe enemy activities throughout the entire northern half of the province capital. General Hung approved my recommendation and sent the 5th Reconnaissance Company to reinforce the defenses of Dong Long Hill.

I withdrew 254th RF Company, which was then providing security for Van Hien village seven miles east of the province capital, and stationed it atop Hill 169, adjacent to the 492-foot-high "Windy Hill," located about three miles southeast of the province capital.

I recommended that General Hung send a company of the 52nd Ranger Battalion to help 254th RF Company defend Hill 169, from where our troops could monitor all communist troop movements east and south of the province capital. It was because of the successful defense of this hill by 254th RF Company and the Ranger Company that on April 14 elements of 1st Airborne Brigade and 81st Airborne Ranger Group had a secure landing zone from which they then deployed to establish a fire support base for their advance into the city to rescue it from enemy attack.

I also recommended to General Hung that he send 5th Division reconnaissance units deep behind enemy lines to collect information to enable us to put together a more effective plan of defense because my own province intelligence and reconnaissance elements were only capable of operating in the area of the province capital. However, General Hung did not approve this recommendation.

There was more than a little tension between General Hung and me. He controlled all the regular forces in and around An Loc, while I controlled the RF, PF, and PSDF troops. We did not always see eye to eye during the battle and this would cause some difficulties once the fighting began in earnest.

On the afternoon of April 7, the Chon Thanh district headquarters was shelled heavily by enemy artillery. The chief district military commander, Lt. Col. Pham Quang My, received minor wounds and the deputy district military commander, a major, was killed. I decided to send Maj. Nguyen Ai Quoc, deputy chief of staff for operations and logistics, down to replace them that very night in order to calm the fears of the people of Chon Thanh and to provide the district with a commander capable of coordinating with and supporting friendly units trying to clear Highway 13.

At this time, one event in particular made many hearts stand still, especially among members of my family. Colonel Truong Huu Duc, commander of the 5th Armored, 18th Division, was in a helicopter observing the battle when antiaircraft fire shot his helicopter, killing only him. His body was flown back to Lai Khe. A number of newspaper journalists waiting there for reports of the battle assumed I had been killed. This was because Colonel Duc, like me, was a large man, had a mustache, and was a member of the tenth class at the military academy. (He was later given a posthumous battlefield promotion to brigadier general.)

That night a number of these newspapers went to press with the news of my death, including my friend Nguyen Ang Ca's paper *Tin Som*. My wife was out visiting relatives at the Old Market. When she was getting in the car to return home, our driver, Thi Ton, hesitantly asked: "Madam, have you heard the news?" My wife was surprised at the driver's unusual tone of voice, so she asked: "What news?" "I read in the paper that the colonel, your husband, has been killed." My wife sat there in shocked silence. When she got home, she received phone calls from Col. Chau Van Tien, province chief of Gia Dinh, and from Lt. Gen. Nguyen Van Minh, 3rd Corps commander, telling her not to worry and that the news was incorrect. My wife grew more worried because she thought they were just trying to calm her down before the official report of my death in battle arrived.

The Binh Long province telephone network and the province headquarters military telephone network had both been completely paralyzed by communist shelling attacks that had damaged all the antennas, leaving only the military's UHF radio circuits in operation. I had no way to call home and talk to my wife.

The next day, relatives from Kien Hoa, Dinh Truong, and friends and acquaintances arrived at my house to pay their condolences to my wife, who was in shock and despair. She had to worry about receiving these guests, arranging housing for relatives until the funeral, selecting the date of burial, and so forth.

Finally, when telephone service was reestablished the next afternoon, I telephoned home. When she heard my voice, my wife was overwhelmed with joy. Later I decided to move the province Office of Post and Communication's long-range telephone switchboard into the military sector's operations center in order to provide us with additional channels of communications with the outside world. I could now talk to different ministries about food and medicines, and even call the presidential offices. These channels would remain open even as communist forces surrounded An Loc.

Despite the efforts of the defenders and their American advisors, Loc Ninh fell on April 7. The communists then turned their attention to An Loc, the Binh Long province capital.

Initially, the forces defending the An Loc front totaled about 6,500 ARVN soldiers and twenty-five American advisors. This number included troops from the 5th Division and attached units, as well as Binh Long Sector forces. The 5th Division total included: Headquarters: 500 men; 7th Regiment (-): 850 men; 8th Regiment (-): 900 men; 9th Regiment (-): 50 soldiers who managed to escape from Loc Ninh; 3rd Ranger Group: 1,300 men; Regimental Task Force 52 (-) from 18th Division: 300 men; 5th Division artillery battalions: 300 men. The total strength of Binh Long Sector forces was 2,000 soldiers, including RF and PF units, PSDF forces, a platoon of V-100 armored cars, and one 105mm howitzer platoon.

American and ARVN intelligence realized the communists had overwhelming superiority, in both manpower and in modern weapons, over our forces. They had massed the following units for the attack on Binh Long: the Viet Cong 9th Division, consisting of the 271st, 272nd, and 95C Regiments, a total of 7,200 men, all of them North Vietnamese; the 5th Division, consisting of the 274th, 275th, and E6 Regiments, a total of 5,200 men; and the 7th Division, consisting of the 141st, 165th, and 209th Regiments, a total of 7,000 men. In addition to the three divisions, the PAVN forces also included the 202nd and 203rd Armored Regiments, equipped with hundreds of T-54 and PT-76 tanks and BTR-50 armored personnel carriers, plus M41 tanks and M113 armored personnel carriers captured from 5th Division at Loc Ninh, with a total strength of 500 men.

Providing support for the infantry and armored units was the 69th Artillery Division reinforced by a number of our own guns the communists had captured at Loc Ninh and from Task Force 52, 18th Division, with a total strength of 4,000 men. In addition, 11th Antiaircraft Artillery Regiment, a force of 1,800 men, was attached to 7th Division for this operation. Seventh Division was responsible for maintaining the roadblock at Tan Khai and preventing our reinforcements from reaching the city from the south. Rounding out the PAVN forces was the 429th Sapper Brigade, with 1,100 men.

A total of twenty thousand North Vietnamese troops were committed to the attack in Binh Long, meaning the enemy outnumbered us three to one. Our forces, on the other hand, had air superiority and were determined to resist the North Vietnamese aggressors. The stage was set for a desperate battle to the death.

8

An Loc

Ninety-four Days and Nights of Shells and Bombs (April 5, 1972–July 7, 1972)

ONLY SIXTY-FIVE miles from Saigon, An Loc, the capital of Binh Long province, was one of the newest and smallest province capitals in South Vietnam, and therefore, the local defense forces assigned to it were extremely weak.

If the communists had been smart and had analyzed the situation properly, they could have captured An Loc rather easily during the first few days of the offensive. If they had used their 9th Division to make a surprise attack on An Loc and then used their 5th Division to attack and besiege Loc Ninh while cutting our line of communications at Tan Khai with their 7th Division, they would have created tremendous problems for the ARVN because we would have been forced to try to recapture An Loc, relieve Loc Ninh, and at the same time clear Highway 13 at Tan Khai.

Perhaps the communists wanted to be certain of victory and not take any risks. That was why they decided to take Loc Ninh first, to ensure that their supply lines and rear areas near Snoul and the Fishhook area were secure before they launched the attack on An Loc. This strategy gave us the time we needed to realign our forces and reinforce our defenses at An Loc.

On April 5 our intelligence reported that the NVA 9th Division was northwest of the city, but they had to wait until they had captured Loc Ninh before the NVA 5th Division could move down from the north to join 9th Division in a coordinated attack on An Loc. Meanwhile every soldier and civil servant, as well as local civilians, worked to strengthen our defenses as we pulled our units back from remote areas to redeploy them in defense of the city. The province government also worked feverishly to provide housing, food, medicine, and blankets to the tens of thousands of refugees from outlying villages and hamlets that were streaming into the city under a barrage of enemy artillery fire.

The sector's defenses did not become relatively solid until April 10, when the troops of 8th Regiment (-) arrived by helicopter. The families of soldiers and city officials feverishly dug strong bunkers and stockpiled food and other essentials for a hard and protracted fight. The Sector Logistics Administrative Center issued one PSP section to each family for use in building bomb shelters (PSP—pierced steel plating—sections are interlocking steel plates used by military engineers to build tactical aircraft runways). We also equipped our PSDF soldiers with M72 antitank rockets and trained them in their use.

Communist artillery pounded the city relentlessly, day and night. A number of fires broke out and the shrill screams of ambulance and fire engine sirens never stopped. The enemy's heavy artillery barrage and antiaircraft defenses did not deter our pilots. American helicopters landed continuously to evacuate nonessential personnel and civilians. Only a few American officers and NCOs remained behind to handle communications, liaison, and coordination duties.

That same day, the 5th Division commander, Brig. Gen. Le Van Hung, who had just received a battlefield promotion to brigadier general in spite of 5th Division's heavy losses at Loc Ninh, arrived in An Loc. He established his division forward headquarters at the former headquarters of Binh Long sector. Provisions were also made to establish forward headquarters for III Corps in the same location if that became necessary.

For the initial attack on An Loc, the North Vietnamese forced a large number of the residents of Quan Loi village to storm their way into the city through the eastern gate, with communist troops right behind the civilians. The RF unit defending the gate did not know how to respond to this flood of civilians and asked for instructions. I ordered the unit to fire over the peoples' heads and just past both flanks of the crowd. The RF was authorized to fire directly into the crowd only if the crowd refused to stop or if we could verify that communist infantry was following them to take advantage of the confusion to attack the city.

I then asked my American advisor, Lt. Col. Bob Corley, to call in Cobra helicopter gunships to strafe the area right behind the crowd, to block the advance of any enemy troops following the civilians. The crowd scattered in terror and a large number fled to our lines. I directed our village and hamlet chiefs to go to the gate to identify residents of their areas and allow only persons they knew to enter our temporary refugee camps.

Amid this confusion, artillery shells continued to rain on the city. A heavy artillery attack preceding a ground assault is a time-honored communist tactic. Before sending in their infantry and tanks to overrun An Loc, the communists bombarded the city relentlessly. By the time the battle was over, every square inch of ground in An Loc bore the scars of their 82mm mortars, 122mm rockets, 130mm long-range guns, and even 105mm and 155mm howitzers captured at Loc Ninh and Hung Tam.

The high point of the artillery barrage was the night of April 12. More than ten thousand artillery shells pounded the city. After midnight, the lead troop columns of the NVA 9th Division, led by tanks, seized the northern part of An Loc. When the artillery barrage ended, the entire 9th Division surged forward in an attempt to capture the city.

Because of my ten years of combat experience in the marine corps and as commander of the 18th Division Training Center and the 43rd and 48th Regiments, I had experience in repelling communist human wave attacks. I ordered my soldiers to stay low in their bunkers and foxholes as long as the communist artillery barrage continued. I told them to use this time to close their eyes and get some rest to prepare for our own counterattack. As soon as the artillery fire lifted, I said, our troops should stand up, get into firing position, and shoot anything and everything they saw moving in the darkness. I was on the radio constantly, contacting my RF and PF units deployed on the northeastern, southeastern, and southwestern perimeters of the city, to monitor the situation so that I could make the appropriate battle decisions as quickly as possible.

At about six o'clock on the morning of April 13, the enemy artillery barrage ended. Shortly thereafter, communist tanks and infantry penetrated our defensive line on the city's northeastern perimeter (which was held by the 3rd Ranger Group), captured the airfield and Dong Long Hill, and slowly advanced southward into the city. Machine guns and rockets fired by our helicopter gunships shattered the infantry columns that followed the tanks. The skillful and courageous American and South Vietnamese pilots of our Cobra helicopter gunships became the "angels of death" for the attacking enemy troops on the ground below.

The infantry force accompanying the communist armored vehicles broke and ran back to the rear even as the enemy tanks continued to advance. We later learned from prisoner interrogations that there was no coordination between the tanks and the infantry, and furthermore that the armor and infantry had two separate command structures. Without infantry to protect them and with no underground agents to guide them, the enemy asked local civilians to give them directions. Because the civilians never liked communists, they gave them the wrong directions or directed them into ambush positions manned by our troops. Instead of giving them directions toward province headquarters, the civilians directed the tanks toward combat positions held by our RF and PSDF forces. Three PSDF members destroyed a heavy T-54 tank with three M72 LAW antitank rockets. News that PSDF soldiers had destroyed a T-54 tank swept through the city. Our defenders gained confidence in the destructive capabilities of the magnificent shoulder-fired M72 rocket.

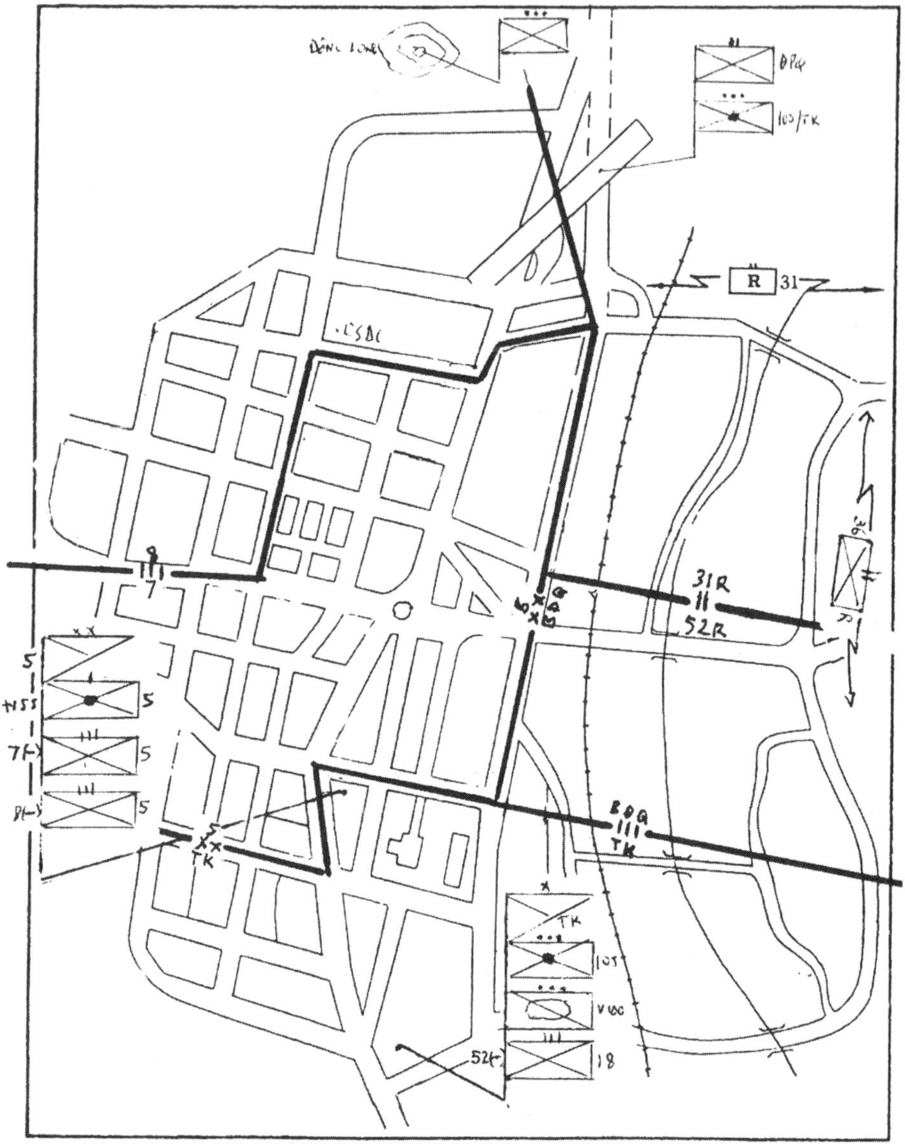

Friendly Disposition at An Loc Before the First Attack, April 13, 1972

At 10:30 a.m., another T-54 tank, with no guides to direct it, wandered aimlessly through the streets, smashing any obstacles in its path. Its tracks eventually became entangled in strands of concertina wire. Unable to move, it sat motionless, like a gigantic pile of junk, south of sector headquarters. I issued an order to Captain Khai, commander of sector artillery: "*Major* Khai," I said, "you must destroy that T-54 for me."

Captain Khai ran to our lone remaining 105mm howitzer, which was sitting abandoned in the middle of the sector headquarters parade ground because enemy artillery shrapnel had flattened its tires and destroyed its gun sight. Sighting along the barrel, he aimed the gun directly at the tank and fired, turning it into a pile of useless iron scrap.

I had just given Captain Khai a battlefield promotion to major.

The T-54 tank driver was taken prisoner. He was a corporal in 226th Company of Battalion M72. He said his name was Van Mai. Under interrogation, he told us that his tank company, a total of nine T-54s, had infiltrated from North Vietnam to Cambodia in February 1972. On April 13, his unit, together with 272nd Infantry Regiment of the NVA 9th Division, had attacked An Loc. His commander had told them that when their tanks attacked Loc Ninh, all our troops defending the district capital had fled in terror. His commander therefore decided to send his tanks into An Loc first and bring the infantry in only after the tanks had frightened the defenders away.

The communists made no arrangements for direct coordination between infantry and armored units. All communications between units had to go through Group 301, the code designation for COSVN headquarters. This was the first time the enemy had used tanks in great numbers and had no experience in tank-infantry coordination.

In addition, the communist troops had been told that when they entered An Loc, the people would greet them with open arms. Each comrade carried one new uniform to wear in a parade when An Loc would be captured. Mai's admissions were consistent with the arrogant announcement made by Madame Nguyen Thi Binh, foreign minister of the NLF and one of the North Vietnamese negotiators at the

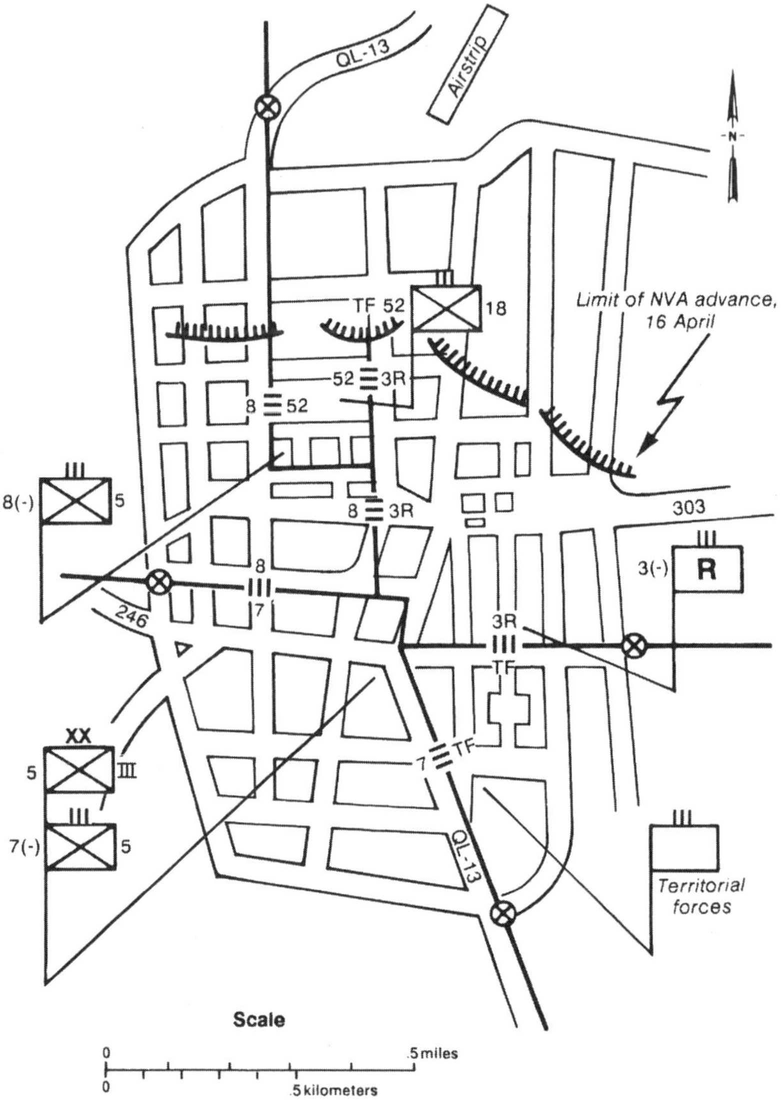

Note: All advisers used sketch maps of An Loc similar to this one, with each block numbered for ease of identification.

Source: Major John D. Howard, "An Loc: A Study of U.S. Power," *Army*, 25 September, 1975.

First Attack on An Loc. *Map from "An Loc: A Study of U.S. Power" by Major John. D. Howard. From* ARMY *Magazine, September 1975. Copyright 1975 by the Association of the U.S. Army. Limited reprint permission granted by AUSA.*

Paris peace talks. She had boasted on April 13 that, within a few days, An Loc would become the capital of the "Provisional Revolutionary Government of South Vietnam." She is one of the very few people left from the NLF and is a puppet vice president of Vietnam.

Our troops destroyed nine T-54 and PT-76 tanks (including one command vehicle) inside the city, while Vietnamese and U.S. Air Force pilots destroyed several more armored vehicles outside the city. Ferocious platoon-sized clashes raged inside and outside the city perimeter. Enemy antiaircraft guns put up a curtain of fire around the city, preventing medical evacuation helicopters from evacuating our wounded. The military situation was critical, but the resolve of our soldiers and civilians to resist the enemy attack remained high.

We learned valuable lessons about combating enemy tanks. Our defenders were no longer terrified when confronted by enemy armored columns. Through Lieutenant Colonel Corley, I requested that the latest version of the M72 antitank rocket be supplied to our defenders. I ordered my troops to check all bunkers and foxholes and repair all fighting positions to prepare for the next round of communist attacks.

Determined to support our brave ARVN troops in spite of the heavy communist fire, our skilled Vietnamese and American pilots flew daring missions to deliver supplies to the city. C-123 and C-130 aircraft would fly in very low, at treetop level over the rubber plantations. When they reached An Loc, they would climb suddenly, dumping pallet-loads of supplies out the open rear ramp doors of the aircraft onto the province soccer field. In this way as much as 90 percent of the rations and ammunition fell within our lines.

In response, the enemy massed their antiaircraft guns as close to the perimeter of the city as possible, and a number of cargo aircraft were shot down. The supply drops had to be made from above eight thousand feet to avoid antiaircraft fire, but then the parachutes were scattered by the wind. More than half of the supply pallets landed outside our perimeter, and some pallets were ripped apart by antiaircraft shells as they dangled on the ends of their parachute shrouds. Only a small portion of the supplies actually reached our forces in the city.

Later, the United States brought in an experimental version of parachute that could be dropped from above ten thousand feet to avoid antiaircraft fire and SA-7 SAM missiles. The parachute descended very fast when dropped from the aircraft, lessening the scattering effect of the wind considerably. At an altitude of three hundred yards, a drogue chute would pop out, extracting a large parachute, which would slow the descent of the supply pallet and allow it to float gently to the designated landing point. Using this new parachute, two-thirds of the supplies now reached friendly hands. A few pallets were destroyed when the drogue parachute failed to deploy, and a small number of pallets landed behind enemy lines.

Whenever a supply drop was made, every unit would send its own personnel out to wait at the soccer field and fight for possession of the supply pallets. To avoid this problem, 5th Division headquarters ordered Col. Bui Duc Diem, assistant for logistics to the commander of 5th Division, to work with Maj. Nguyen Dinh The, sector staff chief, and Maj. Nguyen Kien Diem, the sector headquarters S-4 officer, to coordinate the collection, control, and distribution of supplies to combat units and to the civilian population. Those assigned to this duty were truly worthy of commendation.

The enemy shelled the soccer field heavily to destroy the supply pallets and to prevent our troops from recovering them. Our soldiers learned to wait several hours for the artillery barrage to lift before sending teams out to recover the supplies. Some soldiers took advantage of this situation to sneak onto the soccer field and recover supplies for themselves. I recommended to Col. Le Quang Luong, the Airborne Brigade commander, to assign one of his units the responsibility for recovering supplies. We were finally able to thus stabilize An Loc's supply situation.

According to records kept by the joint general staff, during the siege An Loc received a total of 3,686 tons of food rations, ammunition, and medical supplies, as well as 31,330 gallons of fuel. These supplies eased the concerns and increased the confidence of the soldiers and

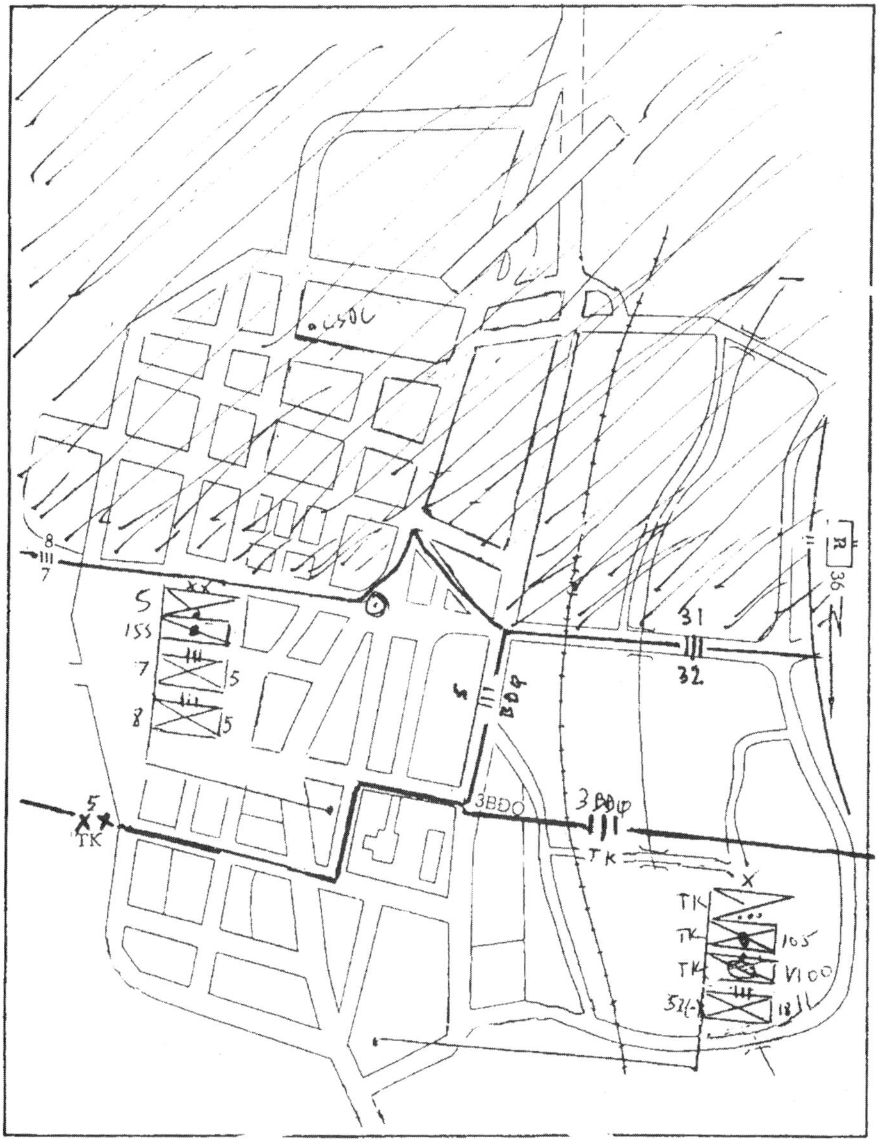

Situation After First Attack, Northern Part of An Loc

civilians defending An Loc. Everyone now focused on strengthening their bunkers, bomb shelters, and fighting positions.

The enemy was exhausted after April 14, and their shelling gradually decreased. Long strings of heavy bombs dropped by B-52s on enemy troop concentrations and armored vehicles destroyed a large proportion of his combat capabilities. In addition, our soldiers and civilians destroyed a number of enemy tanks and killed many of his infantrymen. The enemy needed time to regroup, bring in reinforcements, and to re-equip his units before launching new attacks. Information obtained from Montagnard tribesmen provided us rather precise information about the type of heavy weapons the enemy had as well as the location of communist infantry and armored units. Through our American advisors, I requested immediate U.S. air strikes against communist units before they could launch a new round of attacks.

After repelling the first wave of communist attacks, the morale of our soldiers and civilians improved enormously. Our greatest fear, the fear of attack by tanks, had now been somewhat alleviated. We were no longer overcome with terror at the sight of armor. When tanks appeared, we knocked them out. When communist troops surged into the city, our aircraft bombed them.

During the initial attack of April 13 and 14, the ARVN had sustained losses of twenty-eight killed, fifty-three wounded, six missing. One hundred seventy of the enemy had been killed and two captured. In addition, our forces captured three crew-served weapons, five individual weapons, and two radios. Sixteen enemy armored vehicles were destroyed. We did fare well in the first enemy assault, but the battle was far from over.

As expected, enemy artillery barrages shook the ground and shattered the air on the night of April 15. Several city blocks caught fire. We could hear the blast of guns firing, then the sound of the shell whistling through the air, ending in a resounding explosion when the shell hit the ground. The sounds enabled us to tell from which direction the shells were coming. Our soldiers gradually learned to identify each type of enemy artillery round from the sound alone.

At dawn the next day, the enemy fired more than one thousand rounds of artillery into An Loc. The artillery barrage focused particularly on two locations: General Hung's 5th Division headquarters and my own Binh Long sector headquarters. In spite of the continuous heavy shelling, our troops were able to rest through the barrage because of our efforts to strengthen our bunkers and combat fortifications. Both headquarters maintained a constant stream of radio communications, verifying the latest intelligence reports from our forward reconnaissance teams on enemy movements and positions and requesting immediate air strikes.

Communist assault forces opened fire at six o'clock in the morning, launching the second wave of attacks on the city. Our troops and civilians came out of their bunkers, guns at the ready, to repel the attack. This time the NVA 9th Division attacked with 272nd Regiment in two columns from the north and west, each supported by tanks and heavy artillery. Eighth Regiment, 5th Division, was unable to hold against the enemy tide and pulled back to a line on the south side of Tran Hung Dao Avenue.

The entire northern end of the city was now in the hands of the enemy. After capturing the northern part of the city, the communists installed nests of antiaircraft guns on top of a number of tall buildings, threatening our air support. Our gallant pilots, both Vietnamese and American, were undeterred by the enemy antiaircraft cannon and heavy machine guns. Waves of daring, precise bombing attacks not only silenced the communist artillery, but also turned communist armored vehicles into blazing hulks strewn across the battlefield. With their armor destroyed and their artillery support removed, the communist attack bogged down. North Vietnamese assault troops now tried just to hold their ground while waiting for our forces to counterattack and annihilate them.

Along An Loc's western perimeter, the NVA 9th Division threw the entire 271st Regiment into the battle. Our intelligence detected the enemy movement and reported it to the operations center. U.S. Air Force B-52s rained thousands of tons of bombs on the regimental assembly area in the Xa Cat rubber plantation 2.5 miles west of An Loc. Grievously wounded, 9th Division broke and ran, abandoning the assault. We later captured the minutes of a meeting held on June 17, 1972, during which 9th Division admitted that 271st Regiment headquarters and one entire battalion had been annihilated by B-52 strikes and that this was why they had abandoned their attack on An Loc's western perimeter.

In spite of air strikes throughout the area, in the second attack communist forces managed to capture one-third of the city.

During the second wave of attacks, our forces suffered eighteen soldiers killed, eighty-nine wounded, thirty-eight missing. In addition, we lost a number of individual weapons. One U.S. AH-1 Cobra helicopter was shot down. The communists left thirteen bodies on the battlefield and carried away many others. Ten enemy armored vehicles were left burning in the streets and on the outskirts of An Loc.

* * *

The enemy forces still vastly outnumbered our defenders, and we were running low on ammunition. We could not evacuate our wounded, who continued to pile up in greater and greater numbers. Our stocks of medical supplies were so low that Doctor Nguyen Van Qui, a medical corps captain, took nylon threads from sandbags, boiled them thoroughly, and used them to stitch up soldiers' wounds. Sector headquarters set aside two large underground bunkers to serve as a surgical hospital and to treat our wounded. Every time I visited the wounded, I had to hold my nose because of the stench of wounds left unattended too long.

I knew most of our soldiers were addicted to cigarettes. Although I do not smoke, I always took along several packs of military-issue cigarettes, and I would light a cigarette and hold it to the lips of our wounded so they could take a puff. Afterward, I ordered the sector Supply Office to distribute all our commissary items, including milk, sugar, cigarettes, and so on to our frontline units. Later, when I was sent to Military Region One, Lt. Gen. Pham Quoc Thuan, newly appointed III Corps commander, requested an investigation of me, alleging that I had abused my authority and wasted approximately 200,000 piasters'

The author as a military cadet

The author and his wife after their wedding, November 27, 1957

Lt. Gen. Nguyen Van Hinh, chief of general staff, and light infantry battalions at Soc Trang

The author and his battalion staff, Demilitarized Zone operation

Maj. Tran Van Nhut, deputy and chief of staff, Vietnam Marines, 1963–64

Gen. Tran Van Nhut and Maj. Gen. J. J. Wagstaff, III Corps advisor

President Nguyen Van Thieu at An Loc, July 7, 1972. In the background are the author (center) and Lt. Gen. Nguyen Van Minh (right)

President Thieu and the author

Brig. Gen. Le Van Hung, the hero of An Loc

The author (left) and Lt. Gen. Nguyen Van Minh, commander, III Corps and Military Region Three

Left to right: Lieutenant General Minh (back to camera), President Thieu, Colonel Miller (advisor to the 5th Division), the author, Col. Cua Binh Duong, and Brigadier General Hung

North Vietnamese Army T-54 destroyed by regional forces at Xa Cam

The author and Hoang Duc Nha, special secretary to President Nguyen Van Thieu

Maj. Gen. J. F. Hollingsworth and Col. Walter F. Ulmer, senior advisor to the 5th ARVN Division

Brigadier General Hung and Colonel Ulmer with Maj. Ron Skarupa and Lt. Col. Ray Gunderson, other members of Advisory Team 70

Photographs on this page courtesy of Lt. Gen. Walter F. Ulmer's collection.

Every man, whether regional force, provincial force, or self-defense force, was equipped with at least two or three M72 rocket launchers ready to kill enemy tanks

North Vietnamese Army PT-76 destroyed by South Vietnamese–U.S. forces

Destroyed An Loc

Col. Nguyen Thong Thanh, An Loc deputy sector chief and later province chief in Phuoc Long (killed in early 1975)

Lt. Col. William B. Nolde (right), Binh Long advisor after July 7, 1972, the last American killed in action in Vietnam, two hours before the cease-fire of January 28, 1973

The author at Chu Lai, November 1972

The 2nd ARVN Division on board ship, being evacuated to Binh Tuy

worth of logistics supplies. I made a detailed report to the president and prime minister, with copies to Thuan. I said that I was prepared to reimburse the government if in fact I had misused public funds for my own personal benefit. Apparently, the president understood why I had distributed the supplies and nothing ever came of Thuan's charges.

Conditions in the civilian hospital were even worse. So many civilians were killed that the province had to use bulldozers on several occasions to dig mass graves. Province headquarters selected a plot of empty ground in front of the hospital to use as a cemetery to avoid the risk of infection.

Our troop strength at An Loc had shrunk as a result of two savage waves of attacks. Many wounded soldiers still stood by their comrades, determined to repel the enemy. Our prospects were bleak. If we did not receive reinforcements soon, An Loc would inevitably fall into communist hands within the next few days.

During the days we spent crouched in our bunkers, we listened to BBC and Voice of America for news of the outside world. BBC Radio broadcast an opinion that was unfavorable for our forces. It said: "If An Loc holds, it will be a miracle." Because I had commanded the soldiers, civil servants, and civilians of the province for almost three years, I felt my stomach tighten. I prayed that if the situation got worse, I would be able to fight and die beside my soldiers and my people.

Sometimes communist radio operators broke into the sector's radio communications network and demanded to speak to me. An arrogant voice once shouted over the radio: "We have located your position. Surrender or die!" I laughed and replied: "So it's you again, huh, Big Mouth? Just look around. Wherever you see our yellow flag with three red stripes, that's where you will find me. Just come on over, and I'll arrange for you and your big mouth to fulfill the dream of 'being born in the North to die in the South' that your uncle Ho Chi Minh had for all of you." I tried to keep him talking, but he turned off his transmitter, afraid our radio directions finders would pinpoint his location so we could call in artillery and air strikes on his position.

The miracle mentioned by BBC did in fact take place. The situation improved with the arrival of the 1st Airborne Brigade. An initial contingent of paratroopers landed safely by helicopter at the foot of Windy Hill, with an immediate and visible effect on the morale of the defenders. One day later, the entire 1st Airborne Brigade, under its gallant and skillful commander, Col. Le Quang Luong, completed its helicopter movement into the An Loc area.

As soon as he landed on Windy Hill, Colonel Luong initiated a lightning operation. Leaving a light brigade headquarters element, together with 6th Airborne Battalion, one 105mm artillery battery, 3rd Airborne Reconnaissance Company, and 3rd Airborne Engineer Company stationed on Windy Hill, he advanced toward An Loc with his 5th and 8th Airborne Battalions divided into two columns.

The 8th Battalion, under the command of Lt. Col. Van Ba Ninh and supported by the Ranger and RF companies stationed atop Hill 169, advanced on the left to the hamlet of Phu Hoa. Ninh's column met no significant resistance and quickly linked up with troops defending my sector headquarters at seven o'clock on April 17.

The righthand columns, under the command of Lt. Col. Nguyen Chi Hieu and made up of 5th Airborne Battalion and headquarters, 1st Airborne Brigade, advanced toward the hamlet of Soc Gon. Hieu's airborne troopers encountered a unit of the NVA 5th Division at the hamlet. They captured an enemy soldier who told us that they had been hurriedly moved down from Loc Ninh to replace the NVA 9th Division, which had failed in its attempt to take An Loc. The 5th was charged to continue the attack and overrun and destroy An Loc. When the vicious and bloody battle that ensued was over, eighty-five enemy bodies were left strewn across the battlefield. Our forces captured seven crew-served weapons and twenty AK-47 rifles. Three airborne soldiers were killed and thirteen wounded.

On April 16, the soldiers of the 81st Airborne Ranger Group were transported by helicopter from our base at Lai Khe to the area next to the landing zone held by 1st Airborne Brigade on Windy Hill. Trained to conduct independent, long-range operations, the soldiers of 81st Airborne split into small teams to move forward to relieve the siege of An Loc. During their move toward the battlefield, the Airborne

Rangers were mistakenly bombed by our air force. Because they operated in small formations, only two soldiers were wounded. Both these casualties were immediately picked up by our helicopters and transported to the hospital at Lai Khe for treatment.

Fifth Airborne Battalion continued to advance toward An Loc. Communist forces fought to halt Lieutenant Colonel Hieu's relief force, but the NVA 5th Division forgot they were facing the "angels in red berets," as the airborne soldiers, one of ARVN's most elite units, were known. The communists could do nothing to halt their advance.

Just before daybreak on April 16, the NVA 5th Division launched a new attack against the airborne front line. Thirty of their soldiers died instantly in a fusillade from the airborne guns. Our forces captured six crew-served weapons, one 12.7mm antiaircraft gun, and five individual weapons. Airborne losses were five soldiers killed and seventeen wounded.

The airborne advance continued. At ten o'clock, just as 5th Airborne Battalion reached the forward perimeter of the city, the enemy launched yet another new attack. This time the communists had an advantage—they now held foxholes and fighting positions that our forces had dug earlier to protect themselves against communist artillery fire. The airborne were surrounded, caught between a hammer and an anvil.

Lieutenant Colonel Hieu came up with an unusual solution to the problem. He decided to use the enemy's own "sapper" tactics against them. Airborne troopers assaulted each foxhole separately, leaping into the foxholes suddenly and killing the communist troops holding them with hand grenades and bayonets. The close-quarters combat was excruciating. Our soldiers and the enemy were inches apart in broad daylight. Grenades flew back and forth, followed by screams of agony. The small area, black with gunsmoke and reeking with the stench of burned flesh, became a tiny corner of hell, filled with sounds of savagery. After two hours of hand-to-hand fighting, the airborne troops eliminated the last pockets of enemy resistance along the line of foxholes.

At one o'clock in the afternoon, Colonel Luong gave a warm handshake to General Hung. After Hung outlined the situation for him and after assigning a defensive position to each of the airborne units, Colonel Luong visited the province sector headquarters. He decided to co-locate his 1st Airborne Brigade's headquarters with mine to facilitate the coordination of our operations.

Colonel Luong had been a classmate of mine in high school. We had also worked together on operations when I served in the marine corps. Now as we met once again to fight side by side, I gave him a quick briefing of the situation in An Loc, including the terrain, the refugees, the food situation, medical evacuation and treatment of casualties, our defenses, and the operations of our provincial reconnaissance units.

The ferocity of the battle continued unabated. The fighting was in close quarters as the two sides scratched and clawed for possession of every house, every foxhole and bunker, every square inch of ground. The communists kept up a continuous artillery bombardment of the city.

After arriving safely within our perimeter, 8th Airborne Battalion, led by Lt. Col. Van Ba Ninh, used Tran Hung Dao Avenue as the starting point for an advance into the western part of the city. When the battalion was about six hundred yards beyond the Phu Lo Gate, communist forces suddenly opened up with a tremendous barrage of 82mm mortar and 75mm recoilless rifle fire. During the first few seconds, before there was time to react, twelve of our soldiers were killed and sixty-two wounded. In spite of these casualties, Ninh calmly redeployed his forces and launched a counterattack. The communist troops wavered and were forced to retreat. Ninh's attack expanded our perimeter on the western side of the city.

Meanwhile, the fighting on An Loc's southeastern perimeter continued with equal intensity. Two companies from 6th Airborne Battalion, left behind to hold Windy Hill and cover the southern approaches to the city, were struck by wave after wave of assaults.

On April 17, at one o'clock in the afternoon, communist troops attacked 63rd Company at the intersection of Route 245. To support 63rd Company, 64th Company was ordered to move up from Srok Ton Cui. The battle went on all night. On the morning of April 18, U.S.

and South Vietnamese aircraft mounted ferocious air attacks to support the airborne defenders. Enemy troops fell in droves, but our side also paid a heavy price for this battle. Sixty-third and 64th Companies were ordered to withdraw to Hill 150, and 61st Company was sent in to replace them. Throughout the rest of the day, the situation remained relatively quiet. The communists needed time to replace their losses, re-equip, and reorganize their units.

Lieutenant Colonel Pham Van Huan, commander of the 81st Airborne Ranger Battalion, was a classmate of mine from the tenth class at the Dalat Military Academy. Huan was ordered to coordinate closely with 8th Regiment, 5th ARVN Division, and 3rd Ranger Group to organize the recapture of the northern portion of An Loc that had fallen into communist hands. The terrain in this area was extremely difficult. The houses were reduced to rubble, there were many solid bunkers and bomb shelters the residents had built before the battle, and barbed wire fences surrounded every city block. After conducting reconnaissance and analyzing the situation, Huan issued assignments and objectives to each of his units.

At exactly midnight of April 18–19, the units of the 81st Airborne Rangers stood ready to carry out their assigned missions. They were instructed to use only grenades and bayonets whenever possible. Throughout the attack, all friendly units at An Loc were strictly forbidden from firing illumination flares to avoid exposing the fighters of the 81st. The assault teams were ordered to move slowly in order to make as little noise as possible, especially when they tried to avoid obstacles and the many open holes and wells in the area. Sometimes they were forced to crawl across the putrid, rotting bodies of the dead as they crept forward. A scream would ring out occasionally as a bayonet stabbed an enemy soldier. A blast would be heard as a grenade was thrown into a foxhole held by communist troops.

For three hours, the Airborne Rangers exterminated communist troops one by one while losing not a single one of their own. At four in the morning, there was an accident that left a soldier severely injured. In the space of a few hours, 81st Airborne Ranger Battalion advanced north about 450 yards. This may have been a short distance in terms of the enemy's advance into An Loc, but it was a great leap forward by the 81st Airborne Rangers in the effort to relieve communist pressure on the city.

I now became gravely concerned about the situation on Windy Hill. The area had been relatively calm in the morning. But at about two o'clock in the afternoon, the enemy discovered the positions of 6th Airborne Battalion atop Windy Hill and began a heavy artillery attack that lasted for hours. Friendly forces on the hill were completely paralyzed by the enemy shelling. The only support we could give them was air strikes.

Meanwhile, a C-130 transport delivering supplies was hit by communist guns and burst into flames. The pilot was able to crash-land the aircraft south of the city. U.S. Army helicopters rescued the entire American flight crew, two of them wounded.

In An Loc, the tension increased steadily, minute by minute. On April 19, the communists intensified their artillery bombardment of the city. Between six in the morning and seven in the evening, almost two thousand artillery rounds hit the city. Under cover of this bombardment, the communists launched a new attack with three regiments. The fighting was intense, but the defenders held on tenaciously. The 5th and 8th Airborne Battalions had taken up positions in the rubber plantation just south of the city, and they were able to block the NVA thrust from that direction.

One of the reasons we were able to withstand the repeated communist attacks was the effective air support that we received almost around the clock. Our pilots had to fly through a heavy curtain of antiaircraft fire, but that did not stop them. To avoid being hit by our air strikes, communist troops tried to get as close to our lines as possible. On many occasions, our aircraft dropped bombs only one to two hundred yards from our troops. As the situation became critical, I made the most daring and dangerous decision in this life-and-death struggle; I recommended, through U.S. advisory channels, that we bring the B-52 strikes closer to our lines to break up the enemy attacks. Lieutenant General Hollingsworth approved my recommendation. We would learn later that this played a major role in the defeat of the communists at An Loc.

The 81st Airborne Ranger Group was ordered to cross Tran Hung Dao Avenue and retake the New Market, the bus station, and the hamlet of Thanh Mau (Blessed Mother). They had to take down walls and move through homes and buildings, advancing step by step to avoid being seen by enemy observation teams and targeted by the enemy's direct-fire weapons. When the advance reached the Buddhist pagoda and the Police Field Force barracks, the communists launched a ferocious counterattack using every heavy weapon at their disposal. Because the Airborne Rangers operated in small teams, their losses remained extremely light. Throughout their advance, I stood next to Lieutenant Colonel Huan on the second floor of a building next to the cemetery where the Airborne Ranger dead were buried, observing the course of the battle.

The Airborne Rangers used grenades and M72 rocket launchers to destroy bunkers and fighting positions held by communist forces. The enemy began to waver and retreat to the north. By mid-day, however, after regrouping his forces, the enemy launched a counterattack against our flank. But his forces were too few and too widely dispersed to hold the entire area that had just been recaptured. Lieutenant Colonel Huan pulled back a short distance to regroup and consolidate. During the night of April 19, as communist troops went to sleep along the line they had just recaptured, 81st Airborne Ranger Group retook most of the key positions.

As the situation in the city became stabilized, the situation on Windy Hill to the east of An Loc was growing desperate. After locating the positions of our troops, who were holding a perimeter eight hundred yards long and eighty yards wide, the communists concentrated a ferocious artillery barrage on the position, exploding a stockpile of more than one thousand rounds of 105mm ammunition and crippling the position's six 105mm howitzers. Sixth Airborne Battalion's primary mission of defending the artillery became meaningless. The battalion's only responsibility now was to hold the high ground.

At nine o'clock that evening, Colonel Luong gave Lt. Col. Le Van Ngoc, the deputy brigade commander, who was located with light brigade headquarters elements on Hill 169, complete authority to deal with the situation. Ngoc ordered 6th Battalion headquarters and 62nd Company to move down off the hill and join 61st Company at the hamlet of Srok Ton Cui. Sixty-third and 64th Companies, under the command of the deputy battalion commander, Pham Kim Bang, would remain behind to defend the hilltop.

Before dawn on April 20, with Windy Hill under heavy communist pressure, the Red Cross asked the North Vietnamese battlefield commander to stop the artillery shelling to allow evacuation of the wounded. The request was rejected. The communists continued shelling the city, firing almost five hundred artillery rounds into An Loc that day. They also made exploratory attacks against 5th Airborne Battalion southeast of the Xa Cam Gate. Six of our soldiers were killed and twenty-one wounded, while the enemy left thirty-five bodies behind as he withdrew. We captured six crew-served weapons and six individual weapons.

Windy Hill continued to be pounded by enemy artillery. The NVA mounted an infantry attack up the side of the hill at sunset. They sent four T-54 tanks in two columns in the darkness, from the east and the northeast. Their headlights blazing, the tanks slowly advanced up the slope. The Airborne troopers waited until the tanks were about fifty yards away before opening fire. The two lead tanks burst into flames and the demoralized infantry retreated.

After several more barrages of artillery fire, more assault waves swarmed up the hill, supported by the two remaining tanks. The airborne troopers knocked out the last two tanks. However, our troops were now exhausted. A number of their commanders were dead or wounded and their lines had been pierced in several places. Sixty-third and 64th Companies were overrun. Some survivors fled to the top of Hill 169, where they joined the light headquarters element with Lieutenant Colonel Ngoc. This position subsequently came under heavy artillery attack. Ngoc received permission from Colonel Luong to retreat to An Loc. The brigade reconnaissance and engineer units, together with a number of soldiers from other units, arrived in An Loc on the morning of April 21 after following the route taken by 8th Airborne Battalion four days before. After taking Hill 169, the communists temporarily ceased firing to regroup and consolidate their ranks.

At this time, 6th Airborne Battalion (-), with its 60th, 61st, and 62nd Companies and sixty wounded, was still located at Srok Ton Cu. At 1:30 a.m. on April 21, with no food and almost out of ammunition, the battalion quietly withdrew to the southeast under cover of darkness. To clear a route for the withdrawal, three B-52 cells dropped bombs north, east, and south of the banks of the Be River. The battalion was to be picked up by helicopter when it reached the designated landing zone. After repeated attacks during its withdrawal, it was attacked again just as it reached the landing zone. The unit collapsed into disorder. A number of troops were picked up by helicopter and taken to Lai Khe at 5:45 p.m. Only 106 men made it back to our lines, among them the 6th Battalion commander, Lt. Col. Nguyen Van Dinh, and fourteen artillerymen. Over the next few days, a few of the missing troops filtered back to friendly lines.

News of the loss of Windy Hill worried soldiers of all ranks. After their previous trials by fire, though, every soldier, official, or civilian was confident of our resolve and our ability to stop any new enemy attack, especially now that we had been reinforced by two of the best fighting units in the ARVN, 1st Airborne Brigade and 81st Airborne Ranger Battalion. Also, in addition to intelligence provided by our reconnaissance teams, we received a great deal of information from citizens and tribesmen. Captain Thiet, the sector S-2 officer, and Captain Dao of the province Phoenix Committee, debriefed these sources thoroughly and used the information effectively. These sources allowed us to identify precisely enemy troop movements, troop assembly areas, artillery firing positions, and armored vehicle staging areas. The South Vietnamese and American Air Forces were able to shatter the enemy's units before they reached our positions. Besides, 265 B-52 bombing missions (a total of 865 sorties) flown from Thailand and Guam provided massive support.

But conditions inside the city continued to deteriorate. There were difficulties with aerial resupply and critical shortages. Too many soldiers had been wounded. The civilians were living underground, and many of them had been wounded, too.

* * *

On April 24, the North Vietnamese launched a powerful attack in the central highlands and destroyed half of the ARVN 22nd Division. On April 27, the NVA mounted new attacks and destroyed the ARVN 3rd Division. Quang Tri fell. Pleiku was in peril. The communist forces were on the outskirts of the imperial city of Hue. President Thieu rushed his big battalions away from the Mekong Delta to check the offensive in other parts of the country. The Viet Cong rapidly filled the vacuum created by these redeployments, occupying the abandoned government posts in the Mekong region. South Vietnam's existence became questionable.[24]

It was time for a decision in Washington. Nixon addressed his nation by television on May 8, 1972, at nine o'clock in the evening. He described the military situation in South Vietnam and a deadlock in the negotiations with the North Vietnamese. Then he announced:

> I have ordered the following measures which are being implemented as I am speaking to you. All entrances to North Vietnamese ports will be mined to prevent access to these ports and North Vietnamese naval operations from these ports. United States forces have been directed to take appropriate measures . . . to interdict the delivery of any supplies. Rail and all other communications will be cut off to the maximum extent possible. Air and naval strikes against military targets in North Vietnam will continue.

He then demanded a cease-fire throughout Indochina and the return of all American prisoners of war. If these conditions were met, all American forces would be withdrawn from Vietnam within four months.

The reaction in the Soviet Union and China was restrained. There was no rush to the barricades in either Moscow or Peking. The Soviet leadership was unwilling to permit the war to interfere with détente or the scheduled summit meeting with Nixon. The Chinese even exerted pressure on Hanoi to settle with the United States.

The American people felt that the North Vietnamese invasion of South Vietnam justified Nixon's response and that bombing was a better alternative than the reintroduction of American ground forces. They rallied around the decisive presidential initiatives. Nixon's public approval rating shot up dramatically. His scheduled twin Summit meetings in Moscow and Peking had created a new atmosphere of "peaceful coexistence" in the world that was against Hanoi's interests.

The blockade of North Vietnamese ports caused a huge disruption in deliveries. Supplies had to be routed through China by rail. Thousands of railroad cars were backed up on the Chinese side of the border, while the lines on the Vietnamese side were being cut by American air attacks. Transportation by trucks was time-consuming and relatively inefficient. Supplying three fronts in South Vietnam became too complicated and impossible to synchronize. On the other hand, Saigon's small strategic reserve could be switched easily to meet each threat as it developed.

* * *

On the night of May 6, 1972, during an ambush set by the 212th RF Company near the Quan Loi Gate, our soldiers captured communist Sublieutenant Hoa, who said he had been sent to reconnoiter this area in preparation for an attack. He also revealed that COSVN had held a criticism session to review the reasons for their inability to take An Loc on April 20 and 21. The 9th Division had been severely criticized for its poor combat performance. The main effort in the coming attack would now be made by the communist 5th Division, supported by the 9th Division and armored units.

From this moment on, the communists intensified their artillery bombardment of the city and moved their antiaircraft positions in as close as possible to our defensive perimeter. On May 9, a helicopter carrying troops of 2nd Battalion, 8th Regiment, which was being brought in to reinforce the city's defenses, was shot down, forcing us to halt our effort to bring in additional reinforcements.

The Border Defense Ranger outpost at Tong Le Chan reported that they had detected the movement of communist armored vehicles toward An Loc. Reports about an imminent attack led to an agreement between III Corps headquarters and its senior American advisor, Lt. Gen. James Hollingsworth, that the maximum possible air support, including B-52s, would be provided for the defense of An Loc. As he flew over An Loc observing the situation, General Hollingsworth called me often on the U.S. advisors' radio network to see how I was doing and to reassure me. I once told him: "Danger 79 (the general's call-sign), why don't you come down here and have a drink with me? Then you can see for yourself how secure things are." The general laughed and answered: "Thanks, M72 (my call-sign), maybe another time." Later, after I came to the United States as a refugee, the general and I used these same call signs when speaking to each other on the telephone.

Based on the information provided by interrogations, all units defending An Loc redoubled their preparations for battle. Bunkers and foxholes were strengthened and ammunition and food were stockpiled for the coming offensive. RF and police units were given their own individual defensive sectors. Barbed-wire barriers and obstacles were strengthened, additional mines and booby-traps were laid, claymore mines were set out, and we issued as many of the new, extremely effective M72 rocket launchers as we could lay our hands on.

Montagnard tribesmen had always provided us with extremely accurate information on the enemy. The ones assigned to our reconnaissance teams were even more useful. Dressed in civilian clothes and claiming that they had been fired at and pursued by our troops, they crossed into enemy territory, then sneaked back to report on what they had seen and heard. We used this information to call in fighter-bombers, B-52s, and AC-130 Specter gunships equipped with 105mm cannon, to attack the identified targets.

During the night of May 10–11, 1972, the enemy bombarded An Loc with several thousand rounds of artillery. Not a minute went by without the sound of an exploding shell, and not an inch of ground was left untouched. Our bunkers shook violently with the repeated explosions. Based on our experience from previous attacks, the entire population, soldiers, officials, and civilians, hid underground in bunkers and holes. We knew the communists would attack only after the shelling stopped. Just as they had done during the two previous attacks, when the artillery bombardment stopped at 4:30 a.m., in the faint light before dawn, their infantry and tanks began their assault. When the tanks neared our lines, they sped up because they were afraid of being destroyed by our M72 rockets if they moved too slowly. As they left their infantry support behind and crossed our front lines, our troops were waiting to knock them out.

The enemy attacked with five regiments from four different directions. The 274th Regiment, 5th Division, attacked from the north; the E6 Regiment, 5th Division, attacked from the northeast; the 272nd Regiment, 9th Division, attacked from the west (the Phu Lo Gate); the 271st Regiment, 9th Division, attacked from the south (the Xa Cam Gate); the 275th Regiment, 5th Division, was held back in reserve.

The attack was carried out exactly as our prisoner, Sublieutenant Hoa, had told us. The main enemy effort, directed by the 5th Division headquarters, focused on the north, while the supporting attack from the south and west was meant to tie down our forces on that part of the defensive perimeter. Six to eight tanks supported each attacking column. The distribution of the attack columns revealed the aim of the communist plan. If they succeeded, they would have cut An Loc into four separate pockets. They could then gradually tighten their grip on the defenders, squeezing our perimeter in until our forces were completely overwhelmed and destroyed.

The fighting was intense. On the northern perimeter, the 274th Regiment attacked the perimeter held by the 81st Airborne Rangers. Several enemy tanks penetrated our lines but were destroyed by the 8th Regiment, which held backup positions to the rear of the paratroopers. In spite of valiant efforts by the 81st Airborne Rangers, part of the northern perimeter fell into enemy hands.

On the northeastern perimeter, the E6 Regiment, attacking in two columns, penetrated the line held by 52nd Ranger Battalion. Although our troops destroyed one enemy PT-76 tank, the Rangers were forced to fall back to the south, splitting our position in two.

On the western perimeter, 272nd Regiment flooded through the Phu Lo Gate. ARVN troops from the 7th Regiment knocked out two PT-76 tanks, but communist infantry surged forward to the Re-Education Center and captured the province Public Works Office. At 9:30 a.m., unable to resist the enemy attack, 3rd Battalion, 7th Regiment, was forced to pull back. Communist forces occupied the western part of the city.

On the southern and southeastern perimeters, the 275th Regiment, 5th Division, which the communists had planned to hold back in reserve, was sent forward to attack in two columns. The first column attacked the sector Political Warfare Company. When a PT-76 tank appeared in front of our positions, Sgt. La Trong Thang knocked it out with an M72 rocket and the enemy infantry retreated. The second column struck the Xa Cam Gate in the area assigned to 1st Airborne Brigade. It was defended by 1st Battalion, 48th Regiment, from Task Force 52 of 18th Division, a unit that had escaped to An Loc from its base at Hung Loc and had been placed under the operational control of 1st Airborne Brigade.

Because of our prior preparations for the battle, fighter-bombers, helicopter gunships, and B-52s were constantly overhead to provide support for our units from four o'clock in the morning onward. Our aircraft struck areas on the outskirts of the city and sometimes even sections of the city itself. The situation became critical at ten o'clock, when the enemy captured the Police Field Force Station on the northern perimeter and overran the province Chieu Hoi Office on the northwestern perimeter, only five hundred yards from ARVN 5th Division headquarters.

This desperate fight for the city coincided with the start of SA-7 firings by the enemy. By late afternoon of May 11, a VNAF A-1 and an A-37, a Cobra gunship, and two FAC aircraft had been shot down. Although not all of them had been SAM victims, FACs were handicapped to working from six thousand feet or higher. Considering the antiaircraft situation and the available targets on the ground, the remaining Cobras were sent home by the senior advisor to the 5th ARVN Division, Col. Walter Ulmer. The SA-7 surface-to-air missiles added another level of difficulty to the dangerous job of USAF FACs (forward air controllers). First Lieutenant William Carruthers Jr. (known as Sundog 39) was one who flew the unarmed O-2A aircraft, which carried two pods of white marking rockets, seven in each pod. Carruthers later remembered those perilous days: "When somebody called out on the radio 'missile, missile, missile,' we would turn and dive toward the ground."

On the western perimeter, the communists captured the Province Public Works Office, only three hundred yards from 5th Division headquarters. On the west and southwest, the communists managed to penetrate sections of our perimeter. On the southeast, after being reinforced by the 8th Airborne Battalion, our troops recaptured the Xa Cam Gate area and, together with friendly aircraft, knocked out six enemy armored vehicles, including one BTR-50 amphibious armored personnel carrier.

After gaining control of the situation on the southeastern perimeter, the 1st Airborne Brigade commander, Colonel Luong, sent 63rd Company (a 6th Airborne Battalion unit that had withdrawn from Windy Hill) to the southeast to replace 8th Battalion, which immediately moved over to support province sector forces in retaking those portions of the southern and southwestern perimeter that had been penetrated by communist troops. After accomplishing this mission, 8th Battalion left its 82nd Airborne Company behind to reinforce the defenses of the newly recaptured area.

At ten o'clock, 5th Airborne Battalion was split into two elements. The first element established a defensive line to block enemy troops trying to advance from the Public Works Office. Meanwhile, the other element of paratroopers established a defensive line at the Montagnard Elementary School to prevent the enemy from advancing past the province Chieu Hoi Office. Third Airborne Reconnaissance Company was sent in the afternoon to help protect 5th Airborne Battalion headquarters. While this action transpired, 1st Airborne Brigade remained with me, co-located with my sector headquarters.

During the period from four o'clock in the morning until dark, there were a total of 350 tactical air support sorties and twenty-six B-52 Arclight missions. General Hollingsworth later told me a number of the

B-52 missions had originally been intended for other battlefronts but were diverted at the last minute to support the battle to defend An Loc.

Because the air support plan had been closely coordinated between the air planners and our American advisors and us, and because of the great determination displayed by our pilots, especially the American pilots, the communist effort to seize An Loc and to turn it into the capital of the National Liberation Front for South Vietnam was shattered.

Although the tide had turned by the massive application of airpower, the fighting continued. On the northern perimeter, the 81st Airborne Ranger Battalion, faced with a strong communist attack, was forced to withdraw temporarily from the area of the Police Field Force Station, destroying four enemy armored vehicles as it pulled back. Later, it counterattacked and recaptured the same area.

After May 11, the communists tried to hold on to the areas they had captured. They reinforced bunkers and fortifications and prepared for a long struggle. Our soldiers did the same. We strengthened our defensive positions, regrouped and reorganized our units, and sent teams to the rear of the enemy to surround them and cut off their supply lines.

On the night of May 12, despite their heavy losses, the communists launched a new, two-pronged attack. The 272nd Regiment attacked from the west and 274th Regiment attacked from the northeast. Even though armored vehicles supported both units, these attacks were repulsed and the enemy suffered heavy losses.

The third wave of enemy attacks had come close to taking the city, but the defenders prevailed. It had been costly for both sides. ARVN and sector forces suffered 137 killed and 136 missing. We lost one A-37 bomber, one L-19 observation plane, and 142 weapons. We killed 218 of the enemy, captured thirteen crew-served weapons and twenty-three individual weapons, and destroyed twenty-three armored vehicles of all types.

On May 13, Father Minh, the local priest, and a number of other religious and political leaders asked me to allow them to evacuate back to Chon Thanh. I approved it and directed the sector Logistics

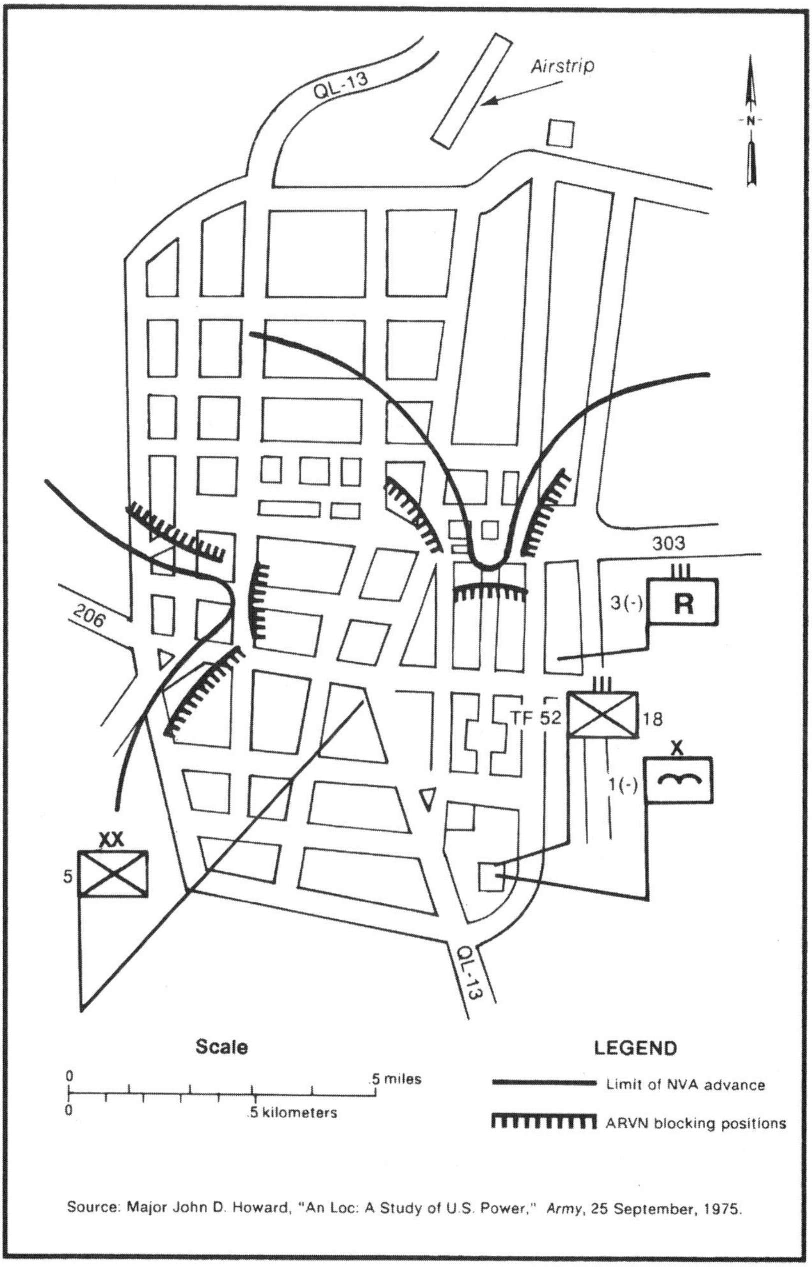

Third Attack on An Loc. *Map from "An Loc: A Study of U.S. Power" by Major John. D. Howard. From* ARMY *Magazine, September 1975. Copyright 1975 by the Association of the U.S. Army. Limited reprint permission granted by AUSA.*

Administrative Center to supply milled rice to the evacuees in preparation for their trip. Sadly and with great emotion, I hugged the government office chiefs, the province government's *chef de cabinet,* the chief of the Province Administrative Office, and other nonessential cadre. If they stayed, they could do nothing to help us, and yet there was no guarantee they would be able to evacuate safely back to Chon Thanh through enemy lines.

My advisor, Lieutenant Colonel Corley, opposed the evacuation. I told him I would take full responsibility in the event anything went wrong. All I asked of him was to arrange for armed helicopters to fly overhead and escort the evacuation column as far as the roadblock at Tan Khai, an area totally under enemy control.

I later learned that communist troops had stopped the evacuation column to "screen" the evacuees. Some civilian evacuees were allowed to continue to Chon Thanh, but a number of the province's senior governmental cadre were detained and taken prisoner. They were released only after the signing of the Paris cease-fire agreement of January 27, 1973. As for Father Minh, he did not accompany the evacuation as he originally intended. Later, for unknown reasons, he left the priesthood. Particular note should be made of the fact that not one single RF or PF soldier broke ranks to join the evacuation column. This was a source of pride to me because it demonstrated the sense of responsibility felt by all of the soldiers.

Over the next few weeks, the situation in An Loc improved dramatically. Technical intelligence reports revealed that 5th Division withdrew from the An Loc battlefield on May 20. It was later learned that the division moved to the vicinity of Chup in Cambodia, where it received replacements and reorganized for battle. By June 9, 1972, it was ordered to redeploy to Kien Tuong province in the Mekong Delta.

The communists did not withdraw all their forces from An Loc. They left elements of the NVA 9th Division in the area. From this time onward, they launched no more large-scale attacks, but instead intensified their efforts to besiege and isolate the city and stepped up artillery attacks with the aim of tying down our forces.

9

Clearing Highway 13

WHILE THE bitter fighting continued in An Loc, a battle that proved just as bloody developed to the south along Highway 13. The highway, which linked An Loc and Binh Long with the northern approaches to Saigon, ran through Tan Khai, Chon Thanh, Lai Khe, and Binh Duong. It was a high-speed avenue of approach that was of crucial importance to both sides.

When the communists began their attack on An Loc, III Corps headquarters became concerned that the NVA 7th Division could not only maintain the roadblock at Tan Khai but also be able to mount attacks in several other provinces near Saigon. Accordingly, Lieutenant General Minh, III Corps commander, requested additional forces from the joint general staff (JGS). The JGS responded by ordering the 21st Infantry Division to move from their usual station in the Mekong Delta to the Lai Khe area.

During the period between April 12 and 22, the 21st Division worked to strengthen and solidify our main bases at Lai Khe and Chon Thanh so they could be used as jumping-off points for future operations by our forces to relieve the besieged defenders of An Loc. The 21st Division initiated operations by ordering the 31st Regiment to

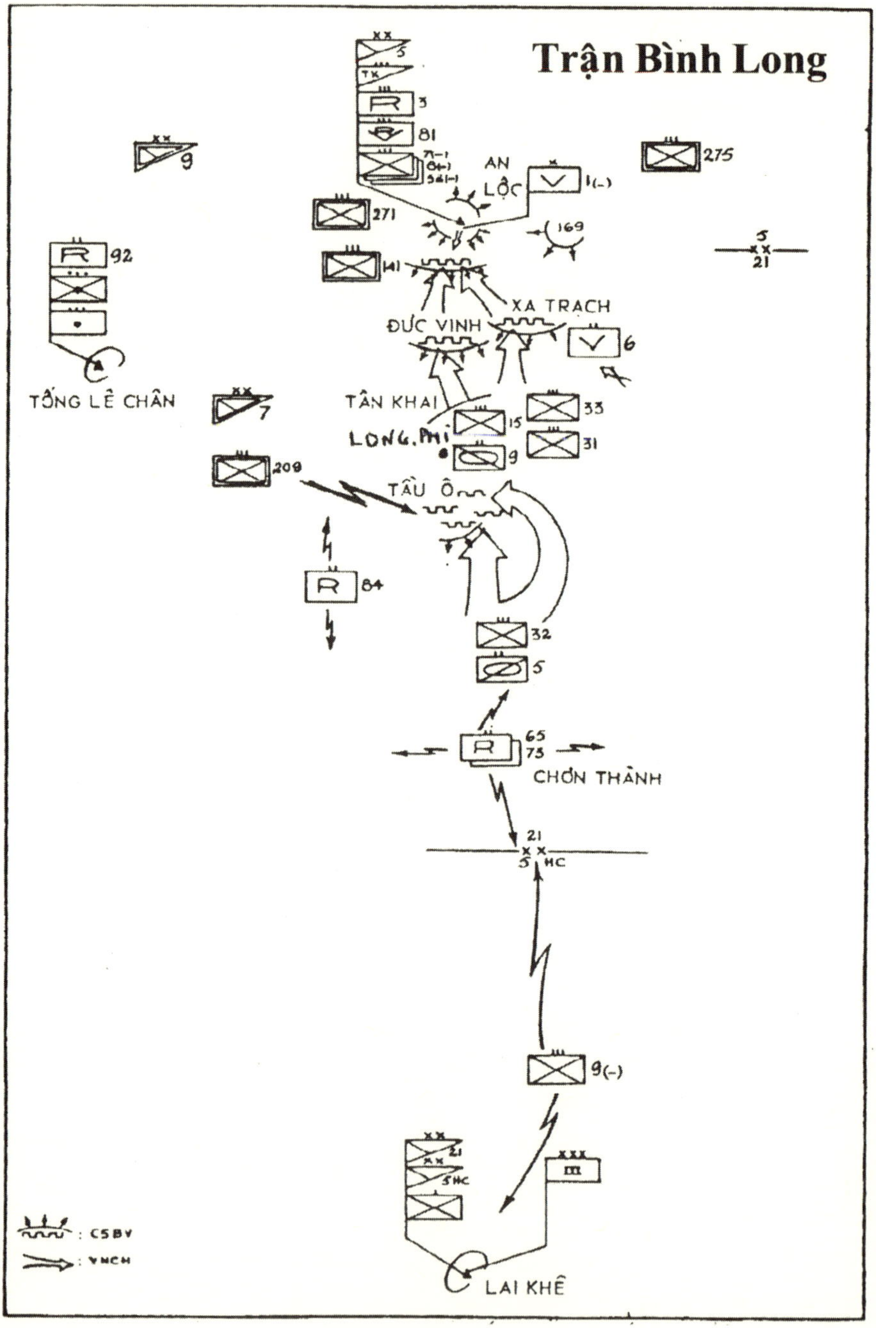

Operation to Clear Highway 13

conduct reconnaissance operations northwest of Lai Khe, while the 32nd Regiment was assigned to defend Chon Thanh. The 33rd Regiment was held back at Lai Khe as a reserve force.

Third Corps headquarters had planned to use 21st Division, 1st Airborne Brigade, and other attached units to launch Operation "Total Victory 72" to clear Highway 13 and relieve the siege of An Loc. After the heavy communist pressure on An Loc forced III Corps to send 1st Airborne Brigade into An Loc by helicopter as an emergency measure to strengthen the city's defenses, the plan to clear Highway 13 had to be revised. When the joint general staff sent the 3rd Airborne Brigade as reinforcements, III Corps headquarters issued new orders for Operation "Total Victory 72D."

On D-day, April 24, 1972, a forward headquarters of the airborne division would be established at Chon Thanh under the command of Col. Ho Trung Hau. Third Airborne Brigade would clear enemy forces and open Highway 13 from Tau O Stream to Xa Cam. Then, 21st Division's area of responsibility would extend from Tau O Stream south to Binh Duong.

The 21st Division was going to have a rough time of it. On April 22 communist troops, firing B-40 rockets, destroyed a bus at Bau Bang, on the road from Chon Thanh to Lai Khe, killing four civilians and wounding twenty. They then established a heavily fortified roadblock at this point to prevent us from sending reinforcements from Lai Khe to Chon Thanh. It took five days and the use of two regiments, the 32nd and 33rd, to finally clear this roadblock.

On April 25, while the 21st Division was trying to clear the enemy roadblock, 2nd Airborne Battalion from the 3rd Airborne Brigade was inserted by helicopter into two landing zones. The first element made a helicopter assault into a landing zone northeast of Tau O Stream, while the second element landed a little less than a mile east of Tan Khai. Immediately after landing, the first column established Fire Base Anh Dung (Hero) with one battery of 105mm howitzers to provide fire support for friendly forces. During the next several days, the battalion was hit repeatedly by heavy shelling attacks, but had only a few scattered clashes with enemy infantry. However, on April 27, communist artillery bombarded the battalion with guns of all types. The artillery firebase was hit by recoilless fire that damaged three of the howitzers, rendering them incapable of firing anything but direct fire missions.

The day before, 1st Airborne Battalion, also divided into two groups, had landed by helicopter in the Duc Vinh area, only a short distance apart. This battalion was shelled by artillery but also had only minor ground contacts with enemy forces.

On May 2, 3rd Airborne Battalion air-assaulted into two landing zones east of Highway 13, approximately midway between Tan Khai and Tau O Stream. Third Battalion's mission was to operate to the west to expand the area under friendly control and to link up with the two other Airborne battalions operating farther north. Between May 5 and 7, 3rd Battalion had a number of rather heavy, battalion-sized clashes with enemy forces, resulting in extremely heavy losses on both sides.

After 3rd linked up with 2nd Airborne Battalion, the two battalions were shadowed by enemy forces. Although they had only scattered clashes with enemy infantry, they continued to be shelled heavily, taking a daily toll of dead and wounded. On May 5, a heavy artillery barrage hit 2nd Battalion as it searched an area south of Tau O Stream. The battalion commander was wounded and Lt. Col. Ngo Le Tinh, the deputy brigade commander, flew in by helicopter to replace him. Third Corps headquarters sent out 21st Reconnaissance Company to reinforce 2nd Airborne Battalion. First Airborne Battalion operated only in the Duc Vinh area and was not ordered to advance northward because the two airborne battalions to the south were still being followed by enemy forces and were unable to clear Highway 13.

Third Battalion, now operating in 2nd Battalion's area of responsibility, was soon in desperate straits. Pushed by communist forces, under constant shelling attack, it was forced to stay continuously on the move. Not a day went by without more casualties. Between May 12 and 14, it was hit by a series of attacks, and once even one of our aircraft mistakenly bombed its position, killing the deputy battalion commander and some other soldiers.

On May 14, while trying to return to the eastern side of Highway 13, the battalion had to cross an open field five hundred yards south of Tau O Stream. The communists were waiting in a prepared ambush with heavy weapons targeted on the open field. In spite of heavy air support, the communists struck when the battalion was almost across the field, killing the 3rd Company commander and many other troops. The battalion had to abandon much of its heavy equipment and leave its packs behind in order to evacuate the dead and wounded. Some of the bodies began to rot and had to be buried on the spot.

On May 15, the battalion was resupplied, enabling it to continue to move east, but the enemy continued to tail the unit, hitting it with artillery and isolated ground attacks that inflicted additional casualties. The battalion spent the night two miles southeast of Tau O Stream, then continued eastward the next day searching for a suitable helicopter landing zone. At this point, communist troops broke contact with the 3rd Battalion. Once on the ground, 2nd and 3rd Battalions moved away from Tau O Stream and marched safely to an assembly area southeast of Highway 13. First Airborne Battalion also received orders to withdraw and pulled back without loss.

During this fighting, friendly forces sustained sixty men killed, 340 wounded, twenty-four missing. Our troops lost twenty-one crew-served weapons and thirty-eight individual weapons. The enemy suffered 254 killed and we captured one prisoner. Additionally, our forces captured twelve crew-served weapons and nineteen individual weapons. The ARVN forces were not able to break through the enemy blocking position to relieve the defenders of An Loc.

* * *

Simultaneously with the siege of An Loc and the fighting along Highway 13, communist forces also surrounded and shelled the small outpost of Minh Thanh, located fifteen miles southwest of An Loc and twelve miles west of Chon Thanh. The outpost was held by headquarters, 3rd RF Inter-Group 25, which was made up of the 987th and 989th RF Companies plus attached units. On April 7, 1972, in light of the serious situation following the loss of Loc Ninh, the inter-group commander, Maj. Vo Van Tay, pulled 989th RF Company and PF and police units back to defend Minh Thanh, raising the total number of soldiers defending the outpost to 170 men. It must be pointed out that, in addition to these troops, a number of government officials and their families also took shelter inside the outpost, adding to Major Tay's burdens.

Communist forces began to shell the outpost on April 8, while conducting strong ground probes against the defenders. The outpost had previously been an American position, and its strong fortifications were capable of withstanding artillery attacks. In addition, the perimeter wire and the network of minefields around the position were extremely solid and the ground beyond the perimeter fence had been cleared of vegetation. These factors enabled the defenders to hold out against repeated artillery barrages and exploratory ground attacks.

After a number of failed attacks, the enemy decided Minh Thanh base was of no tactical importance. They shifted their focus to simply besieging the outpost and hitting it with artillery and occasional ground probes aimed at shattering the morale of the defenders and forcing us to further disperse our fire support resources. Resupply and evacuation of casualties was a large problem. The outpost was so small that parachute drops of supplies fell outside the perimeter in the no-man's-land between the enemy's lines and our own. Both sides crawled out trying to retrieve the supply pallets, resulting in frequent firefights. A large percentage of the outpost's casualties were the result of such engagements.

The situation persisted, day after day, month after month. The casualty count, dead and wounded, rose to almost fifty soldiers. In spite of this fact, morale remained high and never wavered. Many times during my radio conversations with the outpost, I almost broke down in tears because everything they needed was beyond my capabilities to provide. All I could do was call on U.S. air power through my American advisor because there was no advisor at Minh Thanh.

The siege of Minh Thanh lasted more than six months. The defenders held on until October 14, 1972, when III Corps headquarters decided that the outpost was no longer playing a useful tactical role for our forces and ordered Tay to evacuate the base and retreat back to Chon Thanh. But the communists discovered our intentions and launched an immediate pursuit. In the end, Tay made it back with only 50 percent of his men, plus twenty women and children. The enemy captured all the rest, including the commanders of 987th and 989th RF Companies.

* * *

The joint general staff sent 15th Regiment, 9th Division, under the command of Lt. Col. Ho Ngoc Can, to replace 3rd Airborne Brigade, which was being recalled for a new mission. As soon as 15th Regiment arrived at Chon Thanh, it was sent up to Tan Khai to join units of 21st Division in the advance toward An Loc. The 21st Division had been unable to make much progress because of the enemy's heavily fortified blocking positions.

On May 11, 32nd Regiment, reinforced by a troop of armored cavalry; 1st Company, 5th Armored; an element of 1st Company, 18th Armored; and the 65th, 73rd, and 84th Ranger Battalions, began an advance that immediately ran into fairly heavy resistance. The NVA 209th Regiment, 7th Division, reinforced by a reconnaissance company and C41 Antitank Company, was deployed on a line more than two miles long, in thick jungle and rugged terrain that was unfavorable for an attack by our troops. For forty long days, from May 11 to June 21, this column was able to advance a little more than one mile in spite of the use of all available firepower (2,400 105mm and 155mm artillery rounds, thirty-five bombing strikes by tactical aircraft, and five B-52 strikes) against positions on both sides of Highway 13.

Twenty-first Division was from the Mekong Delta, hence unused to combat in rugged jungle terrain. During the initial phase of the attack, facing the enormous power of the communist defenders, 32nd Regiment suffered heavy casualties, losing ninety-five men killed, 455 wounded, four missing, and four M113 armored personnel carriers destroyed. The communists lost 503 men killed, and our forces captured thirty-seven crew-served weapons and seventy-one individual weapons. On June 21, 46th Regiment, 25th Division, replaced the exhausted 32nd Regiment.

Fifteenth Regiment, reinforced by an armored company, was committed to the battle on May 11. On May 14, the regiment was ordered to send one company from 2nd Battalion into An Loc by helicopter to reinforce the city's defenses. Heavy enemy antiaircraft fire prevented the helicopters from landing, and they were forced to return to Lai Khe. That same afternoon, 15th Regiment was ordered to form Regimental Task Force 15, made up of the regiment's own 1st, 2nd, and 3rd Battalions, reinforced by the 15th Reconnaissance Company, the 9th Cavalry Squadron, and one battery of 105mm howitzers.

On May 15, the 1st Battalion of the 15th Regiment, accompanied by 9th Cavalry Squadron and the 105mm guns of 95C Artillery Battery, moved by road from Chon Thanh up to Ngoc Lau, then north along the eastern side of Highway 13 to Tan Khai. On May 16, the 2nd Battalion made a helicopter assault into Bau Nat, 1,700 yards east of Tan Khai, and moved forward to occupy the hamlet of Tan Khai.

Once this was accomplished, task force headquarters and a 105mm artillery platoon landed by helicopter at Tan Khai, where they established Fire Base Flying Dragon. On May 17, 15th Reconnaissance Company made a helicopter assault into the area northwest of Tan Khai to reconnoiter the area. The 3rd Battalion then landed by helicopter at Dong Le, south of Tan Khai. Meanwhile, one battalion from 33rd Regiment, 21st Division, was transported by helicopter to Fire Base Flying Dragon to replace 2nd Battalion, 15th Regiment, which moved forward to link up with 3rd Battaion, 15th Regiment.

On May 18, the units of 15th Regiment, together with 9th Armored Squadron, moved out from the area west of Tan Khai to advance toward An Loc. The deputy regimental commander stayed behind at the fire base, which now included one battery of 105mm howitzers, one platoon of 155mm howitzers, and an infantry battalion from 33rd Regiment, 21st Division.

In parallel with the advance of Task Force 15, on May 18 33rd

Regiment (-), under the command of Lt. Col. Nguyen Viet Can, was ordered to move out from our base at Ngoc Lau and advance north along the eastern side of Highway 13 toward An Loc. On May 18, communist forces began sporadic shelling attacks against Fire Base Flying Dragon. On May 19, Task Force 15 had several small clashes with enemy troops just as it entered the hamlet of Duc Vinh 1. During the next several days, communist artillery continued to shell our troops to disrupt and slow their advance.

Because of the increasingly heavy enemy pressure on Fire Base Flying Dragon, Task Force 15 had to send 1st Battalion, 15th Regiment, back to the rear to assist the battalion of 33rd Regiment in expanding our area of control around the base. The fire base played a critical role, serving as a logistics base and a casualty evacuation point, as well as providing fire support to our troop columns advancing toward An Loc.

At midnight on May 20, as Task Force 15 was silently crossing Xa Cat Creek and moving toward the hamlet of Duc Vinh, our troops heard the rattle of tank tracks and the sound of many large engines, indicating that enemy armored vehicles were on the move in front of them. On May 21, the task force continued to press forward and was constantly tracked by communist troops, who shelled the task force sporadically during the day and fought a few minor ground skirmishes against elements of the task force. Our troops advanced cautiously in successive bounds, the lead unit digging foxholes and fighting positions after each bound forward to support the next unit as that unit in turn moved forward. Enemy antiaircraft fire was rather heavy, and the task force had to be resupplied by parachute drops.

On May 22, when the task force was still half a mile from the village of Thanh Binh, the enemy suddenly blocked its path. The task force was surrounded and attacked and hit by heavy artillery fire. The entire task force was cut off and isolated, and the situation was desperate. Casualties could not be evacuated, and the wounded had to remain at their combat positions. The dead were buried on the spot. On May 23, the communists launched a powerful ground attack supported by artillery and tanks. At six in the morning, enemy armor penetrated the defensive perimeter. Although our troops knocked out the lead vehicle, a PT-76 tank, other enemy armored vehicles continued rumbling forward through our lines. Our troops never wavered and fought back with great gallantry. After two separate assaults during which two enemy tanks were destroyed, the communists were forced to pull back, leaving behind twenty-four bodies on the battlefield. We captured eighteen enemy weapons. Friendly forces lost twelve men killed and twenty-five wounded. During this battle, B-52s heavily bombed enemy positions in Thanh Binh to support our forces.

It was impossible to evacuate casualties or to resupply the task force by helicopter or parachute drop. Only one hundred yards separated our lines from the enemy. Even though our troops were thirsty and could see the water of the Xa Cat Creek flowing in front of them, they could not reach the water because the enemy was deployed along the bank.

On May 23, the task force halted its advance to wait for friendly armored vehicles to clear the way and escort a convoy to bring water and supplies from Tan Khai and to evacuate the casualties. Thirty-third Regiment (-), stationed at the hamlet of Dong Phat, had no significant contacts with enemy forces. Ninth Cavalry Squadron, covering Task Force 15's rear, was deployed along Highway 13. It provided support to the evacuation of casualties.

On May 24, 9th Squadron fought a bitter engagement along this same stretch of road against the 141st Regiment of the 7th Division. Eight of our soldiers were killed, seventy-seven were wounded, and eight went missing. Twenty-two of our M113 armored personnel carriers were destroyed. The communists left twenty dead on the battlefield and we captured fourteen individual weapons. Because the communists knew the route our forces were using, they were able to set up an ambush in which they massed every type of antitank weapon in their arsenal, including B-40 and B-41 rocket launchers, 75mm recoilless rifles, and AT-3 Sagger missiles. Many of these weapons, such as the B-41 rockets, were effective at ranges more than four hundred yards, and the enemy fire was extremely accurate. The 9th Squadron's losses were so severe that the unit had to be pulled back to Fire Base Flying Dragon to re-organize, re-equip, and serve as a reserve force for defense.

On May 25, after building a strongly fortified base about one kilometer south of Thanh Binh, our forces resumed their advance. Task Force 15 immediately ran into heavy contact with enemy forces. It had to hold its position to avoid being overrun. By then, the strength of the task force was down to only around 320 men. Thirty-third Regiment (-), moving up toward An Loc from the hamlet of Dong Phat, ran into ferocious resistance from the enemy and was unable to advance any farther.

On June 4, the reconstituted 6th Airborne Battalion was transported by helicopter to Fire Base Flying Dragon. After landing, the battalion advanced northward, bringing along with it three hundred replacements for Task Force 15. Two days later, 6th Airborne encountered strong enemy positions north of the hamlet of Duc Vinh 2. Even though most of the battalion's troops were new recruits, the cadres were survivors of the earlier battle at An Loc. Its commander, Lt. Col. Nguyen Van Dinh, swore he would return to An Loc to take revenge for the destruction of his unit. Fighting gallantly, 6th Airborne overran the enemy positions with only limited casualties. One Airborne soldier was killed and sixty-four were wounded, while thirty-one enemy soldiers were killed and twelve individual and two crew-served weapons were captured.

After linking up with Task Force 15 at a point only two miles south of An Loc, 6th Airborne turned the new replacements over to the task force. Communist pressure virtually evaporated after their battle against 6th Airborne. On June 7, 33rd Regiment was able to evacuate 210 wounded troops and Task Force 15 evacuated 149 wounded. After being resupplied and completing the evacuation of the wounded, Task Force 15 (-) and 6th Airborne Battalion advanced in parallel toward An Loc. On June 8, while advancing east of the village of Thanh Binh, 6th Airborne had another heavy engagement against communist forces. Riding a tide of victory, the battalion killed seventy-three enemy troops, whose bodies were left on the battlefield. Additionally, thirty-three individual weapons and two crew-served weapons were captured. Friendly losses amounted to eleven men killed and thirty-one wounded.

After this battle, the two relief columns moving up from the south finally reached our lines when they made contact with elements of the 1st Airborne Brigade who had expanded our defensive perimeter to the south of the city. I personally went out to the village of Thanh Binh to meet with Task Force 15. In celebration of the link-up, I gave Lt. Col. Ho Ngoc Can, the task force commander, and Maj. Mandeville Craig, the task force advisor, a bottle of cognac—the last bottle left in the entire province.

During the operation to relieve An Loc, Task Force 15 lost a total of 153 men killed, 592 wounded, and 27 missing. It killed 304 enemy troops, captured forty-one crew-served weapons and eighty-five individual weapons, and destroyed two PT-76 tanks. The fight for Highway 13 had been a bloody affair, but the ARVN forces had finally punched through.

In An Loc, after blunting the enemy attacks of mid-May, our forces in the city had been reorganizing and consolidating. After the link-up with the relief forces from the south, we took advantage of the enemy's weakened state to launch an operation to clear communist forces inside the city. The 81st Airborne Rangers, 8th Regiment, 5th ARVN Division, and 3rd Ranger Group recaptured the northern parts of An Loc. Seventh Regiment (-) recaptured the western portion of An Loc that had fallen into enemy hands on May 11. Communist forces put up only weak resistance and fled as soon as our troops fired on them.

Friendly forces were able to expand the An Loc defensive perimeter by more than one mile. The weakened communist forces gradually pulled back, enabling us to bring in twenty-three helicopter sorties on June 9. These helicopters landed south of the province capital, bringing in reinforcements, delivering supplies, and transporting out hundreds of sick and wounded soldiers who had been awaiting evacuation, some since the battle had begun in early April.

* * *

In early June, Lt. Gen. James Hollingsworth and Sir Robert Thompson, special advisor to President Richard Nixon, made a surprise visit to An Loc. I escorted the two guests around the city to let them see with their own eyes the most magnificent victory in ARVN's history. I paid particular attention to the communist tanks that had been destroyed in the area defended by RF and police units. As the party prepared to depart, Sir Thompson shook my hand and expressed his admiration for the courageous fighting spirit of the soldiers, the government officials, and the people of An Loc. He said this was the greatest victory won by free world forces in the battle against communism since World War II and that, in his opinion, it was a greater victory for the South Vietnamese than that of the Viet Minh at Dien Bien Phu.

On June 16, Lieutenant General Hollingsworth returned, accompanied by Lt. Gen. Nguyen Van Minh, III Corps commander. During a visit to the 5th Division headquarters, General Hollingsworth suddenly stopped in front of Lt. Col. Art Taylor, advisor to 1st Airborne Brigade, and pinned a Silver Star on his chest. The Silver Star is the third highest U.S. award for valor on the battlefield. I saw tears of pride and emotion fill Lieutenant Colonel Taylor's eyes, and I was so moved I felt I was about to cry myself.

On June 18, 1st Airborne Brigade was ordered to withdraw from An Loc on foot. It took the brigade nearly two weeks to reach Tan Khai. After arriving there on June 31, it was lifted by helicopter to its rear base to rest and regroup before being sent to I Corps, where the fighting continued around Quang Tri. During its march to Tan Khai, 1st Airborne Brigade had a number of clashes against communist forces and suffered heavy casualties.

I remember that the night before he left with his troops, Colonel Luong, commander of 1st Airborne Brigade, confided in me:

> My brigade was spread thin to defend An Loc. We were deployed on the eastern, western, and southern perimeters. A fair number of my troops were killed here, and we had to bury them all where they fell,

> all around the province capital. We were not able to collect all the bodies together and build a memorial to them, as the 81st Airborne Rangers have done. I have a favor to ask of you. After the situation improves, as the province chief and as an old school friend from the time we were boys, please help me locate the bodies of my men killed here, collect them all in one place, and build a memorial to them at the southern end of the city so that, in later years, anyone who drives in on Highway 13 will see it before entering the city, and the 1st Airborne Brigade will thus be remembered.

I shook Colonel Luong's hand and promised I would do my best to fulfill his wish. Unfortunately, a short time later, I had to leave An Loc for I Corps to take over command of the 2nd Infantry Division and was unable to fulfill my promise.

On June 24, 81st Airborne Ranger Battalion was airlifted out of An Loc back to its rear base in Saigon to rest and recuperate. On June 29, Lt. Col. Nguyen Viet Can, commander of 33rd Regiment, 21st Division, was killed in the hamlet of Dong Phat by an enemy artillery shell as he moved with his regiment up the eastern side of Highway 13 toward An Loc. He received a posthumous promotion to colonel. Colonel Can was the younger brother of Lt. Gen. Nguyen Viet Thanh, who was killed in a helicopter accident in 1970 during the Cambodian incursion. Colonel Can was also one of my classmates from the military academy.

On July 7, Lieutenant Colonel Corley informed me that we were about to be visited by "senior officials." When a group of helicopters arrived, I was shocked to see President Nguyen Van Thieu, wearing a khaki safari suit and a black cap on his head, jump off a helicopter. Dozens of Cobra gunships patrolled the skies overhead to protect the president and to deter enemy artillery attacks.

The president was accompanied by Gen. Cao Van Vien, chief of the joint general staff, retired French General Vanuxem, General Hollingsworth, Mr. Hoang Duc Nha, dozens of foreign and Vietnamese journalists, and Lt. Col. Nguyen Dat Thinh, a very close friend whom I had met on many battlefields from the DMZ in the north to the Ca Mau Peninsula in the south.

I drove a jeep escorting the president and his delegation to visit Brig. Gen. Le Van Hung at 5th Division headquarters, less than a mile from my sector headquarters. Our soldiers were all greatly surprised to see their supreme commander appear among them so unexpectedly. They were all shouting: "Mr. President! Mr. President!"

An awards ceremony was held in the 5th Division operations center. General Hung and I were awarded the National Defense Medal, Third Class. Lieutenant Colonel Nguyen Thong Thanh and Lt. Col. Mach Van Truong, commander of 8th Regiment, were given battlefield promotions to the rank of colonel.

The president and his delegation were then taken out to visit each of the units still fighting in An Loc. The city was completely destroyed, reduced to rubble. When the delegation reached "Sunset Boulevard," the east-west boulevard that divided the northern and southern parts of the city, the president ordered his car to stop. He knelt in prayer in front of a large statue of Christ that was still completely intact and undamaged, despite more than two months of shelling and ground attacks.

Later, the president again knelt in prayer at the 81st Airborne Ranger cemetery in remembrance of all the heroes, soldiers, civil servants, and civilians who had gallantly given their lives in the battle to defend our homeland. The president's visit to this memorial also demonstrated to the world that this was a victory won by the forces of the free world over the expansionist schemes of the communist bloc. Although they had been frightened and worried, the soldiers and civilians of An Loc, confident in the justness of their cause, had come together with an iron will to fight and defend themselves and their families against communist aggression.

Then and later, when people asked me why the morale of the soldiers and civilians in Binh Long had remained so high, I replied without hesitation: "It was the result of the proselytizing measures I carried out among the people of the province from the moment I took over as province chief." Since assuming that office, I had worked hard to help the people. I had reduced the corruption in the province government and won the support of the people, even the Montagnards. Everybody wanted to protect the Fatherland. Everybody wanted to follow the patriotic and noncorrupt leader. Furthermore, I had worked hard with the RF, PF, and PSDF. We had no deserters among the province soldiers during the battle; even the wounded stayed and fought the communists.

After taking General Hung back to 5th Division headquarters, I drove the president's delegation back to my sector headquarters to wait for the helicopters. At the sector operations center, the president wrote in large letters on the sector operations map: "HEROIC BINH LONG."

I then invited the president and his delegation to enjoy a bit of dried squid and a glass of whiskey, both of which Lt. Col. Nguyen Dat Thinh had just brought in as a gift for me. While waiting for the helicopter, President Thieu used the province long-range communications radio to call Mrs. Thieu and tell her not to hold dinner for him because he was still in An Loc.

During this call, General Vanuxem pulled me aside to tell me he had recommended to the president that I be given command of an infantry division. I thanked General Vanuxem because I knew it was difficult to secure such an important position if one was not a close friend or the protégé of one of our national leaders. Later in 1973, after I had become a division commander and led the 2nd Division in recapturing areas held by the North Vietnamese communists, General Vanuxem and Sir Robert Thompson visited me; I reminded General Vanuxem of this conversation and thanked him again for his support.

After the president's visit, the situation in An Loc became quiet. Eighteenth Division arrived to replace 5th Division, which returned to Lai Khe to rest and rebuild its forces. Lieutenant Colonel Ngo Minh Hong's 5th Ranger Group arrived to replace 3rd Ranger Group. But An Loc remained dangerous. On July 9, Brig. Gen. Richard Tallman, General Hollingsworth's deputy at Third Regional Assistance Command, accompanied by three other officers, landed by helicopter on the helipad in the southern tip of the sector compound. The enemy opened up with artillery, killing the three U.S. officers and an ARVN sergeant, also mortally wounding General Tallman and critically wounding two U.S. advisors—Maj. Joe Hallum and Capt. James Willbanks—who had gone out to meet the general's party. The general and the two advisors were evacuated by helicopter, but the general died on the operating table in 3rd Field Hospital in Saigon.

For the rest of July, our forces continued to expand the defensive perimeter. Simultaneously, we took on the monumental task of trying to clean up the city and reestablish basic services. We reorganized the hospital and restarted social services. My deputy for administration went to Binh Duong to take care of the refugee center that had been set up there.

The good news was that North Vietnam's 1972 Easter Offensive had stalled and the prospects for South Vietnam had become brighter. The psychologically important imperial city of Hue did not fall. Neither did Kontum. President Thieu remained in power, contrary to the demands of Hanoi's negotiators from their American counterparts.

North Vietnam lost an estimated one hundred thousand men and South Vietnam twenty-five thousand.

An American observer, war correspondent Philip C. Clarke, concluded his report "The Siege of An Loc—A Chronicle of Courage" as follows:

> By halting the enemy's 1972 offensive against Saigon, An Loc's defenders had brought South Vietnam another three years of freedom. They also had helped force Hanoi to the negotiating table so the last of America's servicemen could safely be withdrawn and 590 prisoners of war set free.
>
> Above all, An Loc's unconquerable few had written, in their own blood, a lasting chronicle of courage . . . silent testimony to the indomitable, unconquerable human spirit.[25]

* * *

July 12, 1972, became a crucial date in Vietnamese politics because in the United States on that date the Democratic party convention nominated George McGovern as its presidential candidate. Hanoi had been following American politics for nearly two decades and knew that McGovern did not have any chance of being elected. It was certain that Nixon would be reelected by a landslide and would therefore become more unyielding in the negotiations with North Vietnam. It was better for Hanoi to reach an agreement with Washington before, rather than after, the presidential elections.

The policymakers in Hanoi had a great deal of determination in their pursuit of the conquest of South Vietnam, and they had deep faith in the righteousness of their cause. What they lacked was wisdom. If they had offered, in July 1972, to free the American prisoners of war, the U.S. Congress would have forced the Nixon administration to some kind of an agreement in the negotiations. But Hanoi considered the POW issue such a trump card that they were afraid to play it prematurely. Hence, they missed out on a winning play. They decided instead to be devious, to sign whatever agreement would place the U.S. Air Force on the sidelines, unable to repeat its performance during the Easter Offensive, while Hanoi would not honor its obligations of the agreement and would continue the "liberation" of South Vietnam without U.S. interference.

The policymakers in Saigon, headed by President Thieu, knew how devious Hanoi was, knew that any agreement signed by Hanoi was not worth the paper it was printed on. Therefore, their only hope was to create obstacles to the signing of an agreement between the United States and North Vietnam. Their one and only hope was to make the Vietnamization program a success, enabling our country to resist the aggression of the North with American military assistance.

* * *

On August 25, 1972, all village and hamlet cadres, soldiers, and government officials in the province gathered in An Loc to perform a traditional ceremony at the local temple to thank the gods for protecting the province. It was also an opportunity for everyone to get together and see who had survived and who had not after our ninety-four days in hell. At about three in the afternoon, I received a phone call from III Corps headquarters informing me that I was to report to President Thieu on August 26 to receive command of the 2nd Infantry Division. This division had suffered heavy losses and its commander, Gen. Phan Hoa Hiep, had submitted his resignation. I was instructed to immediately turn over my duties as province chief and sector commander to Col. Nguyen Thong Thanh, the deputy sector commander.

My unexpected departure stirred up considerable emotion among the soldiers, officials, and civilians of the province. As I was waiting for the arrival of my helicopter to take me away, a large number of people assembled at the helipad to beg me to stay. I was greatly touched by this outpouring of affection. The helicopter arrived after about an hour and, as a precaution against communist artillery, took off as soon as I boarded.

As I sat looking down at An Loc, my heart was troubled. I remembered a line from my days as a young student: “Parting is such sweet sorrow.” I was reminded of the painful losses we had suffered. Every war brings death and destruction, but grief caused by emotional losses is the hardest to overcome. Below me, scattered all over the city, were the graves of ARVN, RF, PF, and PSDF soldiers, interspersed with those of the many civilians who had perished in the bitter fighting. Many of the dead were friends I had known and worked with for the past three years. They fought like lions to defeat the brutal communist plot to overrun and capture An Loc. They had gone to their eternal rest so that the people of An Loc could live in freedom and happiness. Their gallant exploits remain with us, the record of their valor etched into the sacred soil of An Loc.

Members of South Vietnam’s valiant Airborne Rangers proudly gave their lives for the sake of our beloved Fatherland and for their fellow citizens. They had returned to the soil of our Motherland, but their images were engraved in a special place in the heart of a young secretary, initials N.T.P., who worked in the province administrative office. Born and raised in Loc Ninh, Miss P. had been the belle of Binh Long province. Her beauty had broken the hearts of countless proud young males of the province, but her heart was unmoved until the gallant forms of our Airborne Ranger warriors came striding down the streets of her beloved city. P. fell in love, a deep, passionate love, with a young Airborne Ranger in the midst of the smoking hell that was An Loc.

The brutal battle, however, gave the lovers no time to enjoy the sweet, private moments that bring beauty and joy to our lives. One day, he braved a storm of artillery shells to visit her as she lay on a stretcher in a house, inside the 81st Airborne Rangers' area of operations, being treated for shrapnel wounds from a communist shell. He returned to his unit to continue his historic mission of defending his lover's home city. After destroying several enemy tanks with M72 rockets, and helping repel wave after wave of enemy assaults on the city, he fell during a hand-to-hand battle. Miss P. had lost her one true love. In grief at the noble sacrifice of her lover, she broke down in tears as she chanted a poem:

Historic An Loc remembers the deeds
Of the Airborne Ranger who gave his life for his country.

P. wept for her lover, for his ever victorious unit, for our nation, for her own noble but fragile love for a man. Her tears merged with the lines of the poem, and the poem became part of our literature forever. History will eternally honor the resolute young warriors who fought the communists, and it will never forget the mothers, the wives, and the young girls like Miss P.

Anyone who has been in combat, no matter under what flag, in what branch of service, and no matter what rank, can ever forget the two lines of this short poem. And everyone is reluctant to take leave of his comrades in arms. We sit around a table, drinking and joking with one another, knowing all the while that we may never see one another again.

As I departed from An Loc, I had my own personal grief. A brutal hunk of communist shrapnel had cut down Uncle Tam Qua, my father's close friend and an outstanding colleague who had helped me tremendously. Uncle Lam Ut, whom I loved so much and who had done so much to support me, had disappeared as he tried to fight his way back to An Loc from the village of Khanh Lam; he was listed as "missing in action." And there were more, many more, countless friends and acquaintances who died in An Loc or were reported missing.

As Binh Long gradually receded in the distance, I thought about the future and about my family. I knew my entire family, especially my wife and my mother, would worry when they learned I was being sent to I Corps to take over 2nd Infantry Division at Que Son, in the distant and unfamiliar territory of central Vietnam and in a dangerous and difficult situation.

On the morning of August 26, 1972, I reported to President Nguyen Van Thieu to receive his instructions. He had no specific instructions other than sketching out for me the overall national situation. Then, half-jokingly, he said: "Your fate is still governed by an unlucky star. Try to be patient; you'll get through it." I thought that he had had my horoscope read using the birth date recorded in my personnel file. Thieu suspected everyone, and he always checked the horoscope of anyone he planned to entrust with an important position.

He then told me to report to Lt. Gen. Dang Van Quang, his special assistant for national security. General Quang had little to say other than a few polite questions about my health and my family. He had little experience in combat, so he could not give me any advice.

Then, as required by protocol, I reported to the joint general staff. I saw only Lt. Gen. Nguyen Van Manh, the chief of staff. He also had no special instructions for me other than to tell me to try hard.

I then went to the U.S. military airfield. In addition to my family, a few officers from Binh Long sector headquarters were there to see me off. General Fred Weyand, who had succeeded Gen. Creighton Abrams as Commander of MACV, was also there. After I said good-bye to my family, General Weyand escorted me personally to the aircraft, hugged me, wished me good luck, said a few words to the American flight crew, and stood there waving as my plane taxied slowly out to the runway.

Another chapter in my life was about to begin.

10

Commander of the 2nd Infantry Division

ALTHOUGH THE battle of An Loc was over, the fighting continued in the northernmost provinces just south of the Demilitarized Zone (DMZ). The North Vietnamese Army had overrun Quang Tri province and its eponymous capital city. As a new brigadier general, I was to assume command of the 2nd ARVN Division, normally located at Quang Ngai province in southern I Corps area. The 4th Regiment of 2nd ARVN Division had participated in the fighting to retake Quang Tri, led by Lt. Gen. Ngo Quang Truong, who had become I Corps commander on May 2, 1972. The South Vietnamese counteroffensive had been launched on June 28.

The American U-21 aircraft I was on landed at the Phu Bai airfield at one o'clock in the afternoon on August 27, 1972. I thanked the crew and disembarked, but there was no one there to greet me, just the operations personnel. I saw several units of the 1st Airborne Brigade waiting for aircraft to take them back to Saigon for R&R. I talked to several of the men I recognized who had fought beside me at An Loc.

After a long wait, I hitched a ride to I Corps headquarters, located in the Mang Ca barracks in Hue. I reported first to Maj. Gen. Hoang Van Lac, deputy Military Region One commander, and then to Lt.

Gen. Ngo Quang Truong, commander of I Corps and Military Region One. The American advisor to I Corps, Maj. Gen. Howard H. Cooksey, walked over and shook my hand. He told me that General Hollingsworth had just called him to ask that he "take care" of me.

After discussing the situation in I Corps, General Truong, General Cooksey, and I flew by helicopter to visit several units, including the headquarters of the marine division, a Marine Brigade headquarters, the airborne division headquarters, and the 1st Infantry Division headquarters.

That night, I stayed at General Lac's compound. Although I had been busy all day, I could not get to sleep. I tossed and turned most of the night. I felt proud, but I was also worried. I was proud of being appointed to such an important position, but worried about the responsibilities I was about to assume. I knew a mountain of work was waiting for me. I would not have been so concerned if I had been taking command under ordinary circumstances, but my new unit had been in heavy fighting and was still facing the enemy on the battlefield as it worked to regroup and reorganize its units and to absorb new replacements.

I knew that two of 2nd Divisions regiments, the 5th and 6th Infantry Regiments, had suffered heavy losses and were now receiving replacements called up from a number of RF units. The division's third regiment, the 4th Regiment, was attached to the airborne division in fighting to retake Quang Tri.

The fighting in the area continued, and I was not entirely sure what kind of situation I would be facing when I assumed command of my division. After reviewing all these anxieties and worries for some time, I decided this was an opportunity for me to prove myself, a chance to display my capabilities. The lines of an old poem came to mind:

If the road of life was always a bed of roses,
How could we tell who the heroes are?

I mentally prioritized the things I had to do after I assumed command, and that finally helped me to get a few hours' sleep.

Early the next morning, August 28, an American helicopter took me to Danang, where I reported to Lt. Gen. Lam Quang Thi, deputy I Corps commander. General Thi said he was the one who had recommended to General Truong that I be appointed to replace Gen. Phan Hoa Hiep, who had asked to be relieved of command. I had heard of General Thi, but I had never before met him. I thanked him for his support.

General Thi and I took a helicopter to Fire Base Baldy (Huong An), where the operational headquarters of the 2nd Infantry Division were then located. The division was trying to stop the advance of the NVA 2nd Division, which had moved down from Thuong Duc, captured the capital of Que Son district, and was now overrunning heavily populated lowland areas in Duy Xuyen district, Quang Nam province.

It should be emphasized that at this time 2nd Infantry Division had the dual mission of rebuilding and reorganizing its units while simultaneously preparing a counterattack to retake Que Son district and Fire Base Ross, the highest ground in the area, which dominated the entire district of Que Son all the way down to the sea.

During the change of command ceremony, General Hiep said a few words and then presented the 2nd Infantry Division flag to me. It was a flag with fourteen ribbons representing fourteen meritorious service citations. The entire 2nd Division, officers and men of all ranks, proudly wore a tricolored *fouragier* on their shoulder, denoting that the unit had received eight Gallantry Cross with Palm medals, the highest unit award. In fact, the division had received more such awards than any other division in the Army of the Republic of Vietnam. With pride, I thanked General Hiep and formally assumed command of the division.

Later, I spoke to the division headquarters staff officers, giving them words of encouragement and advice. Several unit commanders who were present gave me short briefings on the situation, both enemy and our own. I learned that 5th and 6th Infantry Regiments, commanded by Col. Lu Nguyen Huu and Col. Pham Van Nghia, respectively, had suffered extremely heavy casualties. Regional Force soldiers drawn from units in Quang Tin and Quang Ngai provinces were being sent to replace these casualties. Fourth Regiment, under the command of Col. Le Ba Khieu, had just been released from the operational control of the airborne division, where it had been temporarily attached for the counterattack on Quang Tri.

In addition to the division's organic units, it also had the 2nd Regiment from 3rd Division under its operational control; this regiment was stationed along the Duy Xuyen district border and had not yet moved into the division's operational area. When the division's 4th Regiment arrived back in 2nd Division's area of operations, 2nd Regiment from 3rd Division would be released and returned to its parent headquarters.

I felt a little uncomfortable because most of the colonels in the division were senior to me. These officers, including the deputy division commander, Col. Nguyen Am; the inspector general, Col. Nguyen Luong Khuong; and the commander of our Chu Lai base camp, Col. Tran Van Tu, had graduated from the academy several classes before me.

After assessing the overall situation, the division staff and I walked over to the headquarters of the 5th and 6th Regiments, which were regrouping and reorganizing nearby. I wanted to learn more about the morale of the troops and to resolve immediately any problems regarding troop strength and equipment, in order to get these units back into the fight as soon as possible. After visiting with the 5th and 6th Regiments, I drove out to visit 4th Regiment, which was just completing its return to our operational area. There I received a briefing from Colonel Khieu. After observing the deployment and the missions assigned to his individual battalions prior to the attack to retake Que Son and Fire Base Ross, my worries abated and I felt confident in the abilities of my combat commanders. Khieu gave a good briefing, demonstrating that he knew both the enemy and the capability of his own troops. His attack plan made good use of supporting tactical air and artillery. Later, Khieu became chief of staff of 2nd Division, then province chief in Quang Ngai, and ultimately G-3 of I Corps.

That night I returned to the division's operational headquarters. Because I was hungry, I asked if there was anything to eat. I was told that there was only the enlisted men's mess, located in a nearby tin-roofed building. I walked over and entered the dimly lit mess, asking for whatever they had left to eat. All the personnel were surprised to see me; the previous division commander had never eaten there. Several times during the meal, I heard the blast of an enemy 130mm round exploding near the mess. The soldiers in the club all took cover, but I just sat there and continued to eat. These few, isolated rounds were nothing compared to the storm of artillery fire I had experienced at An Loc.

After dinner, completely exhausted, I returned to the operations center. I stretched out on a chair and asked the staff officers to brief me on the latest developments. I was shocked to find out that most of the senior officers, including the deputy division commander, the chief of staff, and the deputy chief of staff, were not there. Only Lt. Col. Kieu Van Thanh, chief of the G-3 office, was present to brief me.

After the briefing I asked about the absence of the other officers. Thanh told me that all the senior officers flew back to Chu Lai, thirty miles to the southeast, to spend the night there. I asked Thanh, "If problems developed during the night, who did General Hiep turn to?" I was told that General Hiep always spent the night in Danang.

Later that night, I issued a new order: as of eight o'clock the next morning, the deputy division commander, the chief of staff, the deputy chief of staff, and all staff officers were to work and live at the division's operational headquarters. The only exceptions would be the inspector general and the Chu Lai base camp commander, neither of whose presence was required for combat operations. In addition, division headquarters would immediately establish an officers' mess where the division's staff officers would eat. I also ordered that senior U.S. advisors were to be invited to eat at the mess, so we could discuss over dinner any urgent problems that had arisen during the course of the day.

I am sure not everyone was happy with this order, but later all the senior U.S. advisors assigned to our division told me that they were happy for the opportunity to have discussions and to present their recommendations over a hot meal rather than being forced to eat cold C-rations.

Excluding the southern portion of Quang Nam province, for which the division had been assigned temporary responsibility, our primary area of responsibility covered the two provinces of Quang Tin and Quang Ngai, ninety-three miles from north to south. Only 40 percent of the area was lowland. The rest was covered with jungle and included a number of mountain ranges running parallel to Route 1 all the way down to Sa Huynh on the Binh Dinh province border. The terrain provided good cover for enemy troop movements and concealment of his forces.

Communist Military Region Five headquarters was located in the Do Xa base area at the intersection of the borders of Quang Tin, Quang Ngai, and Kontum provinces. The provinces of Quang Tin and Quang Ngai, which the communists called "Tin-Ngai," had been under continuous communist control from 1945 until the Geneva agreement of 1954. In 1955, when the communists retreated to North Vietnam, they left behind a large number of cadres and cached a large quantity of weapons. Of particular importance, they developed family relationships in the area by encouraging their cadre and soldiers to get married before regrouping north. The proportion of people with connections to northern regroupees was 55 to 60 percent in this area, the highest in the nation. Because of these advantages for the communists, it was easy for them to build an infrastructure and increase their military strength by drafting local youth to defend areas temporarily under their control.

Communist forces permanently operating in this area included two divisions, the 2nd and the 711th, plus sappers, province and district local force units, and village and hamlet guerillas. In addition, the communist 3rd "Gold Star" Division regularly came from An Lao, Binh Dinh province, to support the NVA 2nd Division. In numerical terms, at least, the balance of forces was tilted heavily in the enemy's favor. Thus, our forces in the area had a two-pronged problem. First, they had to worry about local security, protecting the villages and hamlets, defending government offices, bridges and culverts, roads and highways, and so on. This effort tied down most of the RF and PF troops in the area, leaving the ARVN units to conduct mobile operations to confront the main communist forces. Second, they had to worry about the safety of their families with the NVA so close.

With all of its regiments back under our control, I directed the division to attack and retake the enemy-held territory in our area. The operation was called Quyet Thang 72. By the end of the week, 6th Infantry Regiment had recaptured the Que Son district capital. First Battalion, 4th Regiment, under the command of Lt. Col. Che Quang Tao, reinforced by a troop of tanks and armored personnel carriers, made an envelopment attack around the rear of Fire Base Ross, where it captured a number of prisoners of war. Based on a timely interrogation of these prisoners, we called in several B-52 strikes to hit the two communist regiments in the area supporting the enemy troops defending the base. The enemy units suffered heavy casualties and, after putting up only light resistance, withdrew. This enabled 4th Battalion, 4th Regiment, to swing around west of Fire Base Ross to capture the Le Pass, cutting the enemy's supply route and the route he used to evacuate his wounded. The enemy defense became untenable, forcing him to abandon the base. Soldiers of 4th Battalion, 4th Regiment, recaptured Fire Base Ross on D+4, the fourth day of the operation.

For the rest of August and into September, the activity in Military Region One intensified. Taking advantage of the absence of 4th Regiment from Nui An (An Mountain) in Son Tra, and the fact that 5th and 6th Regiments were conducting operations in the Que Son area, communist Military Region Five ordered all units to launch simultaneous attacks on a second front, south of Danang, to reduce ARVN pressure on their forces in the Quang Tri–Thua Thien area.

Just after our troops reoccupied Que Son, enemy forces captured the Tien Phuoc district capital in Quang Tin, besieged the Ba To district capital, and applied heavy pressure on our forces south of Song Ve in Mo Duc and Duc Pho districts of Quang Ngai. Second Division

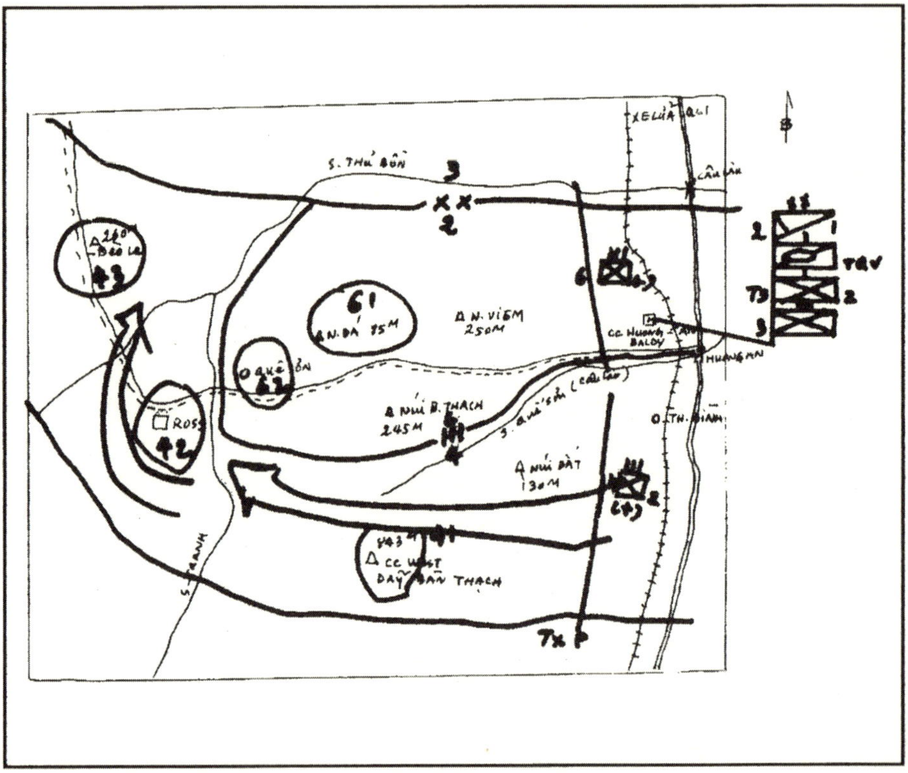

Quyet Thang 72 Campaign to Reoccupy Que Son

headquarters had to send 6th Regiment to block enemy advance west of the Quang Tin province capital. Fifth Regiment was sent in by helicopter to relieve the enemy pressure on the Ba To, Tien Son area (mountain area), and 4th Regiment was pulled back to Quang Ngai to counter the 3rd "Yellow Star" Division's move in the southern part of the province. Second Division returned responsibility for the districts of Que Son and Duy Xuyen to 3rd Infantry Division.

I sent 4th Regiment (-), under the command of Colonel Khieu and reinforced by a troop of tanks and APCs and one artillery battalion, down to the Song Ve district capital. Our forces gradually reduced communist pressure in the area, recaptured the bases west of the Mo Duc district capital that had fallen into enemy hands, and drove the enemy back to the Tien Son area from Thach Tru to Duc Pho and Sa Huynh. During an inspection of the frontlines south of Song Ve, a communist sniper tried to kill me. Fortunately, his bullet hit a fraction of an inch from my foot.

Meanwhile, another element of 4th Regiment (-), commanded by the deputy regimental commander, Lt. Col. Truong Dang Liem, was flown by helicopter from Chu Lai down the coast to the hamlet of Dong Cat east of the Mo Duc district capital. They landed not far from the ancestral home of Pham Van Dong, the prime minister of North Vietnam. In spite of powerful communist antiaircraft defenses in the area, the enemy could not slow the pace of our advance.

The next day, 4th Regiment's two troop columns, coordinating closely with each other, eliminated the communist threat in this area, recaptured the forward outposts that had been lost, and gradually cleared Route 1 all the way to Duc Pho, where the Binh Minh Base Camp, 4th Regiment's rear base, was located.

However, the newly reorganized 6th Regiment, with a newly appointed commander, Lt. Col. Nguyen Thoi Lai, ran into many difficulties while trying to retake the Tien Phuoc district capital. Only after 3rd Division arrived to support the effort was Tien Phuoc finally recaptured.

At the same time, 5th Regiment encountered problems similar to those of 6th Regiment. The 5th Regiment was ordered to eliminate the communist threat to the Ba To district capital, but its efforts did not live up to our expectations. This was in part because the regiment had just been reorganized, and in part it was due to a serious reduction in U.S. support.

Major reductions in air support, including the use of U.S. helicopters to transport heavy 155mm howitzers, U.S. close air support missions, and in particular the very significant reductions in B-52 strikes, became the cause of constant arguments between my U.S. advisors and me. The Paris peace accords had been signed and the Americans were in the final stages of their withdrawal. The support provided to the ARVN was drastically reduced. Because of these problems, the Ba To district capital fell to enemy forces after holding out for more than two weeks.

I pulled 5th Regiment back to its rear base at Tuan Duong to regroup, withdrew 6th Regiment back to our Chu Lai base to regroup and reorganize the regiment, and gave 4th Regiment responsibility for the Duc Pho area because the regiment's rear base area was located there. The regiment devoted particular attention to the Thach Tru area.

From this moment until the day of the cease-fire, there were daily firefights between our forces and enemy units, ranging in size from small unit contacts up to major engagements with entire enemy battalions, as they tried to plant their flags and seize population and territory.

To provide the maximum possible protection to the territory in our area of responsibility, 2nd Division sent nonessential personnel from all noncombat units, including support and logistics units, to join new recruits in the 2nd Division Recruit Training Center to form two additional combat battalions, which were sent out to the villages and hamlets, especially those in the area of Thach Tru, Mo Duc district.

This plan caught the communists off guard and threw them into confusion. They could not understand where we had gotten all these new troops. They constantly monitored 2nd Division's three infantry regiments and had no idea we had formed two new battalions. They were unable to react to this new program in time, and for that reason they failed to seize any more territory in the division's area of responsibility, particularly in the heavily populated areas.

* * *

On the political front, as the negotiations between North Vietnam and the United States went beyond the four-year mark, the prognosis for South Vietnam was not encouraging.

North Vietnam was intent on obtaining a peace agreement before, rather than after, the American presidential election. They expected Nixon to win in a landslide and were afraid Nixon would become more unyielding after the election.

Nixon also preferred a peace agreement before the election because such an agreement would guarantee a landslide win. In either case, American disengagement from the "quagmire" of Vietnam had become the policy of the Johnson and Nixon administrations during the previous four years.

South Vietnam did not want *any* peace agreement, either before or after the American elections, because the fear was that the country and its leadership would not survive the fake peace being engineered by Hanoi. Therefore, Thieu had decided to create obstacles to the signing of any agreement. On September 20, 1972, in a speech in Hue, he declared: "No one has a right to negotiate for or accept any solution [to the Vietnam War] except the people of South Vietnam."

Alexander Haig—assistant to National Security Advisor Henry Kissinger, the chief American negotiator—went to Saigon to convince Thieu that Kissinger was obtaining concessions from the North Vietnamese negotiators. He also told Thieu about some new variations Nixon had approved for the next negotiation session, designed to make the projected peace agreement a "grand design for a generation of peace." But Thieu was not convinced. His view was that the communists' motives were cynical. He bitterly attacked every aspect of the proposed agreement, including segments he had long since accepted. He railed against Kissinger, who did not "deign" to even consider Saigon's views in his negotiations.

Nixon thought Thieu was being unreasonable. "The tail can't wag the dog!" he fumed. Still, he decided that Kissinger would not present the variations rejected by Thieu because he did not want relations between Washington and Saigon to be strained further.

When Kissinger and the North Vietnamese chief negotiator Le Duc Tho met on October 8, 1972, North Vietnam was ready for a final set of concessions:

1. Military and political issues would be treated separately. The United States and North Vietnam would sign an agreement settling the military questions between them—withdrawal, prisoners, and cease-fire—leaving the political problems for a later settlement with South Vietnam.
2. North Vietnam would no longer insist on a coalition government in the South. They would accept an "administration of national concord" so vaguely planned that it was unachievable in practice.
3. American military aid to South Vietnam would continue with a "replacement of armament" clause.

The details of the agreement had all been worked out by October 12. After Nixon's approval, Kissinger planned to obtain Thieu's approval on October 18. Arrangements were made for the official agreement to be signed on October 31, 1972.

Nixon and his cabinet and the Pentagon all approved the details of the agreement. American leaders were convinced that the "replacement of armament" clause would ensure the survival of South Vietnam. American installations were swiftly and secretly transferred to South Vietnamese ownership. Military equipment and material worth $2 billion was flown to South Vietnam from Taiwan, South Korea, and the Philippines. The Saigon regime suddenly had the fourth largest air force in the world.

Nixon the politician was nevertheless concerned about how a negative reaction by Saigon would affect the American elections. In case of disagreements with Thieu, he instructed Kissinger to back off and wait until after the election to conclude the agreement.

But in Saigon, Thieu was furious because he thought Kissinger was going to come and make a crude and arrogant effort to present the South Vietnamese with a *fait accompli* and expect him to sign on the dotted line. Although he had accepted the concept of a standstill cease-fire (also called a cease-fire in place) two years earlier, he had changed his mind on the subject under pressure from his own military, who considered a standstill cease-fire a great disadvantage to the Republic of Vietnam. More than three hundred thousand communists remained in the South; the map was full of "leopard spots" denoting the territory held by the NVA. As the cease-fire neared, the communist bloc poured huge amounts of ammunition and supplies to its forces in the South because the conquered areas would not be returned to South Vietnam after the standstill cease-fire.

Under these circumstances, Kissinger arrived in Saigon on October 19 for a two-day visit, to an icy reception. Meetings were either inconclusive, or postponed, or cancelled. As he reported to Washington: "They are having great psychological difficulty cutting the American umbilical cord. . . . They continue to exhibit awe at communist cunning and a lack of self-confidence." Finally, after four days of negotiations, Thieu rejected the treaty on October 22, thereby enforcing a continuation of the war.[26]

Thieu was flushing down the toilet what Kissinger had accomplished after four years of hard work. "Those whom I regard as friends have failed me," was Thieu's final remark.

Kissinger, humiliated and angry, closed the meeting with deep regret: "We have fought for four years, have mortgaged our whole foreign policy to the defense of one country. What you have said has been a very bitter thing to hear. . . . This is why I leave with such a sense of tragedy." Kissinger had come to Saigon as an ally of Thieu, who could no longer be considered an ally when he left Saigon.[27]

On October 26, North Vietnam decided its interests would be better served by going public. Radio Hanoi began broadcasting the record of their secret negotiations with the United States and demanded that the agreement be signed by October 31. Washington refused: "We will not be stampeded into an agreement until its provisions are right. We will not be deflected from an agreement when its provisions are right."

Nixon won the 1972 election by a landslide of 60.7 percent of the popular vote and 520 electoral votes.

North Vietnam had no choice but to resume the negotiations on November 20, 1972, but their mood had changed to insolence. They kept changing positions and tactics. There were six days of inconclusive negotiations in November and thirteen more days of the same in December. These negotiations could go on forever. Nixon decided that only severe raids could convince Hanoi to change its negotiating strategy. He ordered the resumption of bombing of North Vietnam. It was up to the U.S. Air Force to cut the Gordian knot.

On December 17, 1972, in Operation Linebacker Two, American planes reseeded the mines in Haiphong Harbor. The next day, 129 B-52s bombed North Vietnam. Over the next eleven days, the United States dropped more than thirty-six thousand tons of bombs, exceeding the tonnage during the entire period 1969–1971. About 1,600 civilians were killed. The North Vietnamese air defense system was overwhelmed; their stocks of surface-to-air missiles were exhausted. Their railroad system was brought to a halt. Their electric power facilities were heavily damaged. Warehouses, military complexes, and communication centers were destroyed.[28]

There were definite signs that North Vietnam had had enough. They could no longer react with their usual resiliency. They capitulated and proposed a meeting for January 8 in Paris. Nixon accepted. The "Christmas bombing" was stopped on December 29.

Time magazine selected Nixon and Kissinger as joint "men of the year" for 1972.

Kissinger and Le Duc Tho met on January 8. The draft agreement was completed on January 13. Thieu's approval was received on January 21. The foreign ministers signed the agreement on January 27, 1973. North Vietnam would soon free the American prisoners of war, and the United States would complete the withdrawal of its troops from South Vietnam.

The point of view in Washington was that the Vietnam War was an unhappy chapter in the history of the United States. The point of view in Saigon was that the Vietnam War was about to become a tragedy of indescribable proportions.

* * *

Before the cease-fire took effect on January 28, intercepted enemy radio traffic in 2nd Division's area of responsibility revealed considerable troop movements by the NVA 2nd Division's 52nd and 141st Regiments and the 406th Quang Ngai Sapper Battalion toward Sa Huynh in Duc Pho district. Sa Huynh was a village with a population of more than three thousand people located on Route 1 along the coast near Binh Dinh province border.

On the afternoon of January 27, I flew to Sa Huynh to make a surprise visit to the RF battalion and PF units stationed there, to review plans for the defense of the village. I noticed a strange expression on the RF battalion commander's face when I ordered him to send his troops out to collect information on enemy movements just prior to the cease-fire, which coincided with the beginning of the Tet holiday period.

To guard against any unforeseen problems, on my return flight to Chu Lai I ordered the helicopter to stop at the headquarters of Lt. Col. Tran Kim Dai's 1st Ranger Group at Duc Pho. The Ranger group was providing security for 2nd Division engineers as they repaired bridges, culverts, and the roadway along Route 1 from southern Duc Pho district to Sa Huynh. I gave Dai a quick synopsis of the situation at Sa Huynh and ordered him to immediately send a Ranger company and a battalion forward headquarters element to Sa Huynh to reinforce the defenses there (one Ranger company was already stationed in Sa Huynh). By the afternoon of January 27, a Ranger battalion forward headquarters and two Ranger companies, all under the direct command of 1st Ranger Group headquarters, were stationed at Sa Huynh.

The cease-fire took effect at midnight on January 27. Taking advantage of the fact that our soldiers were preoccupied with the Tet lunar New Year festivities, the NVA launched a surprise attack, capturing Sa Huynh rather easily. They chose Sa Huynh as their target because it had a fairly good harbor. The harbor had been so shallow that only sampans and small boats could dock there. In 1966, however, when the U.S. 11th Light Infantry Brigade arrived and was stationed at Dang Mountain, east of the Duc Pho district capital, the United States dredged and improved the harbor facilities to allow medium-sized ships to use it, turning it into a secondary logistics supply port.

In addition, Route 1 and the railroad tracks were only seven hundred yards from the coastline. If the communists captured and held this area, they would be able to turn the harbor into a naval base at which their forces could receive supplies from North Vietnam, while at the same time cutting South Vietnam in half and severing our nation's two primary north-south arteries, Route 1 and the railroad. Sa Huynh also had excellent salt fields, sufficient to supply all the needs of communist Military Region Five.

Sa Huynh's terrain was rugged, well suited for defense and communist troop movements. To approach Sa Huynh from the north, we would have to go through the My Trang Pass in Dien Truong, and to approach it from the south we had to go through the Binh De Pass across an arm of the Annamite Mountains that stretched all the way out to the sea.

I issued orders to my units to launch "Operation Quyet Thang 36" to recapture Sa Huynh. On D-day minus 1, 5th Regiment drove down to the area of operations by road. We had received a report that the enemy had set up a roadblock, cutting the road between Mo Duc and Duc Pho. I thought the Rangers would have to clear the roadblock first, but the report turned out to be untrue.

First Ranger Group, which was already in Duc Pho, moved to the assembly area and prepared to begin its advance. A division light forward headquarters element moved to Dau Mountain from Chu Lai to control the operation. The main division headquarters and 4th

Armored Squadron (-) remained at Chu Lai, together with 6th Regiment, to serve as a reserve and reaction force for Quang Tin province. Fourth Regiment, at Duc Pho, was placed on alert status as a reaction force in the event the enemy launched another land-grabbing operation in Quang Ngai province.

During Phase 1 of the operation, 1st Ranger Group, with fire support provided by the 105mm howitzers of 21st Artillery Battalion, made the secondary effort, capturing a number of objectives along the coast east of Route 1. Fifth Regiment, reinforced by one troop of armored personnel carriers and with direct fire support from the 105mm howitzers of 22nd Artillery Battalion, launched our main effort, moving down to capture the high ground to the west of Route 1. During this operation, Lt. Col. Vo Vang commanded 5th Regiment. A battalion of 155mm howitzers and a battery of long-range 175mm guns provided general fire support and supported both troop columns when necessary.

For three straight days, the advance moved slowly because the rugged terrain and high mountains made movement difficult. Additionally, the enemy had dug in and fortified his defensive positions rather well. I decided to transport 5th Reconnaissance Company by helicopter to Hill 75, east of Sa Huynh and behind enemy lines, to probe the strength of the enemy resistance and his antiaircraft defenses. The enemy reacted strongly, so we were unable to land these troops.

We ordered our troop columns to use a new tactic when attacking enemy fortified positions. After determining the exact location of the blocking position, we would send small units at night to sneak behind the enemy position to block the enemy's supply and medical evacuation routes. After two or three days, the enemy would be forced to abandon the blocking position. This tactic was effective. It took a lot of time but was very economical in terms of the number of casualties suffered by our forces. On the ninth day of the operation, the enemy's line of blocking positions at the Dien Truong Pass was finally overrun.

Meanwhile, teams from the 2nd Division LRRP (Long Range

Reconnaissance Patrol) Unit were sent in by helicopter farther to the southwest, near the Binh Dinh province border, in an attempt to confirm a number of reports from our radio intercept unit indicating the presence of elements of the NVA 3rd "Yellow Star" Division. On D+12, our LRRPs finally found evidence that 3rd Division was moving forces from An Lao toward Sa Huynh.

Because the NVA 2nd Division was already putting up stiff resistance and was about to be reinforced by 3rd Division, I decided that if I wanted to end this battle quickly I would have to conduct several diversionary operations to induce the enemy to disperse his defenders. We loaded Capt. Tran Van Nho's 1st Battalion, 5th Regiment, into a troop of armored personnel carriers from a newly formed composite amphibious task force, made up of a number of navy LSTs and LCUs (LST = landing ship, tank; LCU = landing craft, utility). Navy captain Nguyen Van Thien, the commander of a former U.S. Coast Guard cutter, commanded this entire force. The amphibious task force sailed in close to shore at Sa Huynh and used naval guns to shell several targets, pretending to be about to land our troops. The enemy did believe that we were preparing to make a real landing and quickly withdrew most of his forces in the west to reinforce his defenses southeast of Sa Huynh. This enabled my two troop columns moving in from the north and the west to capture their objectives with relative ease.

The NVA 2nd Division had only two regiments, the 52nd and 141st, committed to this battle. The division's third regiment, the 142nd, was hiding in the Da Chat area of Ba To district. My division sent an element of 4th Regiment to the Van Ly area in Thach Tru to pretend we were preparing to launch an operation into this area to recapture Ba To district. Our objective was to tie down the enemy's third regiment so we could concentrate our efforts on recapturing Sa Huynh.

On D plus 16 (on the sixteenth day after D-day), one of our LRRP Unit teams monitoring the movement of the 3rd "Yellow Star" Division was able to confirm the location where the enemy force had bivouacked. Colonel Le Thuong, commander of the 2nd Division artillery, concentrated all his guns, naval gunfire, and close air support for a massive bombardment of this large unit. The enemy force was shattered and scattered in all directions, rendering it incapable of sending reinforcements to the NVA 2nd Division. Captain Trong Tuan of my radio intercept unit allowed me to listen to the arguments and accusations being hurled back and forth between the NVA 2nd and 3rd Divisions.

On D plus 17, we knew that, although they were still trying to hold out in the hamlet of Thach Tru and Sa Huynh harbor, the communists were in serious trouble, having received no resupply or reinforcements. Our troops attacked and seized the high ground to the north, east, and west. I decided to commit our reserve, 2nd Battalion, 4th Regiment, and a composite armored troop, including both tanks and APCs. I ordered them to attack right through Sa Huynh, from north to south.

After leaving the Dien Truong Pass, our troops met stiff resistance. The communists fired AT-3 Sagger wire-guided antitank missiles at our armor, but failed to hit a single vehicle. This type of missile is easy to see during flight, so our drivers, who had experience with these missiles, would wait until the missile got close, then suddenly put on the brakes. The missile would fly right by the target vehicle and explode when it hit the ground or when it reached the end of its wire.

To increase the effectiveness of our support to the troop columns, the division fired smoke and tear gas rounds into the enemy defensive positions. The wind usually blew from east to west (from the ocean onto the shore), but at this particular moment it was blowing north to south, so the entire town of Sa Huynh was blanketed in smoke and tear gas. The smoke and gas crushed the morale of the enemy troops, who abandoned their positions and fled in confusion. We completed the recapture of Sa Huynh at seven o'clock in the evening on D plus 17, February 21, 1973, ending a ferocious struggle eighteen days after the cease-fire supposedly first took effect. We captured hundreds of enemy weapons, including fifteen 14.5mm and 12.7mm heavy antiaircraft machine guns, three 75mm recoilless rifles, and six AT-3 anti-tank missiles.

This was one of the greatest victories for the ARVN during the entire post-cease-fire period. It was a joint services operation conducted completely under our command, with no U.S. advisors and no support of any kind from the United States. In a battle between major units on both sides, we once again demonstrated that the Armed Forces of the Republic of Vietnam had truly come of age.

The next day, the International Commission for Control and Supervision (ICCS) arrived to inspect the battle area and determine who had broken the cease-fire. They interviewed the residents and collected evidence at the scene. Even the Polish representative on the ICCS, a communist ally of North Vietnam, reluctantly added his signature to the memorandum stating that it was Hanoi that had violated the Paris peace accord. This was the first instance of a communist representative on the ICCS publicly acknowledging a communist violation of the Paris agreement. However, this cease-fire violation did not meet any punishment or any concrete action by the nations that had signed the treaty guaranteeing the implementation of the peace agreement. The Polish representative who had signed the memorandum was recalled to Poland.

A few days later, President Nguyen Van Thieu came to visit the battle site and reward the soldiers. Looking around Sa Huynh, he said: "The terrain here is really very rugged. The fact that the men were able to retake Sa Huynh is quite commendable."

When we began discussing the strategic situation in my area, I proposed withdrawing my three Ranger battalions to consolidate our position in the populated region of my Divisional Tactical Area. But President Thieu insisted that I adhere to his "four nos" slogan:

No to communism.
No to an inch of land or a single person to the communists.
No to neutrality in the face of communist cynicism.
No to a coalition government with the NLF.

Later, Sir Robert Thompson and General Vanuxem made separate visits to Sa Huynh. Both of them expressed admiration for the combat capabilities and the fighting spirit of our forces. Before leaving, General Vanuxem shook my hand and said: "I am very proud that, during my visit to An Loc with President Thieu on July 7, 1972, I recommended that he appoint you to the command of an infantry division."

My division staff and I took a small boat out to the fleet to reward Capt. Nguyen Van Thien's Task Force. I awarded the Heroism Medal, Division Grade, to Captain Thien and a number of navy personnel who had distinguished themselves during this battle.

To demonstrate our gratitude for the tremendous sacrifices of the wounded and disabled veterans, the 2nd Division headquarters persuaded businessmen from Cho Lon, Saigon, and Danang to contribute more than 1 million piasters to purchase thirty wheelchairs and a number of valuable gifts and provide rewards that were delivered to all servicemen being treated at the Duy Tan Military Hospital who fought so courageously throughout the 1972 "summer of fire" when the communists launched their new round of attacks.

In spite of the fact that its area of responsibility was ninety miles long and thirty miles wide, that the western part of its territory consisted of mountainous jungles, that its terrain was rugged, and that the local population was difficult, 2nd Division had gloriously fulfilled its mission during the 1972 "summer of fire."

For this achievement, from August 1972 until January 1973, 2nd ARVN Division was awarded two more Gallantry Crosses with Palm.

I had reorganized my division by rotating all my battalions through the Division Training Center to undergo basic training and psywar training. I also had to conserve ammunition stocks and other supplies due to declining U.S. assistance.

As for the enemy, after signing the "Agreement on Ending the War and Restoring Peace in Vietnam," the government of North Vietnam worked hard to prove that it was the most treacherous government in the world. They committed two hundred major violations within less than two weeks of signing the agreement.

There was sporadic fighting at the beginning of the cease-fire. As time went on, the communists continually violated the truce and the fighting resumed in earnest.

11

The Last Days of the 2nd Infantry Division

THE FIGHTING continued throughout the rest of 1973 and into 1974. South Vietnam sustained a heavy blow in August 1974 when Richard Nixon resigned the presidency of the United States in the wake of the Watergate scandal. Nixon had repeatedly promised to the South Vietnamese that the United States would come to their aid if Hanoi violated the Paris peace accords by launching a general offensive. With Nixon out of office, Congress slashed military appropriations to South Vietnam and Senator Edward Kennedy insisted it was time to terminate America's "endless support for an endless war." President Thieu was forced to fight a "poor man's war."

These events were not lost on the communist leaders in Hanoi, who came to the conclusion that the United States, having withdrawn from Vietnam and without Nixon at the helm, could not and would not intervene. But they were still afraid of provoking the United States. They stopped short of a large-scale offensive, but encouraged the Viet Cong to engage in armed conflict. By the end of 1974, the military balance had shifted in favor of the communists. The Viet Cong had regained most of the territory lost in the Mekong Delta the previous year. What used to be the primitive Ho Chi Minh Trail was now a gravel-paved two-lane highway. The 285,000 North Vietnamese troops in the South were well supplied and could move to any battlefront within hours.

Still, having been burned twice by American military reaction in 1968 and 1972, they were cautious. They attempted a limited offensive and targeted the Phuoc Long province sixty miles northeast of Saigon. It had a population of about fifty thousand with the majority being Montagnards. The region's main resources were lumber and rubber, but the province was very poor. It was defended by mostly regional and popular forces and was largely ignored by the III Corps commander.

On December 13, 1974, the NVA 301st Corps launched the attack. The province's defenders managed to hold for a brief period, but they were severely outnumbered. Because the airborne and marine divisions were still committed in I Corps, there was no strategic reserve and the joint general staff could send only one battalion from the 81st Rangers to rescue Phuoc Long. It was not enough. Professor Nguyen Tien Hung, the minister of planning, assured President Thieu that the Pentagon had budgeted for contingencies in Vietnam in case the communists violated the Paris agreement. Thieu was reassured and continued to believe that the United States would intervene up to the last minute of his presidency.

Ultimately, the attackers overwhelmed Phuoc Long. They killed or captured three thousand ARVN troops and "liberated" the province by January 8, 1975. The success in Phuoc Long marked the first time that communists had occupied an entire province, with the exception of Quang Tri in 1972.

The U.S. Air Force did not come to the rescue of Saigon. This proved to be the beginning of the end for the Republic of Vietnam.

* * *

On the first day of Tet 1975, I flew to Nui Tron (Round Mountain) to take gifts to Capt. Tran Bao's 1st Battalion, 6th Regiment. The communists began shelling the base as soon as my helicopter landed. An

82mm mortar round that hit nearby fortunately landed inside a foxhole. While the hole stopped the biggest pieces of shrapnel, several small pieces of shrapnel, together with rocks and sand, scattered across the area, slightly injuring the regimental commander, Colonel Lai, several other division staff officers, and myself.

In early 1975, 2nd Infantry Division was ordered to return 12th and 14th Ranger Groups to the control of I Corps headquarters. These two units had been attached to 2nd Division to protect our land-clearing program in the communist secret zones in eastern Mo Duc and Duc Pho districts. The only Ranger unit left in 2nd Infantry Division's area of responsibility was 11th Ranger Group. The 11th Ranger Group's three battalions, the 68th, 69th, and 70th Battalions, had been deployed to defend our border defense posts at Gia Vuc, Son Ha, and Tra Bong. The 2nd Division's own 4th, 5th, and 6th Regiments had been maintained on mobile reserve status ever since the 1973 cease-fire, constantly ready to respond to the requirements of the situation.

Under heavy enemy pressure, the three battalions of the 11th Ranger Group were forced to evacuate back to Quang Ngai to defend the heavily populated coastal lowlands. We sustained fairly heavy losses during this withdrawal operation. After the fall of Minh Long district in early February 1975, 2nd Division sent 4th and 5th Regiments to counter enemy pressure in southwestern Nghia Hanh district of Quang Ngai province, where the North Vietnamese 52nd Brigade was operating. This brigade was a newly formed unit made up of the 52nd Regiment of 3rd "Yellow Star" Division, one artillery regiment, and one armored regiment. The brigade's area of operations was the Ba To–Nghia Hanh–Minh Long region.

In North Vietnam, Gen. Tran Van Tra, commanding general of the Liberation Armed Forces, was called to Hanoi in January 1975 to attend the Armed Forces Central Council meeting for the general offensive to be conducted in late 1975 or early 1976. Le Duan, communist party chief, and Le Duc Tho, chief negotiator at the peace talks in Paris, were presiding over the meeting. General Tra was ordered to cease local attacks in South Vietnam in order to preserve the main forces for the all-out general offensive. It was agreed that the first stage of this offensive would target Ban Me Thuot, in the central highlands, and would be led by Gen. Van Tien Dung, the defense minister.

In South Vietnam, Maj. Gen. Pham Van Phu, commander of II Corps, did not agree with intelligence reports that the North Vietnamese would launch an offensive at Ban Me Thuot. He felt that Pleiku, where his headquarters was located, would be the main objective. Therefore, he increased his defenses at Pleiku and left Ban Me Thuot defended by only the 53rd Regiment of the 23rd ARVN Division, elements of the 21st Ranger Group, and regional forces.

The NVA attacked Ban Me Thuot on March 10 with the F10 and 320th Divisions reinforced with tanks and heavy artillery (130mm and 152mm). In reserve was the 316th Division, which had arrived in February from North Vietnam. Although it became clear that Ban Me Thuot was the enemy's main objective, it was too late to react, and the city fell on March 11, 1975.

We kept control of our area of responsibility, but we were experiencing serious shortages in supplies and ammunition. We knew that the communists were preparing for an even larger attack than the one they had launched in 1972 because they felt that the United States would not get involved this time. The only orders we received were to conserve ammunition and gasoline.

Thieu was in panic. To preserve our forces, he ordered General Phu on March 14 to withdraw only the regular forces in II Corps to Nha Trang. All the province chiefs and their regional forces were to stay behind to protect their provinces. At the same time, he ordered General Truong, I Corps commander, to defend Hue, Danang, and Chu Lai, and also to prepare to withdraw to the south when so ordered. Thieu hoped that these moves would pressure the U.S. government to stage a rescue, but he had misjudged Gerald R. Ford, Nixon's replacement. Ford had several times echoed Nixon's promise that the United States would come to the aid of South Vietnam, but he would not be able to overcome an antagonistic Congress.

The withdrawal from Pleiku and Kontum turned into a panic-stricken rout. As the regular forces withdrew, the local forces and thousands of civilians, who were afraid of being left behind, joined them. The column of soldiers and civilians became strung out along Route 7B toward Tuy Hoa. The North Vietnamese attacked the column with the 320th and 968th Divisions. By the time the lead ARVN units arrived at Tuy Hoa on March 27, the evacuation had turned into an unmitigated disaster. Only twenty thousand of the original sixty thousand troops made it through. Only one hundred thousand of an estimated four hundred thousand civilians survived to reach Tuy Hoa.

We received no specific orders, but could follow the situation through Vietnam Radio, Voice of America, and BBC. We were told to be ready to deal with the situation, but were not sure whether it would be an order to defend Hue and Danang or to withdraw to the south. Saigon sent barges to Danang to evacuate civilians to the south, creating serious morale problems for us. Some ARVN soldiers deserted in order to look for their families.

With the situation deteriorating rapidly in II Corps, 2nd Infantry Division was forced to redeploy its forces in order to deal with increasing enemy pressure in its area of responsibility. We sent 6th Infantry Regiment to Quang Ngai to replace 4th and 5th Regiments, which were pulled back to Chu Lai and Tuan Duong to serve as reserve forces.

On March 9, Col. Dao Mong Xuan, province chief and sector commander of Quang Tin province, reported that the Tien Phuoc district capital had been attacked and overrun by communist forces. This kind of report was common in Quang Tin and Quang Ngai provinces, and in many cases we found that in the face of enemy pressure local RF units had in fact retreated from their area on their own initiative.

Actually, the communist forces were only pressuring the hill positions west of the province capital. I flew hurriedly to Quang Tin to get a clearer picture of the situation and decided to commit 5th Regiment to block enemy forces west of the province capital. Because enemy pressure was so strong, and because we received a report that the NVA

52nd Brigade was moving up from Quang Ngai to reinforce enemy forces in the area, I quickly sent 4th Regiment to strengthen our defenses in southwestern Quang Tin and asked General Truong to return the 14th Ranger Group to defend northwestern Quang Tin.

Information obtained from prisoners and intercepts of enemy radio communications indicated that the entire 2nd NVA Division and the 52nd Brigade, together with an artillery regiment and an armored regiment, were present in Quang Tin province. A few days later, our troops recaptured several hill positions west of the province capital, but reports that enemy forces had blocked the Hai Van Pass, preventing the evacuation of tens of thousands of people fleeing from Hue to Danang, had an enormous impact on the morale of our soldiers.

During this perilous period, countless rumors were spread; some saying that peace was near, that there would be national reconciliation, that South Vietnam would be divided in two, and so forth. These rumors only added to the plummeting morale of the troops. The division had been formed in Danang and most of the troops' families lived in Hue. When they heard a rumor that we were abandoning Hue, a number of soldiers deserted to try to find their loved ones.

On the morning of March 24, 1975, enemy forces, supported by armored vehicles, launched a surprise attack on the Quang Tin province capital. Our units could put up only weak resistance before retreating. 14th Ranger Group and 5th Infantry Regiment withdrew north toward Danang, while 4th Infantry Regiment retreated down the coast toward Chu Lai.

That same morning, Col. Le Van Ngoc, the Quang Ngai province chief, requested permission to withdraw to Chu Lai. I forwarded the request to General Truong, who approved it. Sixth Regiment, 11th Ranger Group, and one armored company would support this nighttime retreat. The retreating forces were attacked at many points along the route of withdrawal; by the morning of March 25, only 50 percent of the troops had reached Chu Lai.

On March 25, the Chu Lai base was flooded with RF units, PF units, police, cadre, and civilians from the provinces of Quang Tin and

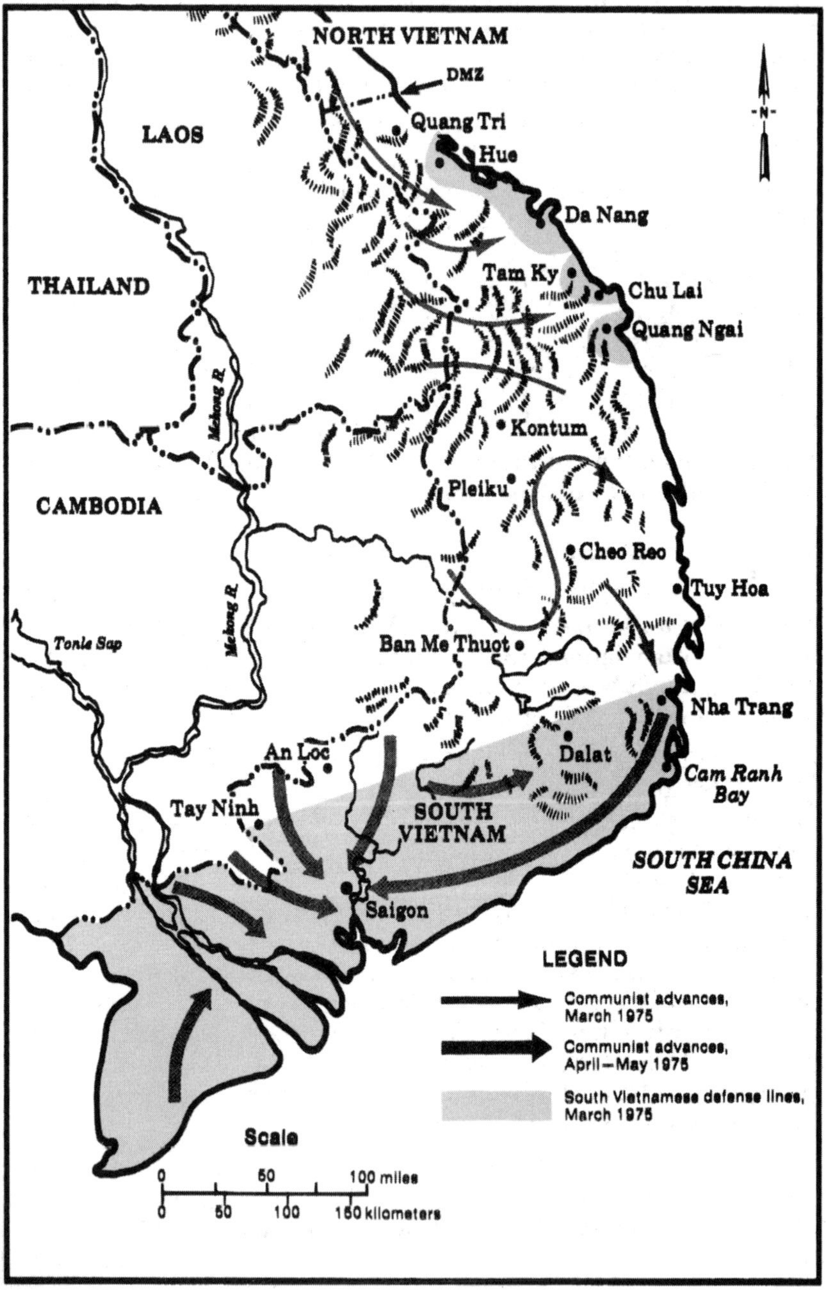

North Vietnamese Army Final Offensive, March–May 1975.
Map from Vietnam: A History *(New York: Viking Press, 1983), by Stanley Karnow.*

Quang Ngai. The dock area swarmed with people who could see an LST troop transport anchored in the Chu Lai harbor. I had to use a bullhorn twice to warn the troops to return to their units and take up defensive positions against a possible enemy attack, but it seemed no one was listening. The soldiers were afraid of being abandoned in Chu Lai, as had happened to other troops during the evacuation of II Corps.

With no other recourse, I telephoned Lieutenant General Truong, informed him of the situation, and asked for permission to use the LST sitting off the coast to evacuate my units to Cu Lao Re (Re Island) to preserve my forces. I also asked that a Chinook helicopter be sent to Chu Lai to evacuate the division's wounded and sick soldiers, together with the wounded from the Quang Ngai sector hospital who had been brought to the Chu Lai hospital a few days before. All these recommendations were approved.

I flew out to the LST to talk to the captain and asked him to land his ship after dark on the beach next to division headquarters in order to avoid attracting civilians and undisciplined soldiers who might try to fight their way aboard. After studying the nautical charts, the captain agreed to bring his ship to the designated spot at about nine o'clock in the evening.

I hurriedly flew back to division headquarters to meet with my unit commanders and assign them their duties. All units were to be at the beach and ready to board at the designated times. The order of withdrawal and boarding was set as follows: division headquarters, training center, artillery, communications, engineers, the logistics battalion, 4th Armored Cavalry Squadron, and last, 4th Infantry Regiment. The artillery was ordered to destroy the breechblocks of their guns, especially those on the 175mm guns. The ammunition dumps were to be destroyed. Oil was to be drained from all electric generators, and the generators were to be left running after our withdrawal in order to burn out the engines.

At nine o'clock, as the LST headed toward the beach, it ran aground more than one hundred yards offshore. The soldiers pushed and shoved one another as they waded out to reach the ship. Armored personnel carriers raced one another out into the sea, running down troops and creating disorder and confusion beyond anything we ever anticipated. In part because of the high waves, and in part because of the disorder among the troops as they fought one another to be the first out to the ship, Col. Hoang Tich Thong, my deputy division commander, told me we could not allow the evacuation to proceed in this manner.

I ordered the LST to back off and dock at the Chu Lai pier. I then ordered all units to move to that location. A helicopter had made several trips to pick up a large number of our wounded at 2nd Medical Battalion, but then a number of soldiers and members of their families swarmed over the landing pad, forcing us to abandon further evacuation of the wounded. Seeing how the situation had deteriorated, I flew up to Danang to meet with General Truong and request more transportation resources for the evacuation. When I arrived, enemy guns were shelling Danang airfield. General Truong was exhausted. After I reported the situation to him, he directed Rear Adm. Ho Van Ky Thoai to order all sea transportation command vessels to stop at Chu Lai and placed them under the command of 2nd Infantry Division.

On the flight back to Chu Lai, I contacted Lt. Col. Hoang Viet Qui, deputy chief of staff for political warfare of the 2nd Division. He told me the situation at the docks was completely chaotic. For security reasons, the captain would not tie up at the dock itself, instead anchoring twenty yards from it. Everyone had to board by rope or rope nets, and most of the weapons had to be left behind. Several soldiers fighting one another to board the ship set off hand grenades, killing a number of soldiers and civilians at the dock and creating a most tragic situation.

Because of the chaotic situation at Chu Lai, I could not possibly land there, so I flew straight to Ly Son Island. Thick fog was covering the island, and several times I thought we were going to crash, but because of the skill and experience of my pilot, we finally managed to land at the bottom of a hill. I used the communications facilities of a relay station on the island to speak to Rear Admiral Thoai directly. I ordered that the convoy of military transport vessels sailing up from the south, which was then off the coast of Duc Pho, contact Lt. Col. Hoang Viet Qui, chief of staff for political warfare, to arrange for the vessels to come in to evacuate the soldiers and their families from Chu Lai.

The evacuation was virtually complete by the morning of March 25, 1975. The soldiers on the LST were taken to Ly Son Island, while those aboard the military transportation command barges and LCMs sailed toward Danang. I think the suggestion I made to General Truong worked out well because, if the entire 2nd Division had been evacuated to Danang, it would have completely disintegrated, as did 1st and 3rd Divisions, because the troops there had lost all discipline and command.

Lieutenant Colonel Qui wanted to go to Danang to assess the situation, so he accompanied the naval convoy. He was later trapped there and captured by the communists.

Hue fell on March 25. On March 26 and 27, the situation in Danang grew more chaotic and violent as evacuated soldiers of 1st, 2nd, and 3rd Divisions, marines, Rangers, and RF soldiers flooded into the city.

On March 28, I flew to Danang. When I walked into the conference room, I saw Maj. Gen. Bui The Lan, commander of the marine division, viciously berating the 1st Division commander, Brig. Gen. Nguyen Van Diem. General Lan shouted that the soldiers of 1st Division were the ones causing the disorder in the streets of Danang. In fact, soldiers caused the disorder in Danang from every evacuated unit, not just 1st Division. I felt uncomfortable in this situation because I was a division commander with the same position and responsibilities as Lan and Diem. Meanwhile, Gen. Le Nguyen Khang and Gen. Ngo Quang Truong sat there quietly, saying nothing.

General Khang was assistant to the chief of the joint general staff. He had flown up to Danang to assess the situation. He ordered me to take 2nd Division (-) down to Binh Tuy to regroup and reorganize in order to establish a line of defense to block the communist advance. Third Division (-) was to return to the Van Kiep Training Center, near Vung Tau in Phuoc Tuy province, to reorganize.

As for 1st Division, it had essentially disintegrated and was no longer combat effective. Its commander, General Diem, was killed in a helicopter crash that night at Son Tra, headquarters of the Navy's 1st Coastal Zone. I flew in to visit 5th Infantry Regiment and picked up a quantity of weapons and ammunition to equip my units that had been evacuated to Ly Son Island. On March 29, the soldiers and civilians of Danang evacuated. Nha Trang and Cam Ranh Bay were later abandoned before they were even threatened by the enemy.

Meanwhile, an emotional debate was taking place in the United States. The "hawks" made a last stand, reminding Congress that in the Paris agreement the United States had promised to replace destroyed equipment. President Ford, the commander in chief, gave no thought to the use of naval power or air power. Instead, he asked Congress to throw another $722 million in emergency military assistance on the problem. Congress was not listening either to the hawks or to the administration. It approved only $300 million for the evacuation of Americans and other humanitarian purposes. Ford announced: "The Vietnam War is finished as far as the United States is concerned."

Henry Kissinger appealed to Congress "to do what is right." But his heart was not in it any longer; he had been insulted enough times by Thieu not to give a damn for Thieu's fate or to put up an effective fight for South Vietnam's survival. "The Vietnam debate has run its course," he commented with finality.

We arrived in Binh Tuy on the afternoon of April 1. After establishing radio contact with Lt. Gen. Nguyen Van Toan, the new commander of III Corps, Military Region Three; Brig. Gen. Le Minh Dao, 18th Division commander; and Col. Tran Ba Thanh, the province chief of Binh Tuy, a helicopter picked me up off my ship to take me to a meeting.

Binh Tuy was a place where remnants from units evacuated from Regions One and Two congregated. This was because the communists had blocked Route 1 at Gia Ray, to the south. Everywhere the flood of refugees went, theft, robbery, and rioting followed. The Phan Rang province chief, Col. Tran Van Tu, abandoned his position and fled the province. General Toan asked me to select someone to replace him. I immediately appointed Col. Truong Dang Liem, commander of 4th Infantry Regiment, to the position of province chief. Lieutenant Colonel Che Quang Thao took over command of the regiment. Unfortunately, for Colonel Liem, there was nothing he could do with a province capital that had sunk into such a state of chaos and disorder. All the military and civilian governmental organizations of the province, together with most of their personnel, had unilaterally evacuated the province after Colonel Tu's departure. A few unfortunate incidents occurred in Phan Thiet when the flood of refugees passed through, but the province chief, Col. Ngo Tan Nghia, maintained control of the situation.

To get back to the situation in Binh Tuy, at midnight on April 2, when the flood of refugees and fleeing military personnel reached the Binh Tuy province capital, I ordered the highest-ranking officers in the group, including one Ranger lieutenant colonel, to come see me in the province chief's office. I explained to them that the communists had blocked Route 1 at Gia Ray and that Binh Tuy was the last point at which we could safely gather the evacuees together, to send them back to Saigon by ship or plane. If Binh Tuy collapsed into chaos, the consequences would be extremely serious. I asked them to explain the situation to the refugees traveling with them. Everyone would be required to hand their personal weapons over to our units at the temporary holding area. All tanks, APCs, and artillery would be turned over to units of the 2nd Infantry Division. After that, the soldiers and their families should wait while I requested transportation to take them south.

I told these officers that, if any disorder broke out, they would be held responsible; their entire evacuation group would not be given an opportunity to return to Saigon. As for the undisciplined elements committing rapes, robberies, and other crimes, who might even be communists trying to stir up confusion and disorder, they would be executed on the spot.

As for the officer cadets from the Dalat Military Academy, I asked

Col. Nguyen Thuc Hung, chief of military affairs for the academy, to collect all at the airfield to await transportation. I went out to the airport to speak to them about the difficult situation facing our nation. As a special dispensation, cadets were allowed to retain their individual weapons.

I radioed General Toan to request the urgent supply of dry rations to feed the evacuee population in Binh Tuy.

Order was thus maintained in the area. On April 5, the cadets were transported by C-130 aircraft to Long Thanh, near Bien Hoa. The refugees were all picked up by navy ships and transported farther south to safety. A number of wealthy evacuees hired sampans to take them to Vung Tau.

* * *

On April 9, the communists launched an attack on Xuan Loc in Long Khanh province with the NVA 341st Division, followed by the PDF (People's Defense Force) 7th Division on April 23. After putting up a valiant defense and suffering heavy casualties, the 18th ARVN Division under Brig. Gen. Le Minh Dao withdrew to the south and moved to set up a defensive line at Long Binh.

On April 11, Gen. Nguyen Van Toan brought Lt. Gen. Nguyen Vinh Nghi to Binh Tuy. He told me General Nghi, former IV Corps and Military Region commander, who had been appointed III Corps commander, would command the forward command post at Phan Rang. The reason General Nghi agreed to serve as the forward headquarters commander was that he had been promised two full-strength infantry divisions to hold the line at Phan Rang. Unfortunately, he was given only units that had already suffered considerable losses and were still in the process of regrouping and reorganizing.

I did not know much about General Toan and had never previously served under his command. When he became commander of II Corps and Military Region Two in 1974, Toan realized the communists planned to launch an offensive in the strategically important western highlands and use it as a springboard for their effort to seize all of

South Vietnam. He prepared to send 22nd Division, 23rd Division, and supporting units to attack Duc Co, the headquarters and logistics complex where the B3 front was located. However, he was accused of corruption and forced out of his post as II Corps commander, leaving the operation unfinished. If this operation had been carried out, the enemy's combat capabilities would have been damaged and they probably would not have been capable of attacking and capturing Phuoc Long and Ban Me Thuot in early 1975.

When I finally sought the truth from different sources and understood the facts, I felt sorry for General Toan and began to sympathize with him and respect him. No other general worked as diligently and energetically as he did during the last days of the Republic of Vietnam. President Thieu granted him virtually unlimited authority over Military Regions Two and Three. He ordered the helicopter evacuation of Col. Le Van Phat's 3rd Airborne Brigade from Khanh Duong, sent Colonel Luong's 2nd Airborne Brigade to Phan Rang, and evacuated the Ranger group from Lam Dong. He rebuilt and reorganized the units evacuated from Regions One and Two (2nd Division, 3rd Division, and 22nd Division). Of particular importance, he deployed and maneuvered airborne and marine units, Lt. Col. Nguyen Manh Hung's 8th Regiment, 5th Division, 18th Division, and Gen. Tran Quang Khoi's 3rd Armored Brigade to stop the communists at the Ho Nai–Dau Giay–Xuan Loc defense line.

General Toan personally approved the use of two 15,000-pound Daisy Cutter bombs (only two because we had only two fuses for these bombs) to support the Xuan Loc front. This type of bomb, which was dropped by a C-130 aircraft, was extremely destructive. It exploded twenty yards above the treetops and was used to flatten areas of jungle to create helicopter-landing zones to deliver supplies and evacuate the wounded. The Vietnamese Air Force could use this weapon, and it would be as effective as a B-52 strike. Unfortunately, by the end of April 1975, we had received only six of these bombs, and for some unknown reason we received only two fuses.

On April 12, 6th Regiment, under the command of Lt. Col. Ton

That Ho, was transferred to Phan Thiet to strengthen the defenses there. The next day, Col. Hoang Tich Thong, deputy division commander, and an element of 5th Regiment were transported to Phan Rang. On April 14, the division headquarters, together with 5th Regiment (-), moved up to Phan Rang.

On April 15, Lt. Gen. Tran Van Don, deputy prime minister and minister of defense, came to visit Phan Rang. I reported to him on the difficulties my division faced: low troop strength, equipment shortages, and low morale among our troops because they were all worried about the families they had left behind in Quang Ngai, Quang Tin, and Hue. General Don was concerned. He counseled me to try to accomplish the mission and said that if we could hold at Phan Rang he would transfer me back to replace General Lan as marine commander to supervise the rebuilding of the marine division.

Out of all our generals, General Don was perhaps the one who suffered the most in the history of the Army of the Republic of Vietnam. He was second in seniority only to Gen. Nguyen Van Minh and played one of the most important roles in the 1963 coup against Ngo Dinh Diem. After the coup, however, he remained a lieutenant general until the fall of South Vietnam, while some of his subordinates were promoted from colonel to four-star general without a single military achievement to their credit. General Don was polite, refined, resourceful, and energetic in the performance of his duties. He was intelligent and had a great breadth of knowledge, but because he did not play politics and did not get involved in factional in-fighting as did the other generals, he was stuck at the rank of lieutenant general. General Don died in Paris early in the twenty-first century.

Early in the morning of April 16, General Nghi ordered me to move the 2nd Division forward headquarters over next to his headquarters at the Phan Rang airfield to simplify coordination and support efforts. I set up the 2nd Division headquarters in an aircraft hangar next to the hangar where General Nghi had his joint headquarters alongside that of the 6th Air Division commander, Brig. Gen. Pham Ngoc Sang, who had moved his command to Phan Rang from Pleiku after the evacuation of Military Region Two. The 2nd Airborne Brigade commander, Colonel Luong, was also located in General Nghi's headquarters.

At eleven o'clock, General Nghi informed me that communist forces had overrun Col. Nguyen Van Biet's 3rd Ranger Group, stationed north of the airfield. Nghi ordered a general withdrawal, telling everyone to get out any way they could and evacuate to the south. I assumed he intended to retreat back to Phan Thiet. In fact, communist troops had already captured the Phan Rang province capital at six that morning, after penetrating the line held by 3rd Airborne Brigade, but no one told me of this development.

When I rushed out of the hangar, I could not find my jeep, so my entire division headquarters ran with me down the runway. After running for about one hundred yards, we found the jeep with the green flag on my radio antenna sitting on the runway. At this point, we heard communist AK-47s firing throughout the airbase. A huge number of soldiers and their families were running all over the runway. The sky was filled with aircraft of all types because they had been evacuating nonessential air force personnel and their families all morning.

Suddenly, Capt. Vuong Huu Danh, my aide-de-camp, saw my helicopter flying over the airfield. Danh quickly established contact with Col. Nguyen Khoa Bao, the 2nd Division chief of staff, who was aboard my helicopter. I directed Colonel Bao not to land on the runway to pick me up because the runway was covered with fleeing personnel. The jeep circled around the airfield until we found a deserted spot, then the helicopter landed and picked up everyone in the jeep. There were more than thirty people on the grossly overloaded helicopter.

I had learned to fly a helicopter because of my experiences as a battalion commander, regimental commander, and province sector commander. I tried to learn to fly so that if I saw the enemy, I could personally take the controls, turn the aircraft, and follow the enemy in order to call in air or artillery strikes. Furthermore, my aide-de-camps all knew my emergency radio frequency, so if my helicopter crashed, search aircraft could use that frequency to contact me, thereby avoiding enemy interference.

After boarding my helicopter, I ordered the pilot to fly over Phan Rang to attempt to contact General Nghi and General Sang on the PRC-25 and Motorola radio frequencies General Sang had given me, but there was no reply. The helicopter was so overloaded that it did not have enough fuel to stay aloft for long. I told the pilot to fly out off the coast of Phan Rang so I could find a way to contact the joint general staff to inform them of the situation in Phan Rang.

There was a navy WHEC-class vessel sitting off the coast, but it had no helicopter pad. I told the pilot to fly down right alongside the vessel, then I jumped out into the sea with my bodyguards. The crew of the ship threw us life preservers and hauled us aboard. I used the ship's radio to call navy headquarters in Saigon and asked them to pass my report to the joint general staff that Phan Rang had fallen. I also established radio contact with my deputy division commander, Colonel Thong, who had retreated to Phan Ri in An Phuoc district. I ordered that all 2nd Division personnel withdraw to Phan Thiet so we could reorganize. My plan was not successful, however, because the communists had established a blocking position at the Ca Na peninsula.

The North Vietnamese had kept only one division in the North. Everything else had been sent south. The communist forces in Phan Rang at this time included 325th NVA Division, 3rd VC Division (Yellow Star), and 968th Group (Local) supported by tanks, artillery, and antiaircraft weapons. Our forces in Phan Rang included the 6th Air Force Division (-), which had been withdrawn from Pleiku; 3rd Airborne Brigade (-) withdrawn from Khanh Duong (Nha Trang), replaced by 2nd Airborne (-) later; 2nd ARVN Division (-) withdrawn from Chu Lai; and 31st Ranger Group (-) withdrawn from An Loc. All these units were exhausted due to the fighting and withdrawal. Their morale was low. Their strength was less than 60 percent.

As I saw it, the JGS underestimated our situation in Phan Rang. They should have sent to Phan Rang at least one division from the Delta, where the situation was calm, instead of depending on the "understrength" of the demoralized units already there. Things might have turned out differently.

While I was speaking on the radio, the ship I was on was sailing south to meet Rear Adm. Hoang Co Minh's navy warship HQ-03, sailing north to pick me up. After I transferred to Minh's vessel, we returned to Phan Thiet, where I reported to General Toan on the situation in Phan Rang. I then met with the headquarters of 6th Regiment, 2nd Division, which was still stationed at Phan Thiet.

To tell the truth, the combat spirit of our troops had completely collapsed. They were worried about their families left behind in areas under communist control, and they lacked sufficient weapons and equipment because of the careless, undisciplined nature of the earlier evacuation. How could anyone maintain the will to fight in such circumstances? I was certain that Phan Thiet would be the next city to fall, so I privately instructed Lieutenant Colonel Ho to assemble a number of civilian fishing boats to use when evacuation became necessary. I told him to sail to Vung Tau when the time came.

Third Corps headquarters gave me a U-17 observation aircraft to fly over Phan Rang to establish contact with units of 2nd Division. I was able to contact several small groups. Carefully using double-talk, I instructed them to try to locate fishing boats and sail south to be rescued. Once, a small navy combat vessel tried to move in close to shore at Ca Na to pick up 2nd Division troops, but it encountered such intense communist artillery and rocket fire that it was forced to turn back.

On April 18, I flew back to Binh Tuy because 2nd Division's rear headquarters was still located there. Colonel Thanh shared my opinion that we must prepare to evacuate from Binh Tuy. On April 19, Phan Thiet was evacuated, and after that Binh Tuy fell.

President Nguyen Van Thieu and ARVN Chief of Staff Cao Van Vien should have made more public appearances during this period to reassure our soldiers, government officials, and civilians. Unfortunately, the silence of these two leaders seemed to give tacit approval to the haphazard evacuation of one province after another. When they finally made a move, it was only to make sure they would be the first to abandon a sinking ship. General Vien ordered his men to fight to the death, and then fled the country. President Thieu resigned, nominated Vice

President Tran Van Huong as his successor, and fled to Taiwan. *Après moi, le deluge.*

On April 19, Phan Thiet was evacuated and Binh Tuy fell. I went to visit Colonel Thong in Phuoc Tuy on April 20, after which he returned to Saigon to take care of his family.

On April 21, a group of about one hundred soldiers of the 2nd Division—all that was left of the division with a normal strength of between eleven and twelve thousand men—carrying only their individual weapons, arrived in Vung Tau. I called them together to talk to them and thank them. They needed to be free to go search for their loved ones. I asked the joint general staff to send someone to pay their salaries. I also asked that they be allowed to take all the dry rations they needed for the long trek home to their families. This was the most emotional moment in my entire military career because it was highly unlikely I would ever see any of these men again. I was so moved that I hugged and kissed 1st Lt. Nguyen Van Giau, commander of the 2nd Reconnaissance Company, one of the bravest and most outstanding officers in the army of the Republic of Vietnam, a man who had been at my side for almost three years.

I was also concerned about other people who were dear to me. I used my personal helicopter to transport Colonel Bao and a number of other soldiers to Saigon to take care of their personal affairs. Colonel Nguyen Thoi Lai, deputy chief of staff for operations and logistics, agreed to remain behind in Phuoc Tuy with his wife's family. We lost contact with Col. Can Ngoc Huan, commander of the 5th Regiment. I later learned that he made it back to Saigon after the fall of Phan Rang by walking overland via Dalat, Lam Dong, and Ho Nai. He was captured by the communists and spent sixteen years in their concentration camps.

Colonel Huan was an interesting fellow, a member of an ethnic minority tribe from the piedmont region of North Vietnam who spoke excellent Thai. Earlier in his career, while serving with the Special Forces, he had been dropped into an area under Pathet Lao control on an operation. He was captured and everyone thought he was dead. His wife even received his death benefit payment, twelve months' salary. However, by pretending to be Thai, he was able to take advantage of an opening to escape and get back to Vietnam. Colonel Huan was also a member of my own Tran Binh Trong (tenth) class at the academy.

On April 22, I met with Rear Admiral Thoai in Vung Tau, and then with Rear Adm. Vu Dinh Dao, commander of the 3rd Naval Region. They told me that if my family needed to be evacuated, they were prepared to help. I felt as if a heavy load had been lifted off my shoulders and rejoiced that I had such good friends.

On April 26, Phuoc Tuy fell into enemy hands.

On April 27, I brought my family, Maj. General Hoang Van Lac and his family, and the wife of Rear Admiral Thoai back to Saigon. We went to the U.S. Defense Attaché Office (DAO) to request evacuation for our families. Most of the wives of senior officers had already left the week before on civilian flights and were staying temporarily in four-star hotels in Manila. DAO informed us that at that time they were not providing priority evacuation status to anyone. Only General Lac's family was able to board an evacuation flight because they had made earlier arrangements.

On April 28, Lieutenant General Don, deputy prime minister and minister of defense, asked me to report to him. When I arrived, he said: "The situation is wonderful now. General Duong Van Minh has become president. He will stay here and work, and later, when the situation stabilizes, we can have anything we want. I am going to assign you to work for Lt. Gen. Nguyen Van Minh, who is now commander of the capital special zone."

I was amazed at his unbridled optimism. I had previously had contact with Minh during the coup against Diem on November 1, 1963. After the coup, if he truly was a capable leader, when we had the support of the entire population and when the Viet Cong was still weak, General Minh could have turned our nation into a better place than it had been under Diem. However, Minh failed to seize the moment, shattering our hopes. So now how could I have any confidence in him when the nation was in such a bleak situation? Our American allies had turned their backs on us, and the North Vietnamese were tightening the noose around our necks.

I called Gen. Nguyen Van Minh from General Don's office. When Minh picked up the phone, he said: "Nhut, is that you? Report in here to me, and I will put you in charge of the defenses in northern Gia Dinh province." I thought to myself: *Where are the troops to put up a defense, and where will we get the support and equipment we need?*

Professor Vu Van Mau, who had been appointed prime minister in Minh's new government, had just asked the United States to leave Vietnam within the next twenty-four hours. This could only mean that the new president intended to negotiate with the communists from a position of weakness. I knew the North Vietnamese communists were not stupid enough to negotiate with General Minh at a time when their forces were surging forward on the tide of victory. If I stayed behind—without troops, without the necessary resources, without our American ally—I would be staying only to submit to a humiliating surrender. I, therefore, asked General Don to intervene with the Defense Attaché Office at the American embassy to evacuate my family. DAO officials reiterated that there were no longer any priority slots, but promised to help should an opportunity present itself.

When I returned home, the communists were attacking the Newport bridge, which was very close to my house. I immediately took my family, the family of Rear Admiral Thoai, and Gen. Hoang Van Lac back to Vung Tau. Fortunately, the 3rd Air Division commander, Brig. Gen. Huynh Ba Tin, continued to keep one command helicopter reserved for my personal use. At the Nguyen Van Nhut naval base at Vung Tau, my family, Mrs. Thoai, and General Lac boarded one of Admiral Thoai's fast patrol boats that had sailed south from Military Region One. Also aboard this patrol boat were Gen. Hoang Xuan Lam, Gen. Phan Hoa Hiep, and a number of other officers.

I visited 2nd Division's rear base in Phuoc Tuy. By this time, only a few soldiers remained at the base. They did not know where to go because the communists had captured Phuoc Tuy and Long Thanh. That night, DAO telephoned to say that they had booked my family on an evacuation flight scheduled for the next morning. Later that same night, however, they told me that, because Tan Son Nhut airfield was being shelled by enemy artillery, all evacuation flights had been cancelled.

On the morning of April 29, General Tin of 3rd Air Division landed his helicopter at the Nguyen Van Nhut base. He told us that III Corps headquarters had been evacuated to Go Vap and that he had lost radio contact with the headquarters. General Tin then led all his helicopters south, evacuating them to IV Corps. By this time, communist artillery was shelling Vung Tau. Rear Admiral Thoai and I flew out to sea in a helicopter and landed on a barge anchored in the middle of the Vung Tau harbor. Admiral Thoai then radioed for a fast patrol boat to come pick us up. As we sailed out to South Vietnamese Navy LST HQ-805, I watched as wave after wave of U.S. helicopters flew in from the 7th Fleet to evacuate foreigners and Vietnamese from Saigon. In a chaotic operation, the United States managed to get its own people out as well as one hundred fifty thousand South Vietnamese. It was to mark the first mass exodus of Vietnamese refugees.

General Don later told me that because he had been promised priority evacuation, he tried to reach the U.S. embassy on April 29 to be evacuated but had been unable to fight his way through the crowds surrounding the embassy. While he was there thinking there was no way out, a young girl approached him and whispered: "You will never be able to get into the embassy, General. Follow me." She drove him to an empty villa and said: "I am supposed to be picked up by a helicopter from this house, but I will relinquish my seat on the helicopter to you. I will have no problem if I remain behind, but if you stay, General, you will be in great danger." As she said this, she pushed him through the gate of the villa and walked away.

General Don asked my wife and me on several occasions to try and help him find his unknown benefactor. I told this story to many of my friends in the hope that this lady would eventually hear that General Don was looking for her. Regrettably, General Don died in France without ever having a chance to thank this good samaritan.

Late in the afternoon of April 29, the communists shifted their artillery fire out to sea, where hundreds, perhaps thousands, of ships, boats, and sampans filled with refugees were gathered trying to board American warships anchored there. The American ships were forced to weigh anchor and sail farther out to sea.

My family and I had to join the Vietnamese Navy at Vung Tau in the evening of April 29 to escape the imminent takeover. As I stood on the deck, watching the land disappear in the distance, my eyes filled with tears. Before me was the land where I had been born and had grown up. After twenty-three years in uniform, fighting from one end of the country to the other, I now felt like a coward for leaving behind family members and abandoning my comrades-in-arms, living and dead, who had fought and bled at my side.

During my military career, I had traveled abroad many times, boarding ships and sailing away from many docks. Often, after a landing operation, warships would pick us up and sail out to take us back to our rear base. This time, however, I felt I might never again return to the land of my ancestors.

Then, suddenly, the words General MacArthur spoke when he boarded a torpedo boat in the Philippines to escape the Japanese during World War II came to mind: "I shall return!"

* * *

On April 30, 1975, Gen. Duong Van Minh signed the unconditional surrender of South Vietnam to the communists. The Vietnamese fleet, with my family on board, left Vietnam and headed toward the Philippines. From there, we were transported by air to Guam.

On May 1, 1975, the Soviet-built tanks of the triumphant North Vietnamese smashed through the wrought-iron gates of Independence Palace in Saigon. The city's name was changed to Ho Chi Minh City. The whole campaign had lasted less than two months, not the two years Hanoi's planners had been expecting.

China supported the National Liberation Front as an entity separate from North Vietnam. In celebration of the supposed NLF victory, the Chinese business center of Cho Lon hoisted the flag of Red China after the occupation of Saigon. But soon all the flags were gone; the NLF did not exist much longer.

My wife Lang Kim Tran, our children Tran Tuan Nguyen (seventeen years old), Tran Huu Nghia (fifteen years old), Tran Van Nga (thirteen years old), Tran Van Ngan (twelve years old), and I arrived at Camp Pendleton on May 6, 1975. The 1st U.S. Marine Division was kind and diligent in its care for us, feeding us good American food. I gained ten pounds during our two-week stay at Camp Pendleton, enjoying the goodwill and generosity that are hallmarks of the United States of America.

12

A Few Thoughts

THE LOSS of South Vietnam, Laos, and Cambodia was a psychological and geopolitical setback for the United States. Twenty-one years earlier, Eisenhower's secretary of state, John Foster Dulles, had put American prestige on the line in a nation-building project that meant intervention in Vietnam. Three succeeding administrations tried but failed to sustain that commitment.

With no "ugly Americans" to hate, the communists turned on one another and their own people. The Vietnamese had fought Chinese domination for two thousand years and they were not going to put up with "Chinese hegemonism" now. In the deepening Sino-Soviet split, they sided with the Soviet Union and started mistreating the Chinese living in Vietnam.

In Laos, the Pathet Lao stayed subservient to Vietnam. They started a campaign of genocide against their own Hmong tribesmen who had collaborated with the Americans. In his book *America's Longest War,* George C. Herring writes: "In one of the great human tragedies of the Indochina wars, America's loyal allies, the Hmong, were the victims of Pathet Lao genocide. Roughly 100,000, including the legendary Vang Pao, escaped." Based on allegations by Hmong refugees, Herring asserts that "another 100,000 were killed in a systematic campaign of extermination that employed bombing, artillery, and possibly chemical-biological weapons." However, historians have been unable to verify these statistics.

In Cambodia, the Khmer Rouge, under the infamous Pol Pot, renamed the country Kampuchea, put an end to Hanoi's dream of an Indochinese federation, and became the enemies of Vietnam and the allies of China. Pol Pot was as devout a communist as the North Vietnamese and had no intention of playing second fiddle to them. He was the author of a bizarre, cruel, and subhuman plan of evacuation of Cambodian cities that resulted in the death of 2 million Cambodians—one-third of the country's population—for the sake of some political abstraction. In response to Khmer Rouge cross-border raids, the Vietnamese invaded Cambodia, drove out Pol Pot, and established a puppet regime. In retaliation, the Chinese decided to "teach Vietnam a lesson" and invaded Vietnam for a short war.

The government of reunited Vietnam consisted of men full of hate who did hateful things to their countrymen. Their aim was to "re-educate" the South Vietnamese to become as dour and sullen as the communists. In the process, they proved the inherent evil of communism. Amnesty International condemned them as violators of human rights. Even Buddhist leaders, former allies of the Viet Cong, were imprisoned or murdered. Vietnamese with any connection to the Americans or to the Thieu regime had to be punished in so-called re-education camps, which were in fact concentration camps.

A large number of professionals, such as doctors, dentists, and engineers, left the country. Children of Vietnamese mothers and American fathers were scorned and called "dust children." Compassionate people all over the world shed tears for the 1.5 million Vietnamese "boat people" who escaped from the country in flimsy boats, looking for sanctuary in any nation other than their own. Even a former justice minister of the Viet Cong was among the boat people; five hundred thousand of them perished at sea.

Refugee camps dotted the countryside of Vietnam's neighbors. The one million South Vietnamese refugees who managed to settle in the United States were considered to be the lucky ones.

The American antiwar activists read the newspaper reports of how millions of Vietnamese endangered their lives fleeing the "communist paradise" but remained blind. John McAulif, an antiwar activist, wrote in 1983: "U.S. postwar policy toward Indochina has been a moral travesty." He denied the obvious: "The bloodbath that the U.S. government so often predicted . . . did not occur." The atrocities committed by the communist Vietnamese on millions of noncommunist Vietnamese was explained away in one small phrase: "Injustices and mistakes." To solve the problems of Indochina, Mr. McAulif's advice was: "A fundamental change must be made in U.S. policy." His conclusion: "We have denied ourselves the opportunity to mourn and regret and learn."

The centrally planned economy of a newly unified communist Vietnam became a basket case, with a per capita income of around $100. It was one of the poorest countries on earth, yet it had one of the world's largest armies, which swallowed nearly half its GDP. As the inflation rate climbed to reach 800 percent in 1988, they realized that, instead of conquering South Vietnam, they would have been better off financially if they had surrendered to the Americans.

They decided to move away from strict communist ideology to some capitalist incentives, which they called *Doi Moi* (Renovation), even seeking foreign investments. They began talking like capitalists, declaring 1990 to be the "year of the tourist." Per capita income rose to $200, but the recovery was threatened by corruption and a population explosion. However, the tourists and overseas Vietnamese helped; the dollar became the currency in which most goods were traded. One tourist was a U.S. veteran, a former corporal, who observed: "I received a warmer welcome as an American vet returning to Vietnam than I did as a Vietnam vet returning to America."

In 1983, the distinguished author Douglas Pike painted an accurate picture of the failed leadership of the Hanoi politburo: "The party-state *apparat* created in wartime was a fighting machine, totally hierarchical, tightly knit, disciplined—exactly what was needed. But in peacetime, these virtues became vices. The party-state institutions are over-organized, excessively centralized, full of cross-purpose—all of which smother initiative, prevent flexibility, and mitigate against innovation."

In his book *Vietnam: A History,* Stanley Karnow writes about two interviews he had in Ho Chi Minh City in 1990 with disillusioned former communists.

Tran Bach Dang, a top communist advisor, said candidly: "Our belief in a communist utopia had nothing to do with reality. We tried to build a new society on theories and dreams—on sand. Instead of stimulating production by giving people incentives, we collectivized them. Imagine! We even collectivized barbers. It was preposterous. We were also consumed by vanity. Because we crushed the Americans, we thought that we could achieve anything. We should have heeded the old Chinese adage: "You can conquer a country from horseback, but you cannot govern it from horseback."

Doctor Duong Quynh Hoa, a pediatrician, had been named a "heroine of the revolution." She was equally frank. "I have been a communist all my life, but now I have seen the realities of communism and it is a failure—mismanagement, corruption, privilege, repression. My ideals are gone . . . communism has been catastrophic. Party officials have never understood the need for rational development. They've been hypnotized by Marxist slogans that have lost validity—if they were ever valid. They are outrageous."

* * *

Before 1975, about three hundred thousand Vietnamese lived outside Vietnam, mainly in France. After 1975, communist atrocities raised the number of diaspora Vietnamese to more than three million. They called themselves either Overseas Vietnamese or Free Vietnamese or Viet Kieu.

According to a recent census, they are distributed as follows:

1,223,736 in the United States
600,000 in Cambodia and Laos
300,000 in France
174,200 in Australia
151,410 in Canada
150,000 in the Russian Federation
85,528 in Taiwan
83,526 in Germany
35,000 in the United Kingdom
25,000 in the Czech Republic
20,000 in the People's Republic of China
18,333 in Norway
12,965 in Japan
10,000 in Poland
400,000 elsewhere

The hard-working 85 million people of Vietnam and the free-market reforms of the Renovation program of 1986 have made Vietnam one of the fastest growing economies in the world. Growing at an annual rate of 7 percent from 2000 to 2005, Vietnam's gross domestic product (GDP) reached $251.8 billion in 2005, ranking it 36th in the world. The Goldman Sachs investment bank placed the country on its "next 11" list of eleven countries that have a promising outlook for future growth. However, Vietnam's per capita GDP of $3,025 ranked it only 123rd in the world.

The disparity in international rankings between total GDP and per capita GDP shows that Vietnam is still one of the poorest nations on earth. This is due primarily to the fact that much of the money gained from the growth of the economy does not trickle down to the people. The Communist party of Vietnam retains control over all organs of government, politics, and society. While its leaders luxuriate in wealth, they have failed to create a society that allows its people to live in comfort.

Communist party members have become a caste, what the people of Vietnam call the "Red capitalist caste." With a mixture of capitalist economics and communist politics, they are imposing a "market Leninism" on Vietnam. The army runs hotels; ministries rent cars; government agencies develop real estate. The only concern of their ideology is money, not the proletariat. They are only interested in the competition between state-owned companies and foreign-owned companies.

Do Muoi, the Communist party general secretary, said in December 1995: "As Lenin taught, we are not afraid of capitalist enterprises, but not being able to supervise and control them." The 8th Communist party Congress stated in June 1996 that market-oriented reforms "must be accompanied by the strengthening of the role of state management along the socialist line."

The Communist parties of the Soviet Union and China failed miserably when they attempted to create successful centrally run businesses and industries. I am convinced that communist Vietnam will not have a better outcome than its former patrons. Only the free world, following the American system of free enterprise, has been able to improve the living conditions of its people.

That is why I regret that the South Vietnamese twenty-one-year experiment with a free economy did not succeed. But I still believe that it was the better system. Therefore, I hope that communist rule will be temporary and will not survive the next generation of the Vietnamese nation.

* * *

I have a vision for the 3 million diaspora Vietnamese to finish *the unfinished war* of my generation by working for *a peaceful revolution* inside Vietnam to create what Vietnam lacks and needs: *a vibrant middle class.*

Communism is a dying ideology. The two behemoths of communism—Russia and China—realized that they were pursuing a mirage. Both nations are now trying to discard communism and replace it with middle class values. Russia already claims that communism is dead and that a new middle class has already taken over the country. China still pretends that communism is not temporary and that they can hold on to political power, while in fact signing the death warrant of communism by strengthening the middle class.

It is regrettable that a few countries with failed economies, such as North Korea and Cuba, try to fight the inevitable death of communism, only because they hold the political and military power to stay in charge. Vietnam belongs to this class.

I believe the three million diaspora Vietnamese can use the power of the ballot to convince the authorities of the United States, France, Australia, and Canada to pressure Vietnam to adopt conditions that will allow a middle class to emerge in that country. Politicians in democratic countries are attuned to the feelings of all constituent groups, large or small.

If all the Vietnamese voters in the United States announce that they will vote *only* for candidates who have a valid plan to pressure Vietnam to liberalize its policies, all politicians from coast to coast, in local or national elections, will find it convenient to study the situation in Vietnam and offer equitable solutions. And when politicians in other nations also see the voting power of the Vietnamese electorate, most democracies will begin pressuring Vietnam for the just cause of liberalization. No totalitarian regime has ever changed its substance without domestic and international pressure.

During future presidential elections in the United States, I will urge the Vietnamese community of America to declare openly that we will vote *only* for the candidate who is willing to urge a change of mentality in the present-day leadership of Vietnam. The candidate who wants the vote of the Vietnamese community should paraphrase President Kennedy and pressure the Vietnamese government to: "Ask not what Vietnam can do for you. Ask what you can do for Vietnam."

I believe Vietnam, guided by the United States, is capable of surpassing within a decade the per capita GDP of the Philippines, which in 2007 was $4,923. In the decade after that, Vietnam can try to match the economy of Thailand, which in 2007 had a per capita GDP of $8,368. By then, Vietnam will have surely achieved a strong, viable middle class.

Furthermore, the diaspora Vietnamese, who control assets worth about $200 billion, should use their own assets, their connections, and their knowledge in fields such as information technology to start small businesses. They will thus be working to rebuild the country of their birth by creating an ever-widening wage base. Money talks in all countries, communist or otherwise, and even harsh bureaucracies cannot fight it forever.

To be successful, the theme of a *peaceful* revolution should be stressed. In the Vietnam War, the two sides lost a total of 1 million human lives and more than 2 million wounded. Nobody wants to countenance that kind of catastrophe again.

In the final analysis, the struggles of the Vietnamese people since 1945, under the leadership of Ho Chi Minh or Ngo Dinh Diem or any of their successors, are not yet over. They are only an *unfinished war.* They are unfinished because we have not yet fulfilled the aspirations of the Vietnamese people. The next generation must stride forward to reach the final goal of this struggle. When they do, there will be no more civil strife and no more antagonism. There will be only love and development. The only war that must be fought is the one against poverty, ignorance, injustice, and corruption. Then and only then can the Vietnamese people build a free, democratic, and prosperous nation.

The spirit of Ho Chi Minh will be delighted when Vietnam surpasses the economic achievements of the Philippines and Thailand. Our beloved Vietnam can attain that goal only through a closer collaboration with the United States, not through the bankrupt communist system.

Notes

1. Charles Fenn, *Ho Chi Minh: A Biographical Introduction* (London: Studio Vista, 1973), 17, 23, 27.

2. Ho Chi Minh, *Selected Works* (Moscow: Foreign Languages Publishing House, 1960), 34.

3. Fenn, *Ho Chi Minh,* 48, 51, 55, 60, 70.

4. Stanley Karnow, *Vietnam: A History* (New York: Viking, 1983), 153.

5. Ibid., 169.

6. Fenn, *Ho Chi Minh,* 104.

7. Karnow, *Vietnam,* 200.

8. Ibid., 214.

9. Ibid., 220.

10. Ibid., 236.

11. Ibid., 229.

12. Ibid., 245.

13. Ibid., 276.

14. Ibid., 294.

15. Ibid., 357, 360.

16. Ibid., 360.

17. Don Oberdorfer, *Tet!* (New York: Doubleday, 1971), 116–17.

18. Vo Nguyen Giap, *Banner of People's War, the Party's Military Line* (New York: Praeger, 1970), 42.

19. Samuel Zaffiri, *Westmoreland: A Biography of General William C. Westmoreland* (New York: William Morrow, 1994), 283–89.

20. Ibid., 290.

21. Henry Kissinger, *The White House Years* (Boston: Little, Brown, 1979), 275.

22. Ibid., 444.

23. Ibid., 511.

24. Ibid., 1165.

25. *Reader's Digest,* July 1985.

26. Kissinger, *White House Years,* 1375.

27. Ibid., 1386.

28. Karnow, *Vietnam,* 667.

Index

The word *insert* refers to photographs on the unnumbered pages following page 124.